'Highly recommended, not only for the remarkable story itself but also the quality of its research, its presentation and readability.'

Adrian Greaves, Zulu War battlefield guide,
author and *Antiques Roadshow* advisor

'Charlie Harford's entertaining memoirs are among the most often quoted sources for the Anglo-Zulu War of 1879, but a scholarly edition is long overdue. Professor Laband's thoroughly annotated volume fills this gap admirably, and will be an invaluable addition to any Zulu War library.'

Chris Peers, author of *Rorke's Drift and Isandlwana, Minute by Minute*

A NOTE ON THE COVER PICTURE

The Last Sleep of the Brave, chromolithograph after the painting by Alphonse de Neuville executed in 1881. (*Alexander Haimann Collection*)

Harford was a member of Major Wilsone Black's patrol from Rorke's Drift that on 3 February 1879 discovered the bodies of Lieutenant Melvill and Lieutenant Coghill on the Natal bank at Fugitives' (Sothondose's) Drift. De Neuville's iconic but highly sentimentalised portrayal of the event is incorrect in almost every detail except for the depiction of Melvill in his scarlet serge 'undress frock' and Coghill in his dark-blue patrol jacket. Coghill was wearing brown cord riding-breeches and not dark-blue trousers as shown. After nearly two weeks under the summer sun, their bodies would have been in a considerably more advanced state of decomposition than shown. The two officers fell several yards apart and were not found lying protectively next to each other. Moreover, they were not killed on flat ground close to the Mzinyathi River, but high up the steep, rocky slope of the valley. There was no dead horse at the scene because they had lost their mounts when crossing the drift. For picturesque effect, de Neuville includes men of the 17th Lancers in the patrol, but the cavalry regiment did not arrive in Natal until April, two months later. Egregiously, he shows Coghill grasping the Regimental Colour of the 1/24th Regiment that lies across Melvill's body. In fact, Melvill had been attempting to save the Queen's (not the Regimental) Colour and he had lost it in the river. Harford was with the small party that retrieved it on 4 February, the day after the two bodies were found.

Charlie Harford's Anglo-Zulu War

The Memoir of a British Lieutenant, 1878–1879

Edited by John Laband

Greenhill Books

Charlie Harford's Anglo-Zulu War: The Memoir of a British Lieutenant, 1878–1879

Greenhill Books

First published by Greenhill Books, 2024
Greenhill Books, c/o Pen & Sword Books Ltd,
47 Church Street, Barnsley, S. Yorkshire, S70 2AS
For more information on our books, please visit
www.greenhillbooks.com, email contact@greenhillbooks.com
or write to us at the above address.

Publishing History
Colonel Harford's undated manuscript, donated by his daughter in 1937 to the then Local History Museum in Durban, was transcribed and edited by Daphne Child and first published in 1978 by Shuter & Shooter of Pietermaritzburg as *The Zulu War Journal of Colonel Henry Harford, C.B.* In 2008 David Payne and Emma Payne with Adrian Greaves published *The Writings, Photographs and Sketches of Henry Charles Harford 1850–1937* (Wales: The Ultimatum Tree Ltd). Their book incorporated Daphne Child's edition for Shuter & Shooter on pages 107–69 along with new commentary and illustrations. A further edition of Child's transcription was released by Pen & Sword in February 2014. This new edition of the work with an introduction and comprehensive notes by John Laband has a foreword by Ian Knight.

CIP data records for this title are available from the British Library

ISBN 978 1 39907 848 1

Typeset by JCS Publishing Services Ltd
Typeset in 12/15pt Baskerville
Printed and bound in Great Britain by
CPI Group (UK) Ltd, Croydon, CRO 4YY

Contents

'The crime of the naturalist': Commandant Hamilton-Browne expostulating with Harford for having used the officers' precious supply of gin at Rorke's Drift to preserve his entomological specimens. (*Col. George Hamilton-Browne,* A Lost Legionary in South Africa, *T. Werner Laurie, 1912*)

Foreword

At dawn on Tuesday, 21 January 1879, Lieutenant Henry Charles Harford looked back at Isandlwana hill, where the main thrust of Lieutenant-General Lord Chelmsford's invasion of the independent kingdom of Zululand had arrived to set up camp the day before. Harford was part of an extensive reconnaissance party that was being sent ahead of the column, further into Zulu territory, to search out signs of an impending Zulu response. It was a fine southern African summer's morning, not marred by the heavy rains which had brought an end to a long dry spell and which had hampered Chelmsford's preparations. The camp stood out as a long splash of white canvas across the fresh green grass along the foot of the distinctive hill itself, and it must have been coming alive at first light with the military bustle of over 2,000 men – British regulars, detachments of mounted troops, African auxiliaries and civilian wagon-drivers – and thousands of draft oxen, horses and mules. Yet as he looked back at it, excited as he was by the prospect of his own adventures, Harford experienced a sense of foreboding in the evocative landscape:

> As the sun rose that morning there was a very wonderful sky scene. Overhanging Isandhlwana and the camps was a long, tortuous, more or less low-lying dark cloud, based on the horizon, much in the same form as a trail of smoke from the funnel of a steamer and ending immediately above

> Isandhlwana hill, which as the sun got higher was first tinted almost blood red, then passing into ashybrown with broad golden edges, assumed a marvellous variety of tints with the rise of the sun. And there it hung for the best part of the morning, frowning, as it were, over the fated Camp. I have never forgotten it.

It is scarcely surprising that Harford remembered the scene, for his return to the camp on the night of the 22nd would be under very different circumstances. After two days of hard marching in the summer heat, of brushes with the enemy, sudden alarms and intense skirmishes – news of which had prompted Chelmsford to divide his command and march out from Isandlwana with part of it to reinforce the reconnaissance to which Harford belonged – Harford would return to find that the camp had been attacked in Chelmsford's absence, and over-run. Over 1,300 British and auxiliary troops had been killed in one of the worst defeats inflicted upon the British Army during the Victorian era. It was dark by the time Chelmsford – and Harford – returned to Isandlwana, and the bodies of the garrison lay among the looted and burning tents and ransacked wagons, mixed up with hundreds of dead Zulus and slaughtered animals. After a harrowing night spent among the freshly dead on the battlefield, Chelmsford returned across the border to the neighbouring British colony of Natal, from which he had started his invasion just twelve days before, to find that the border post at Rorke's Drift had been defended by a small garrison against a fierce Zulu attack throughout the night.

Henry Charles Harford had not taken a direct part in the two great defining battles of the Anglo-Zulu War – and indeed as a lieutenant, serving moreover with the African auxiliary forces, he was far too junior in rank to have exerted much influence upon them if he had –yet the power of his reminiscences lies in what he observed as they unfolded around him. A regular British officer in the 99th Regiment, he had nonetheless grown up in Natal and spoke a degree of isiZulu, the principle African language locally. Looking for a chance for adventure in a country he knew, Harford had volunteered as a 'special service' officer, and had found himself attached to the 3rd Regiment, Natal Native Contingent, as its adjutant. At such he had taken part in the crossing of the border into Zulu territory at Rorke's Drift on 11 January 1879, and had been in the thick of the skirmishing against the followers of the Zulu border chieftain Sihayo kaXongo the following day. In many ways a typical product of the British officer class – his father had been an army officer before him – he shared the prevailing attitudes of the day but his unusual background at the same time afforded him a unique insight into colonial Natal and the workings of the auxiliary units, whom most regular officers tended to look down upon. Then, with an odd symmetry, he found himself at the very end of the war witness to the arrival of the captured Zulu king, Cetshwayo kaMpande – the man the British had set out to depose – into the British camp. Harford had witnessed the very beginning of the war, it's most shocking and dramatic highlights – and its very end.

Harford's reminiscences were first published in 1978, in time for the centenary of the war, and since then they have become a much-loved part of its the mythology. His propensity for collecting rare insects – allegedly even when under fire – and his courage in action have made him a firm favourite among battlefield story-tellers, and he appeared briefly as a character in the 1979 feature film, *Zulu Dawn* (although oddly shorn of his real-life adventures). That original edition, edited by Daphne Child and published as *The Zulu War Journal of Colonel Henry Charles Harford, C.B.*, has long since been out of print, although his story was revisited and expanded by David and Emma Payne in *The Writings, Photographs and Sketches of Henry Charles Harford 1850–1937.*

Yet, as John Laband points out in this thoroughly annotated new edition, Harford's reminiscences were in need of a proper academic appraisal, in this case from the leading expert in the field. His writings were not, as the Child edition suggested, a true journal, written day-to-day as the events unfolded; in fact, they were clearly written much later, when lapses in memory had allowed him sometimes to confuse and conflate timelines, mistake names, and misidentify geographical features. This edition identifies and corrects those lapses, whilst at the same time removing nothing of Harford's fresh and original eyewitness accounts.

Harford lived to enjoy a long military career, to retire on a colonel's pension, and to die peacefully in England in 1937. One wonders if, as an old man, he nonetheless felt that his military career had been a disappointment, for as luck would have it he was never to see shots fired in anger again after 1879. No doubt that was why his adventures remained so fresh in his mind so long after the event, like that sunrise image of the doomed camp at Isandlwana; and his description of them has made this book one of the great first-hand stories of that extraordinary war.

Ian Knight
Chichester
May 2024

Abbreviations

AAG	Assistant Adjutant-General
ADC	aide-de-camp
AMS	Assistant Military Secretary
AQMG	Assistant Quartermaster-General
CB	Companion of the Order of the Bath
CMG	Companion of the Order of St Michael and St George
DA	Deputy Adjutant
DAA	Deputy Assistant Adjutant
DAAG	Deputy Assistant Adjutant-General
DAG	Deputy Adjutant-General
DAQMG	Deputy Assistant Quartermaster-General
DQMG	Deputy Quartermaster-General
GCB	Knight Grand Cross of the Order of the Bath
GOC	General Officer Commanding
HMS	Her Majesty's Ship
HQ	Headquarters
HRH	His or Her Royal Highness
KCB	Knight Commander of the Order of the Bath
KCMG	Knight Commander of the Order of St Michael and St George
KCSI	Knight Commander of the Order of the Star of India
MB	Bachelor of Medicine
NCO	non-commissioned officer
NMP	Natal Mounted Police

NNC	Natal Native Contingent
NNPC	Natal Native Pioneer Corps
psc	passed Staff College
QMG	Quartermaster-General
RA	Royal Artillery
RE	Royal Engineers
RN	Royal Navy
VC	Victoria Cross

Introduction

Shortly after the death of Colonel Henry Charles Harford in England in 1937, his daughter, Violet Eva Davie, presented the Local History Museum in Durban (now the Old Court House Museum, which is part of the Durban Local History Museums) with an undated manuscript written neatly in black ink in a notebook with ruled pages between soft covers decorated by the author. The notebook vividly described her father's experiences as a young officer while serving in the Anglo-Zulu War of 1879. Mrs Daphne Strutt, the curator of the museum, recognised the historical significance of the manuscript and invited Daphne Child to transcribe and lightly edit it, and it was duly published in 1978 by Shuter & Shooter of Pietermaritzburg as *The Zulu War Journal of Colonel Henry Harford, C.B.* Regrettably, despite diligent search, the original manuscript cannot be found among the museums' holdings, although a typescript does exist among other Harford papers in a box originally donated by Mrs Davie to the Natural Science Museum in Durban.[1] As a consequence, the text presented in this edition is that of Daphne Child's published transcription of Harford's holograph with the exception of her editorial interpolations, which have been deleted.

When W.R. Guest reviewed Child's book in *Natalia* in 1978, he was somewhat dismissive. The journal, he pronounced, 'cannot be

1 Email communication on 20 February 2024 from Rebecca Naidoo, museum officer, Durban Local History Museums.

described as a work of major historical importance, in that it does not offer any startling new information on the subject with which it is concerned ... It is an essentially personal narrative, at times anecdotal, rather than a dispassionate analysis of the Zululand invasion.'[2] Just so. Harford did not pretend to be writing a history of the Anglo-Zulu War. Rather, he was setting down his wonderfully compelling memories of his own experiences as a junior officer facing his first taste of action in the field, and witnessing searing scenes such as the devastated camp at Isandlwana after it had been overrun by the Zulu army, and the fort at Rorke's Drift on the morning after the battle. He was also party to memorable events such as the recovery of the bodies of Lieutenants Coghill and Melvill after Isandlwana and of the Queen's Colour of the 1/24th Regiment. For a few days at the end of the war he was the custodian of the captured King Cetshwayo. Yet, perhaps even more engaging than his descriptions of these memorable events are his more mundane recollections as an officer on campaign, his hectic preparations for going out to South Africa, the myriad discomforts of life under canvas, his vexed relations with Boer farmers while on garrison duty at Rorke's Drift, and encounters with Zulu notables while in pursuit of Cetshwayo.

There is an aspect of Harford's reminiscences that will be noted by every reader sensitive to what are now considered unacceptable racial attitudes. Harford had enjoyed a free and easy adolescence in the Colony of Natal, and he was relatively fluent in isiZulu. Yet, as his notebook reveals, his attitude towards the indigenous African population was contradictory. It veered between the instinctive racial stereotyping of the typical mid-Victorian officer with his contempt for 'barbarous' African customs, and a genuine personal appreciation of Zulu fighting qualities, of the buoyant spirits of the African troops he commanded, of King Cetshwayo, noble even

2 Guest, 'Review of *The Anglo-Zulu War Journal of Colonel Henry Harford*', p. 81.

in defeat, and, above all, of his faithful African servant, Jim, who accompanied him throughout the campaign.

It was Daphne Child who dubbed Harford's manuscript a journal, by which designation it has since been known. Yet it is not a journal as such, not a daily, dated record of events such as General Wolseley's *South African Journal* of 1879–80.[3] Harford did indeed have a small pocket diary for 1879 with him during the war, but its scanty entries were few and far between,[4] and the 'journal' could not have been based on it. Harford's manuscript is therefore what can best be described as a memoir, a history written from personal knowledge and remembered facts and incidents. If indeed, as seems the case, the Harford manuscript was written from memory, the question is: when was it committed to paper?

Daphne Child 'assumed' that Harford wrote his account '*during or just after* [italics in the original] the campaign of 1879, and that he copied the narrative into the note-book … many years later, possibly about 1920, making certain additions'. In proof of this, she adduced that 'the work is a young man's description of, and commentary on, events as they happened, and not an old man's reminiscences of things past.'[5]

To take the last point first, style is no conclusive indicator of an author's age. Take the almost embarrassingly sprightly and colloquial memoirs of George Hamilton-Browne, *A Lost Legionary in South Africa*. He had been Harford's companion-in-arms in the Natal Native Contingent and included several vivid and amusing anecdotes about him. Yet, for all the seeming youthfulness of Hamilton-Browne's authorial voice, his book was published in 1912, thirty-three years after the events it described.

3 Preston (ed.), *South African Journal of Sir Garnet Wolseley*.

4 Email communications on 14 and 15 January 2024 from Dr David Payne, FCA, who has scrutinised the diary.

5 Child (ed.), *Zulu War Journal*, unnumbered page: 'Note for Collectors of Africana'.

What evidence is there, then, for assigning a likely date to the notebook? Harford's fresh and sometimes ingenuous account of his experiences during the Zulu campaign is beguilingly compelling, yet a close reading of the text reveals many instances of faulty memory and muddled chronology that speak to a date of composition many years after the events described, probably in the late 1890s. True – as Daphne Child suggested – his details about the subsequent military careers of individuals mentioned in the text could have been added later as an afterthought. That could also explain why several military units and public institutions are assigned titles and names they would not hold until many years after 1879. But there are also numerous instances which speak to composition after incidents have grown dim with the passing of time. Some officers' names are misspelled, and other officers are placed in the wrong unit or given an incorrect rank. Several senior officers such as General Wolseley and Major-General Clifford are conjured up although they were definitely not present at the time. The names of natural features and places are sometimes incorrectly given. Tellingly, there are several instances where chronology is plainly wrong or confused. Perhaps Harford deliberately manipulated the timeframe for the sake of the story – or it could be put down to the failure of memory after a lapse of time. More concerning, there is at least one instance of an extended anecdote, such as that concerning Deputy Commissary-General Brownrigg, which has no basis in discernible fact and – in the exuberant style of Hamilton-Browne – seems to have been included in the interests of telling a good yarn. This alerts the editor to consider every incident Harford describes with a wary eye and, if possible, to seek verification.

It is for this reason that in this edition Harford's reminiscences are accompanied by detailed footnotes that are in constant dialogue with the text. They firmly locate his account in the historical context, amplify and explain the incidents he describes and flag the errors of fact that have crept into the narrative. It is only by thoroughly buttressing Harford's text in this manner that it can be read with confidence and appreciated for what it is: an eye-witness account of a military campaign recalled in tranquillity, one that can stand as an historical source in its own right.

A proper understanding of Harford's text also requires some knowledge of the man who wrote it, for it is framed in terms of his conventional worldview as a professional soldier of the Victorian era, albeit one whose adolescence in Natal had been out of the usual mould, and whose abiding enthusiasm as a naturalist appeared quirky to his fellow officers. Fortunately, we now know much more of Harford's life than was available to Daphne Child. In 2006 Harford's granddaughter, Audrey Violet, born just two years after his death, made his journals, diaries, sketches and photograph albums and other manuscripts in her possession available to Dr David Payne and his daughter Emma Payne. They transcribed and compiled this material, and with the editorial assistance of Dr Adrian Greaves, published it in 2008 in a sumptuous volume as *The Writings, Photographs and Sketches of Henry Charles Harford 1850–1937.* The following account of Harford's life is heavily indebted to this work.

Henry Charles Harford – always called 'Charlie' by his family – was born on 31 December 1850 at Bangalore in the dependent state of Mysore in British India, where his father, Charles Joseph Harford (1826–74) was serving as a captain with the 12th Lancers. The Harfords of Horton in Northamptonshire were landed gentry and Charlie's paternal grandfather, Henry Charles Harford (1798–1879) lived at Frenchay Lodge and Stapleton House nearby, both country houses within a few miles of Bristol. Charlie's mother, whom his father had married in 1850, was Rose Mathilda Scott, daughter of Lieutenant Robert Scott, RN, whose country house, Outlands, was about four miles out of Plymouth. Charlie was the eldest of their two sons and six daughters.

It was normal practice for the children of officers serving in India to be brought up and educated back in Britain. Accordingly, at the age of five Charlie was taken by his mother to his Scott grandparents at Outlands, along with his sisters Sissy (Florence), born in 1852, and Katherine, born in 1854. His mother returned to India in 1856 soon after the birth of Dozie (Ellen), and Charlie remained at Outlands with his three sisters until the age of thirteen.

Charlie had barely arrived at Outlands when he fell from a second-storey window and was impaled on the railings below. He then spent nearly two years mostly in bed recovering, and the muscles of his left leg became contracted, making it slightly shorter than the other. Charlie was left with an almost imperceptible limp and admitted the whole left side of his body was thereafter 'undoubtedly weaker' than the right.[6] Nevertheless, he was evidently a plucky boy, undeterred by this disability. Nor did it affect his future military career. Once sufficiently recovered, he attended Stoke Grammar School in Plymouth as a day boarder, and took full advantage of what Outlands had to offer. He later wrote:

> Love of all things natural and everything pertaining to nature and outdoor life being innate in me, my bringing up at Outlands gave me every facility for indulging in pursuits which have stood me well in after life, saved me from falling into luxurious and idle ways and enabled me to take an interest in my surroundings wherever fortune or fate may have placed me.[7]

Charlie and his sisters always spent half their holidays at Frenchay Lodge with their Harford grandparents. He gratefully remembered his paternal grandfather as 'a thorough sportsman and a splendid shot' who 'inculcated in me the methods of sportsmanship which have stood me in such good stead all my life'.[8]

6 Payne et al., *Harford*, p. 6.
7 Payne et al., *Harford*, p. 7.
8 Payne et al., *Harford*, p. 11.

Thanks to his upbringing at Outlands and Frenchay Lodge, as a young teenager Charlie was already a good shot with a dedicated love of the outdoors. But he would not stay in England much longer. His father had decided to sell out of the service and settle in the Colony of Natal to farm. With that intention, in 1861 he exchanged out of the 12th Lancers into the 85th Regiment because it was stationed in Natal. By 1863 Captain Harford had completed his arrangements, and the whole family set out on the sailing vessel *Lady of the Lake* from Dover to Durban, a journey that took 109 days. Harford later recorded his 'indescribable feeling of pleasure' in the possibilities of 'wild life and sport which then as now appealed to me above everything' that awaited him in his new home.[9] This was a 300-acre farm which his father purchased near Pinetown in the hills twelve miles to the north-west of Durban, where he farmed coffee and tobacco and built a house called Stapleton Grove after the Harford house near Bristol. With his social status and connections, Captain Harford moved in the highest circles of colonial society. He represented Durban County in the Natal Legislative Council from 1867 to 1872, was a justice of the peace for Durban County and a member of the Chamber of Agriculture for Natal. In 1854 Natal settlers had been given the authority to raise their own volunteer military units for service within the colony, and on account of his military experience, Captain Harford raised and was Captain Commandant of the Pinetown and New Germany Volunteers. For several years during his late teens Charlie served as a private in his father's volunteer regiment and gained his first military experience during its camps which were held quarterly to practise drill.

As Charlie had hoped, the wild and unspoiled countryside around Stapleton Grove, and up the north coast of Natal, where he spent his holidays on the farms of his father's friends or with the British garrison at Fort Williamson at the mouth of the Thukela

9 Payne et al., *Harford*, p. 19.

River, gave him every opportunity to ride, shoot and camp out. This life of outdoor adventuring made him tough and self-reliant. It also gave him the opportunity to acquire a reasonable fluency in isiZulu, the language spoken by the Africans of Natal and the neighbouring Zulu kingdom, an attribute which would stand him in good stead when he served during the Anglo-Zulu War.

Charlie's lifestyle as teenager in Natal also allowed him to give full rein to his lifelong interest in zoology and entomology which had begun on his grandparents' estates in England, and he assiduously collected specimens of birds, butterflies and moths and made drawings of them. In 1869 Mrs Colenso, the wife of the Bishop of Natal, wrote of him to a friend that her sons Robert and Frank had 'just a few friends amongst the selectest [sic] of the young military, and one youth who had a passion for natural history, son of a Captain Harford, who lives in the country. Excursions to the mountain for the sake of collecting birds and insects seemed latterly the great object of life.'[10] Charlie would never lose his 'beetle-mania' and throughout his life he was never without his butterfly net, always adding to his knowledge as a naturalist wherever his regiment was stationed around the world, be it the United Kingdom, Natal, Bermuda or India, or subsequently in retirement in Malta and Switzerland. He meticulously assembled collections of his specimens and donated them to natural history museums in Britain and Natal.

Charlie could not run wild as a colonial boy forever, and as he approached his twentieth year his family decided that his must follow in his father's footsteps and adopt the army as his career. On 17 August 1869 Grandfather Harford approached the Horse Guards to have Charlie placed on the list of candidates for the purchase of a direct commission. Most generously, he undertook to pay the

10 Frances Bunyon Colenso to Mrs Lyell, 17 July 1869, in Rees (ed.), *Colenso Letters*, p. 202.

purchase price of £450 (purchasing power today of about £69,300). The Horse Guards supported the application conditional on Charlie passing the army examination, which he duly did in June 1870. Charlie was gazetted Ensign in the 99th Regiment on 8 November 1870,[11] and sailed from Natal early in 1871 to join his regiment at Parkhurst on the Isle of Wight. His way into the regiment was smoothed by letters of introduction to his brother officers by Captain H. Townsend, formerly of the 99th, who was a close friend and associate of his father in Natal. No officer could afford his regimental expenses and mess bills on his pay alone, and Grandfather Harford settled an allowance of £100 a year (purchasing power today of about £15,400) on the fortunate Charlie.

Harford (Charlie's adult dignity as a military officer requires that henceforth he should be referred to by his surname) took well to soldiering and was gazetted Lieutenant on 28 October 1871. In 1872 the 99th Regiment was stationed at Aldershot in Hampshire, and then from 1873 to 1874 at Shorncliffe in Kent on the Channel coast. While there, Charlie attended a course of musketry at Hythe School of Musketry and on 4 July 1873 was awarded a First Class Certificate in the Theory and Practice of Musketry. He also secured the extra certificate for those officers who hoped for regimental and other staff appointment. At the Garrison Class at Shorncliffe, he passed the C & D examination, which established his eligibility for promotion to captain, although in practice promotion continued to be based on seniority within the regiment and the opening of a vacancy.

From Shorncliffe the regiment was posted in 1874 to Fort George at Moray Firth in the north of Scotland. Charlie was delighted because he 'longed to get to a place where there was some

11 In 1874 the 99th (Lanarkshire) Regiment of Foot received the new style of the 99th (Duke of Edinburgh's) Regiment of Foot and was permitted to bear on its Regimental Colour HRH's coronet and cypher.

shooting, and away from towns and crowds'.[12] From Scotland the regiment was next stationed in Ireland, first at the Curragh (1875–7) in County Kildare, and then at Templemore (1877–8) in County Tipperary. In 1878 the regiment returned to England and was stationed at Chatham in Kent, where on 2 February 1878 Charlie was appointed Adjutant.

With the prospect of war in Zululand, Harford, who was anxious to prove himself on active service and was keen to revisit the scenes of his boyhood, resigned his adjutancy and in November 1878 proceeded on Transport Service to Durban, where he arrived on 2 December 1878. On account of Harford's fluency in isiZulu, Lieutenant-General Lord Chelmsford immediately appointed him Adjutant to the 3rd Regiment, Natal Native Contingent. In that capacity Harford took part in the advance of No. 3 Column, Natal Field Force, into Zululand on 11 January 1879, and on 12 January fought in the sharp skirmish at kwaSogekle. He was with the reconnaissance-in-force Chelmsford despatched south-east out of his camp at Isandlwana on 21 January, and the following day took an active part in the skirmish on the Phindo heights. This action was the last time in his entire military career that Harford would be under fire.

While part of No. 3 Column was involved in skirmishing in the region where Harford was engaged, the main Zulu army fell on the camp at Isandlwana and obliterated the garrison. The Zulu reserve then went on to unsuccessfully attack the British depot at Rorke's Drift. Harford was with the troops Chelmsford marched back to the stricken Isandlwana camp, and he spent the night bivouacked among the dead. The following day he was with the force that relieved the garrison at Rorke's Drift.

On 24 January the demoralized 3rd Natal Native Contingent was disbanded, and Harford, along with its other white officers

12 Payne et al., *Harford*, p. 82.

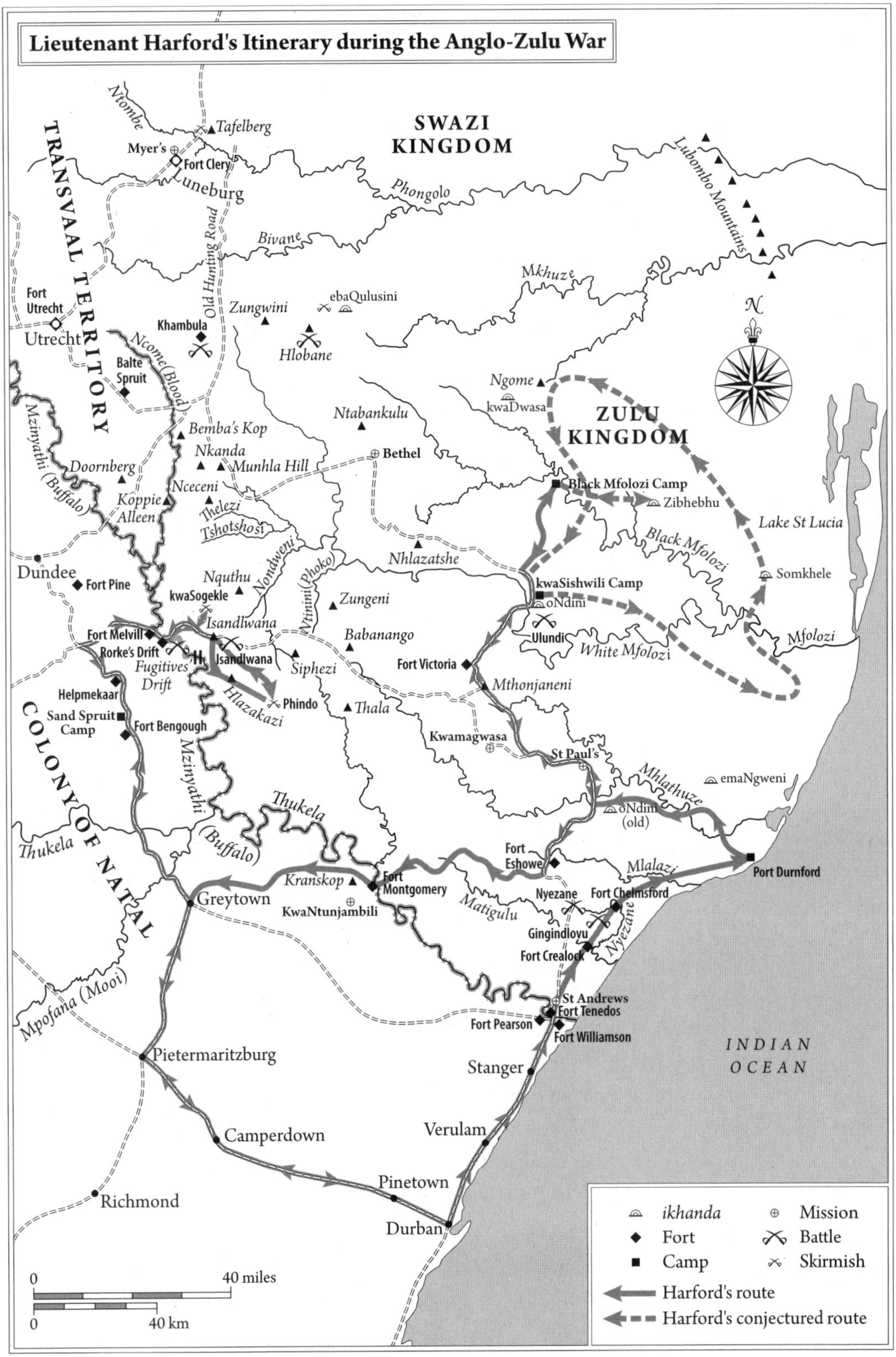
Lieutenant Harford's Itinerary during the Anglo-Zulu War
SWAZI KINGDOM
ZULU KINGDOM
TRANSVAAL TERRITORY
COLONY OF NATAL
INDIAN OCEAN
Ntombe
Tafelberg
Myer's
Fort Clery
Luneburg
Phongolo
Bivane
Old Hunting Road
Lubombo Mountains
Mkhuze
ebaQulusini
Zungwini
Fort Utrecht
Utrecht
Khambula
Hlobane
Ncome (Blood)
Balte Spruit
Ngome
kwaDwasa
Mzinyathi (Buffalo)
Bemba's Kop
Ntabankulu
Nkanda
Munhla Hill
Bethel
Doornberg
Nceceni
Black Mfolozi Camp
Zibhebhu
Koppie Alleen
Thelezi
Tshotshosi
Lake St Lucia
Black Mfolozi
Nhlazatshe
Dundee
Fort Pine
Nquthu
Nondweni
Ntinini (Phoko)
kwaSishwili Camp
Somkhele
kwaSogekle
Zungeni
oNdini
Isandlwana
Ulundi
Mfolozi
Fort Melvill
Rorke's Drift
Babanango
White Mfolozi
Fugitives' Drift
Siphezi
Fort Victoria
Helpmekaar
Mthonjaneni
Hlazakazi
Phindo
Sand Spruit Camp
Fort Bengough
Thala
Kwamagwasa
St Paul's
Mhlathuze
emaNgweni
Thukela
oNdini (old)
Mzinyathi
(Buffalo)
Fort Eshowe
Mlalazi
Port Durnford
Kranskop
Fort Montgomery
Greytown
Nyezane
Fort Chelmsford
KwaNtunjambili
Matigulu
Gingindlovu
Fort Crealock
Mpofana (Mooi)
St Andrews
Fort Tenedos
Fort Pearson
Fort Williamson
Pietermaritzburg
Stanger
Verulam
Camperdown
Pinetown
Richmond
Durban
0
40 miles
0
40 km
ikhanda
Mission
Fort
Battle
Camp
Skirmish
Harford's route
Harford's conjectured route

and NCOs, remained at Rorke's Drift as part of the garrison stationed there to patrol the border. On 3 February Harford was with the patrol that discovered the bodies of Lieutenants Coghill and Melvill, who had been killed on the Natal bank of the Mzinyathi River while escaping from Isandlwana. The following day, Harford was on the patrol that retrieved from the river the Queen's Colour of the 1st Battalion, 24th Regiment, which Melvill had attempted to save.

On 18 April 1879 Harford left Rorke's Drift to join the garrison at Helpmekaar. It was there, in late May or early June (the precise date is unrecorded) that he was summoned to resume the adjutancy of the 99th Regiment, which had been sent to Natal in January 1879 and had taken part in the operations of No. 1 Column, Natal Field Force. The regiment was now encamped at the lower Thukela as part of the 1st Division, South African Force, and Harford took part in its laboured advance up the Zululand coast towards Port Durnford. Following the decisive Zulu defeat at Ulundi on 4 July, on 23 July the 1st Division was broken up and the 99th Regiment returned to Natal. But Harford joined Lieutenant-Colonel Clarke's Column engaged in pacification operations as Staff Officer. Between 17 and 24 August he took part in an extensive patrol in fruitless pursuit of the fugitive King Cetshwayo. Harford was in Clark's camp on the Black Mfolozi when, on 30 August, the captured king was finally brought in, and he was put in charge of the prisoner until the next day, when Cetshwayo was sent on his way to exile in Cape Town. On 2 September Clarke's Column began its march back to Natal. It was broken up on 7 October, and Harford rejoined the 99th Regiment in Pinetown, close to his boyhood home. His family were no longer there; in 1872 his father had left Stapleton Grove to try his luck at the Diamond Fields and had died in Kimberley in 1874, and his mother and siblings had returned to England.

After the Anglo-Zulu War, Harford would never again be on campaign, and henceforth it would all be peacetime soldiering and promotion through seniority. The 99th Regiment was stationed in Bermuda from January 1880 until June 1881. While there, Harford was gazetted Captain on 30 March 1881. On 1 July 1881 the regiment was redesignated the 2nd Battalion, The Duke of Edinburgh's (Wiltshire Regiment) and was stationed in Cape Town, where it remained until 1882. Thereafter, Harford was with his regiment at various stations in India until 1894: Rawalpindi, Nowshera, Peshawar, Sabathu, Lahore, Jhansi and Kasauli (all in what is now Pakistan or northern India), and was gazetted Major on 7 January 1886. India gave him every opportunity to go shooting and collecting specimens. Inevitably, he succumbed to disease: he was on seven months' sick leave for dysentery in 1892, and once more from November 1894 to January 1896 with 'remittent fever', or malaria.

Fortunately for Harford's health, the 2nd Battalion, Wiltshire Regiment ended its tour of foreign service later in 1896. It left India for Portsmouth before being stationed in Guernsey in 1898. While there, on 7 January 1898 Harford was gazetted Lieutenant-Colonel and succeeded through seniority to the command of the 2nd Battalion.

While officers were discouraged from marrying young, a colonel was expected to have a wife at his side. Accordingly, on 4 March 1898 Harford married Florence Pearson Page, the daughter of Dr W. Page, MD, of the prestigious Indian Civil Service. Born on 18 June 1875, Florence was nearly half Harford's age, but such a discrepancy in age was not at all unusual in the service. Their daughter, Violet Eva, known as 'Sweetie', was born on 15 February 1899.

With a growing family to support and with the financial drain of the open hospitality expected of a colonel, Harford found it increasingly difficult without sufficient private means to meet the expenses of Home Service. At the end of 1899 he arranged an exchange with the commander of the 1st Battalion, Wiltshire Regiment in India, who wanted a home command. However, as Harford later admitted, he made 'a very false step' by organising the exchange because within six months the 2nd Battalion was ordered out to fight in the Second Anglo-Boer War, and he lost his only chance to command in a field campaign. 'This was crushing bad luck,' he wrote, 'but it was the Will of Fate.'[13]

More ill-fortune attended Harford when he was stationed at Quetta (now in Pakistan) in command of the 1st Battalion; his new wife of only twenty months succumbed to enteric fever on 12 November 1900. He was left with the nine-month-old Sweetie to bring up alone, for he never remarried.

Harford's tenure in command of the 1st Battalion expired at Peshawar on 8 January 1902. He was gazetted Colonel the previous day and sent home to Britain on half pay. Fortunately for him, on 15 December 1902 he was appointed in command of the 62nd Regimental District at Devizes. This command expired in turn on the last day of 1905 and on New Year's Day 1906 he was appointed to Pontefract as the Colonel in Charge of Records for the Yorkshire Grouped Regimental Districts.

Harford held the South Africa Medal with the date bar for 1879: Zulu campaign, as well as the Duke of Edinburgh's Silver Wedding Commemorative Medal, awarded to him in August 1899 as the Lieutenant-Colonel commanding the 2nd Battalion, Wiltshire Regiment. Then, to his evident surprise, on 15 July 1907 he was invested at Buckingham Palace by King Edward VII as a Companion of the Most Honourable Order of the Bath (Military) – the lowest of the three levels of the order. Charlie did not feel particularly honoured, especially since he believed that, having been mentioned three times in despatches during the Anglo-Zulu War, he ought to have received some honour much sooner. He wrote miffily:

> I was never informed of the services for which the decoration was granted … I take it that on the eve of my retirement and on

13 Payne et al., *Harford*, p. 263.

> looking up my services the authorities came to the conclusion, that I ought to be given something and that the CB would fit the case – however coming so late in the day, the decoration is absolutely worthless.[14]

Harford's command at Pontefract expired on 15 December 1907. Having reached the compulsory age limit, on 31 December 1907 he retired from the army and (as he expressed it) 'through God's grace and merciful providence I was awarded a full Colonel's pension of £500 a year [purchasing power today of about £74,000].'[15] That was just as well, for Harford would live another thirty years in retirement, first in Sliema in Malta, and then from 1911 to 1922 at no. 1 Villa Blanche, Chailly, Lausanne in Switzerland, where Sweetie attended Viney Public School. She married Emile Henry Davie, an illustrator of children's books, on 29 July 1936 and they settled at Wanstead, Crawley Down, Sussex. Charlie died there on 25 March 1937. He never knew his granddaughter Audrey Violet who was born on 10 October 1939.

Harford's notebook contained invaluable pencil sketches executed while he was on active service in the Anglo-Zulu War. Since the Durban Local History Museums have been unable to locate the notebook, they are not reproduced in this edition. Poor-quality reproductions of the sketches can be found in Daphne Child's publication of 1978. However, the Durban Local History Museums do hold a slim, A5 hardcover brown and black leather notebook that contains pencil sketches and watercolours by Harford that were executed while he was stationed in Ireland in 1875–8, and was on his way by sea to Natal in 1878. David Payne, Emma Payne and Adrian Greaves have more than generously put all the myriad illustrations in their book on Harford at my disposal, and many appear in this book.

14 Payne et al., *Harford*, p. 294.
15 Payne et al., *Harford*, p. 293.

Harford's Memoir of the Anglo-Zulu War

NOTE: The correct spelling of names misspelled by Harford, and the correct military units when he has mistaken them, are in square brackets in italics when they first appear. Other editorial insertions (missing names etc.) are in square brackets in roman.

Names to be found in the Biographical Notes are marked with an asterisk (*) the first time they appear in the text. If the name appears first in the footnotes before it does in the text, it is also marked with an asterisk.

CHAPTER 1

Preparations for War

In 1878 we, i.e. the 99th (Duke of Edinburgh's) Regiment[1] were stationed at Chatham whither we had arrived from Templemore, Ireland, in 1877.[2] I had been Adjutant for just a year,[3] when disturbances broke out in Zululand which ended in declaration of war against Cetewayo *[Cetshwayo]** and the Zulu nation.[4] Officers

1 For the full titles of regiments, see List of Cavalry and Infantry Regiments.

2 The 99th Regiment had been quartered at the extensive Richmond Barracks (now McCan Barracks) in Templemore, County Tipperary, Ireland, before being redeployed to one of the several army barracks at Chatham in Kent, England, which had been built to house the soldiers manning the forts protecting the dockyards.

3 Regimental adjutant is a staff appointment given to an officer to assist his commanding officer with administrative duties. Harford's appointment as Adjutant of the 99th Regiment was dated 2 February 1878.

4 In the late 1870s the Earl of Beaconsfield's Tory government in Britain began pursuing a policy of confederation in South Africa. In the interests of imperial strategy, financial savings and economic opportunity, it planned to bring all the British colonies and Boer republics in the region under British rule. At the same time, it sought to neutralise the remaining independent and militarily powerful black states that were perceived as a potential threat to the confederation process. Sir Bartle Frere, appointed in March 1877 Governor of the Cape and High Commissioner for South Africa, saw the Zulu kingdom as the greatest danger. During 1878 he seized on several minor border incidents as an excuse to force a war which he erroneously believed would lead to a rapid military victory and the elimination the Zulu 'menace'.

for special service,[5] as well as troops, were being despatched from Home; and as I had spent the most of my youth, seven years, in Natal and had a very fair knowledge of the Kaffir language,[6] it occurred to me that I should stand a very good chance of getting out if I put in an application. It was an opportunity not to be lost, and although I felt some qualms of conscience in deserting the Regiment after having been so recently appointed Adjutant, I saw the Colonel [Welman]* and asked him if he would have any objection to my sending in an application. At the same time I gave him the name of an officer who was willing to act for me, should my application succeed.

Nothing could have been kinder than the manner in which the Colonel acceded to my request, and after discussing the matter with me at some length, and entering into the problem of my future prospects, being of opinion that I would be certain to get a Staff billet after the War, he advised me to resign the Adjutancy. This I did,[7] and my application for special service was forwarded, with very strong recommendations. Lieutenant Davison,* the officer whose name I had submitted to act for me, was eventually appointed Adjutant.

Time having been given for my application to reach the War Office, I got a day's leave to run up to London and see the Adjutant-

5 An officer anxious for military experience in the field, and for the promotion it might bring, could apply to the War Office for temporary leave from his regiment in order to be attached on Special Service to some other unit on campaign.

6 Harford means isiZulu, the language spoken by Africans in the Colony of Natal and the Zulu kingdom. At the time, white settlers in South Africa and British officials habitually designated Africans as 'Kaffirs', but colonists living in Natal specifically applied the term to Africans living under colonial rule to distinguish them from the Africans in the independent Zulu kingdom, whom they usually (but not always) called 'Zulus'. The term 'Kaffir' is today considered highly pejorative.

7 Harford officially ceased to be Adjutant of the 99th Regiment on 29 November 1878.

General, Sir Martin Dillon,* personally. Arriving at the War Office at 9 a.m., I was the only solitary individual in the waiting-room till 10 o'clock, when I saw the Adjutant-General go into his office. A few minutes later, I gave the porter my card to hand in as soon as the Adjutant-General was disengaged, but unfortunately did not give him a tip as I ought to have done. Officers of all grades, from Generals to subalterns, belonging to all arms of the Service, now began to pour in, and by 11 o'clock the waiting-room was simply crammed. There was scarcely standing room.

Presently the Adjutant-General began to receive the callers, and instead of my being ushered in as I had fondly hoped, having been the first to arrive, some of the senior officers were called upon. Possibly, of course, they might have attended by appointment. However, shortly before twelve noon Sir Garnet Wolseley* arrived,[8] followed by the Duke of Connaught,[9] and until they had taken their departure no further interviews could take place. One o'clock, two o'clock struck, and still there was no sign of their moving, so a good many of those who were waiting, went off. It was not until four o'clock that the Adjutant-General again became available for interviews.

At six o'clock I again found myself the solitary occupant of the waiting-room, so I walked out into the passage, and seeing the porter sitting outside the Adjutant-General's room, said to him, in a fairly loud tone of voice, "Did you present my card to the Adjutant-General this morning? I gave it to you at nine o'clock, and asked you to give it in as soon as he was disengaged; and here I have been

---

8 Harford has mistaken Lieutenant-General Sir Garnet Wolseley for another senior officer, or his memory was playing him false, for between 12 July 1878 and 12 May 1879 Wolseley was High Commissioner and Governor-General of Cyprus, and was not in Britain in November 1878.

9 HRH Prince Arthur, the first Duke of Connaught and Strathearn (1850–1942), was the third son of Queen Victoria. He pursued a military career and in 1878 he held the rank of Colonel and was an ADC to the Queen.

waiting ever since." The man then went into the Adjutant-General's room, and I was ushered in at once.

That my conversation with the porter had been overheard was very certain, for Sir Martin Dillon at once said, "I'm so sorry to think that you should have been kept waiting so long", and then added, "Now what can I do for you ?" After I had explained my reason for coming, he said, "Sit down at my table, and I will dictate a letter for you." This letter was, of course, to himself, which he there and then countersigned, passed in through a little window to an official in the next room, and gave orders for it to be attended to at once. He then questioned me about Natal, and asked me when I would be prepared to start. "Tomorrow morning, Sir", I said, "I'm going back to Chatham tonight." "Very well", he said, "The day after tomorrow, you will get your orders", and bade me "Good night." So, after all, my long wait had been a blessing in disguise; and I left the War Office in a true state of delight at my luck.

Having received my orders, as promised by the Adjutant-General, which gave me three days' grace before sailing, I went up to London to do my shopping, going straight to Messrs Silver & Co., 67 Cornhill, where I got everything I required, except boots.[10] While making my purchases I noticed a gentleman following me up very closely, and presently he asked me if I was going to South Africa, as I seemed to be selecting the very things suitable for a campaign. He said that he also was going out, and as he was at a loss to know what was best to take, would I allow him to accompany me and make similar purchases? So I gave him my list of things, to copy. He (Lieutenant Courtnay *[Courtenay]** of the 21st *[20th]* Hussars) and I subsequently went out together in the *Edinburgh Castle*.[11]

10 S.W. Silver & Co., Army, Navy and Colonial Agency in London, specialised in clothing and equipment for emigrants to Australia and New Zealand.

11 The SS *Edinburgh Castle* was a steamship of the Castle Line established in 1876 by Sir Donal Currie in competition with the older Union Line that

After Silver's I went to Dean's, in the Strand, for a couple of pairs of porpoise-hide boots, the most essential of all my purchases. Only one of all his ready-made pairs fitted me; and, of course, there was no time to have another pair made. While looking round the shop, however, I saw a pair cut quite differently from any other, stowed away in a corner by themselves. So I said, "Mr Dean, what are these?" "Oh", he said, "They have been made specially to order by a gentleman going out to shoot in Algeria; the front parts have been lengthened so as to form a knee-cap, to avoid the knees being pricked in going through gorse, etc." "Well", I said, "If they fit me, would you let me have them?" I was given them to try on, and they fitted me like a glove. So I got my two pairs, and departed. Of this particular pair of boots I shall later on have an interesting story to relate.

Neville *[Nevile]*,* one of our fellows, met me and we lunched together, after which I took the first train to Bristol, to say "Goodbye" to my grandfather and grandmother at Stapleton,[12] returning to Chatham early the next day. The dear old gentleman gave me £100 as he lay in his bed,[13] and I took my last farewell of

---

carried passengers and mail between the United Kingdom and the Cape. The two lines amalgamated in 1900 as the Union–Castle Line.

12 Henry Charles Harford Snr (1798–1879) of Frenchay Lodge three miles out of Bristol, was in 1878 living nearby at Stapleton House with his second wife, Charlotte Jones, whom he had married in 1869. He was a dedicated sportsman and splendid shot, and had taught the young Harford how to shoot.

13 Purchasing power today (reckoned at £1 in 1879 being the equivalent of £154 in 2024) of about £15,400. This was generous, because – as mentioned in the Introduction above – when on 8 November 1870 Harford had been gazetted Ensign in the 99th Regiment, his grandfather Harford had already settled an allowance of £100 a year on him to augment his officer's pay. On top of that, he had paid £450 (purchasing power today of about £69,300) for his grandson's direct commission. Soon thereafter, with effect from 1 November 1871, the purchase of commissions in the cavalry and infantry was abolished by Royal Warrant.

him at an early hour in the morning. It was our last meeting, for he passed away some few months later, at a ripe old age.[14]

On the day fixed for sailing, I railed with all my goods and chattels from Chatham to Victoria Station from whence I made out from the time-tables I should get an early train to Dartmouth, where the *Edinburgh Castle* was lying and due to sail at 4 p.m. Arriving full early at the station, I had the baggage weighed and labelled and placed in a heap on the platform convenient for loading up in the van when the train came in. After strolling up and down for about an hour, a porter appeared, and having had a look at the baggage said, "Is this your baggage, Sir?" I said, "Yes". "I see it's labelled for Dartmouth", he said, "You will never get to Dartmouth from here; you ought to have gone to Paddington!"[15] "Good Heavens!" I said, "What on earth is to be done; I must get to Dartmouth by four o'clock today." Then taking out his watch, he said, "There's a direct train leaving Paddington in a quarter of an hour. You may catch it if you look sharp." Whereupon I said, "I'll give you a halfsovereign[16] and pay double fare for a cart, if you can manage it for me."

In an instant, he hailed a drayman with a two-horsed van in the station-yard, who he informed me was a pal of his; and between the two of them my traps were soon in the van. Whilst loading up, the driver was informed that he would get double fare and that "This gentleman must catch the Dartmouth train leaving Paddington in a quarter of an hour's time!" The porter got his halfsovereign, and I jumped into an hansom cab, following the van. No fire-engine could have gone a better pace than we did, we simply flew through

14 Grandfather Harford died at the age of 81.

15 Both railway stations are in central London, Paddington a little over two miles to the north-west of Victoria. Paddington was the terminus of the Great Western Railway which served Dartmouth.

16 Gold coin worth 10 shillings, or half a pound sterling. Purchasing power today of about £77.

the streets, which, luckily, were pretty empty. At Paddington, happily, there were plenty of porters, and my things, having been already labelled, were soon whipped off. Having paid the driver, I tore off to the ticket-office, and eventually jumped into the train just as it was moving off, the last of my packages being shovelled in while the train was on the move. It was a narrow squeak. As I journeyed along I felt deeply grateful to Providence for coming to my rescue, through the agency of a porter.

On arriving at Dartmouth, I found that the time for sailing had been postponed to midnight; and that a special late train was being run from Paddington for the convenience of passengers to meet this change; so that, really, I need not have hurried as I did. Nevertheless, I had done the right thing, as my baggage was stowed away on board by daylight, and I comfortably settled down in my cabin, whereas the latecomers were wandering about half the night, looking after their belongings.

In the morning I found that Smith-Dorrien, who was in after years to become such a distinguished soldier,[17] was my cabin companion; and I often call to mind his first remark to me, as we met on deck, "I don't know whether I ought to touch my cap to you, or you to me." Anyhow, he was an excellent fellow, and we formed a lasting friendship.

The other officers on board were Cochrane,* of the 32nd Regiment, whom I had known in Natal; Courtnay, of the 21st Hussars,

17 Lieutenant Horace Lockwood Smith-Dorrien (1858–1930), 95th Regiment, was on Special Service in 1878–9. He served initially with the Army Service Corps as a transport officer attached to No. 3 Column. He was present at Isandlwana but escaped to Helpmekaar. Subsequently, he was employed on the lines of communication at Ladysmith, Helpmekaar and Dundee. In May 1879 he took part in the advance of the 2nd Division, and was in the laager at the White Mfolozi during the battle of Ulundi. He went on to serve in Egypt, India, the Sudan, and the First World War, besides holding senior home commands, and died a full general. He was notorious for his foul temper.

my casual shopping acquaintance; Bailey and Mitchell *[Michel]*, of the 57th Regiment;[18] Williams,* of the 27th *[58th]* Regiment, all Lieutenants, and Captain Sprate *[Spratt]*, of the 14th Regiment.[19] Needless to say, we soon got to know each other, and spent most of our time in endeavouring to learn signalling. Of course there were many civilian passengers on board, and altogether we had a very pleasant time. The Captain was one of the very best, and was a great favourite with everyone. Cochrane was simply the life and soul of the ship, always ready to sit down at the piano and sing a good song, or get up concerts, theatricals and other amusements. Scarcely a day went by without something going on under his direction. For the concerts and theatricals a small charge was made, and at the end of the voyage I think it was a little over £60 that was handed to the Captain for charitable purposes.[20]

We touched at no Ports till reaching Cape Town, but had a sight of the Canary Islands, Madeira and Ascension. When off Cape Verde, about 150 miles out at sea, I caught a number of little butterflies, "Blues" of the family Lycaenidae,[21] and a few

---

18 No such officer as Bailey of the 57th Regiment is listed as serving in the Anglo-Zulu War. Probably, Harford meant either Second Lieutenant Louis William Bodé or Lieutenant Ernest Vernon Bellers, both of whom served with the 57th Regiment in the Eshowe Relief Column, were present at Gingindlovu and subsequently served with the 1st Division and Clarke's Column. Lieutenant Cecil Boucher Duff Michel (not Mitchell), 57th Regiment, was on Special Service in 1878–9. He was first attached to the overstretched Commissariat and Transport Department, and afterwards served in the Remount Establishment in the Cape.

19 No officer of the name of Captain Sprate of the 14th Regiment appears in the list of officers employed on Special Service in 1879. Probably, Harford means Captain Edward James Henry Spratt, 29th Regiment, who proceeded on Transport Service to South Africa in November 1878, and in 1879 served on the lines of communication and at the base.

20 Purchasing power today of about £9,240.

21 *Lycaenidae* is the second-largest family of butterflies, with over 6,000 species worldwide. The family comprises seven subfamilies, including the blues (*Polyommatinae*).

wasps. The former simply swarmed at the stern of the vessel, fascinated, apparently, by the churning up of the water by the propeller. It was a lovely day, and very calm. Notwithstanding the great distance that they had flown out from the shore their flight was still very strong, and they preferred to keep on the wing to settling anywhere on the vessel. Whither their instinct was leading them, it is impossible to say; but I am afraid they were doomed eventually to perish in the ocean.[22]

At Cape Town, everyone on board, I think, took a run ashore.[23] Sissy was then living at Kalk Bay, a watering-place between Cape Town and Simonstown *[Simon's Town]*, so I went down to see her; and a more wretched, bare, bleak and uncomfortable-looking place than she was in, it would be almost impossible to find.[24] I then went back to Cape Town to call on Sir Charles Mills* and had a long talk with him. The Major [Erskine]* was still away somewhere

22 While growing up on his father's farm, Stapleton Grove, near Pinetown in Natal, Harford early on became enthusiastic about natural history and began seriously to collect birds and insects, especially beetles. He was encouraged in making his collections by the reclusive, elderly German naturalist, William Gueinzius, who lived nearby in New Germany in a ramshackle house.

23 Cape Town, in 1879 the biggest city in southern Africa, was founded in 1652 as a way station for the ships of the Dutch East India Company, the first colonial settlement in southern Africa. It was the administrative centre while the Cape of Good Hope was under the rule of the Dutch East India Company, and when in 1814 the Cape was ceded to Britain it became the capital of the British colony. During the nineteenth century it remained a strategically vital coaling station for the Royal Navy, with its dockyards in False Bay, and was protected by a permanent British garrison.

24 Emma Florence Mary ('Sissy'), born in Bangalore, Mysore, India in 1852, was Harford's eldest sister. She was the second wife of Major the Hon. David Erskine*; the couple had married on 26 September 1870 in Pietermaritzburg, Natal. Kalk Bay and Simon's Town (the naval station) are on the eastern side of the Cape Peninsular on the shores of False Bay, about 25 miles south-east of Cape Town.

in the Transvaal,[25] getting rid of the £2500 entrusted to him by Mr. Cleland[26] for the purpose of ostrich-farming.[27] Sir Charles Mills pointed out to me the necessity for both the Major and Sissy returning to England as soon as possible, especially as Sissy had been very ill. It was only a matter of finding the money to pay their passages. He said that he would be perfectly willing to pay for the Major, if I would pay for Sissy. So, as Grandfather had given me £100,[28] I handed over £60 for her passage,[29] thankful to think that I was able to do it.

On our way up the Coast, we stopped at Port Elizabeth only to land one or two passengers.[30] While hanging about outside the harbour, another steamer from England passed, conveying a number of Staff College officers to Natal for special services.[31] We at once dubbed them *aasvogels*[32] as we were afraid that, on reaching Natal before us, they would be selected for the best appointments; and as the vessel was close enough for visual signalling, we tried our

---

25 The Transvaal Territory, formerly the South African Republic, had been annexed by Britain on 12 April 1877. Since it was now a British possession, speculators and British settlers saw it as an economic opportunity for trade and farming. The Witwatersrand gold-bearing reef would not be discovered until 1886.

26 Untraced.

27 Purchasing power today of about £385,000.

28 Purchasing power today of about £15,400.

29 Purchasing power today of about £9,240.

30 Port Elizabeth, a seaport lying on Algoa Bay 360 nautical miles east of Cape Town, was founded in 1820 by the Governor of the Cape, Sir Rufane Donkin, who named it after his wife, who had died in India. In 2021 the city was renamed Gqeberha.

31 These officers had been admitted by competitive examination to the Staff College at Camberley, founded in 1858, and there they received advanced instruction preparing them for senior staff appointments. They were resented by less intellectual officers such as Harford, who were focused on a conventional regimental career.

32 Vultures.

skill with the flags. But nobody took the trouble to communicate with us in return.

On arrival at Durban after a most delightful voyage,[33] we at once scattered. Some of the fellows went straight off to Maritzburg *[Pietermaritzburg]*;[34] others remained for a day or two in Durban, to look after their baggage and to obtain their orders from the G.O.C.[35] Knowing the ins and outs of the place well myself, I took young Williams, a nice youngster afterwards killed at Hlobane,[36] with me to report our arrival to General *[Colonel]* Bellairs,* the G.O.C. *[DA]*.

---

33 Harford landed in Durban on 2 December 1878. Durban, 370 nautical miles north-east from Port Elizabeth and situated on the north shore of a great bay at the mouth of the Mngeni River, was the seaport of the Colony of Natal with a population in 1878 of 5,312 whites and 3,500 Africans. In 1824, with the permission of King Shaka, in whose kingdom it lay, it had been established by a small party of hunter-traders from the Cape Colony. Initially called Port Natal, in 1835 it was renamed Durban after the Governor of the Cape, Sir Benjamin D'Urban. Almost all the men and matériel for the British campaign in Zululand passed through the port, but because of the sandbar across the entrance to the bay between the Point to the north and the Bluff to the south, only small ships with a shallow draught could enter the harbour. Most oceangoing vessels consequently had to remain in the outer anchorage and men, horses and supplies had to be brought through the surf by lighter.

34 Pietermaritzburg on the Msunduze River, 50 miles north-west of Durban, was laid out in 1839 by Voortrekkers who had been ceded the territory south of the Thukela River by King Dingane, and was named after two of their leaders, Pieter Retief and Gerrit Maritz. It was the seat of the short-lived Voortrekker Republiek Natalia, but continued after 1842 as the capital of the British Colony of Natal. The headquarters of the British garrison were at Fort Napier that overlooked Government House and the cathedral. Besides being the seat of government, Pietermaritzburg was also the commercial hub of the Natal midlands. It was the largest settlement in Natal, with a population in 1880 of 6,008 whites, 754 Asians and 3,309 Africans.

35 Lieutenant-General Lord Chelmsford was the GOC. Harford in fact reported to Colonel William Bellairs,* his DA and QMG.

36 The battle of Hlobane, 28 March 1879, when the Zulu army routed part of the British No. 4 Column, killing 15 officers and 79 men, along with over 100 African levies.

After getting our instructions to proceed to Maritzburg for final orders, I went with him on a round of calls to old friends, winding up by dining with Phyllis and Mrs Payne,[37] with whom I left the collection of insects I had made on the voyage. I asked them to hand them over to the Curator of the then, in embryo, Museum, which contained other collections of mine,[38] but I am sorry to say Phil forgot all about it and they were all lost.

An early start was made the next morning, and Mr Welch's bus,[39] which was still running as of yore, brought us into Maritzburg about 7 p.m. by the old familiar road, viz. Berea, Rooi Koppies, Cowie's Hill, Pinetown, Field's and Botha's Hills, Padley's and Camperdown, everywhere recalling happy reminiscences of shooting and collecting. One longed to get out of the bus and have a look round again with the gun and net.

With as little delay as possible, I reported myself at Headquarters and first of all saw General Clifford *[Colonel Bellairs]*.[40] He told me that Lord Chelmsford,* who was in the next room, wished to see

37 Untraced, but possibly members of the family that in 1869 founded Payne Bros, the Durban department store.

38 Harford is probably referring, not to the Durban Natural Science Museum which was founded in 1887, but to the Natal (now KwaZulu-Natal) Museum of natural and cultural history in Pietermaritzburg. In 1854 the Natal Society (inaugurated in 1851) began a collection of natural history specimens, housed in the Society Library. In 1894 the society erected a Museum Hall to house the growing collection, and when this proved too small, the Natal government stepped in to build a museum in the Flemish Renaissance style on Loop (now Jabu Ndlovu) Street, opened on 30 November 1904.

39 In 1862 J.W. Welch, who had previously driven mail coaches between London and Worcester, opened a daily horse-drawn omnibus service between Pietermaritzburg and Durban. The journey took 11 hours at the fixed rate of 25 shillings (purchasing power today of about £192).

40 Presumably, Harford means Colonel Bellairs because Major-General the Hon. Sir Henry Hugh Clifford (1826–83), VC, KCMG, CB, appointed in February 1879 as Inspector General of the Lines of Communication and Base in command of all communications between base, the forces operating

me, and I was thereupon ushered in. After the usual formalities the General said, "Now I am going to give you a very good billet, which will give you ten shillings a day Staff pay.[41] I'm going to appoint you Staff officer[42] to Commandant Lonsdale* who will command the 3rd Regiment, Natal Native Contingent,[43] now being organised at Sand Spruit.[44] You will find him an exceedingly nice fellow, and I hope that you will get on well together." Then, after relating to me some of Lonsdale's adventures in the Gaika-Galeka war[45] asked me to lose no time in joining the Natal Native Contingent. Before saying "Good night", I assured the General that he had nothing to fear in regard to my loyalty to Lonsdale; and that nothing would be left undone by me to further the interests of the 3rd Natal Native Contingent in every way, at the same time expressing my gratitude for the appointment.

---

in Zululand and the forces defending Natal, only set up his headquarters in Pietermaritzburg on 22 April 1879.

41 Purchasing power today of about £77.

42 Harford was officially appointed Adjutant to the 1st Battalion, 3rd Regiment, NNC.

43 For the invasion of Zululand, Lord Chelmsford had resolved to augment his regular British troops and colonial volunteers with African levies. The lieutenant-governor of Natal had the right to exact *isibhalo* (or compulsory labour and military service) from the African population. Magistrates accordingly raised Africans for military service from the chiefs in the Natal Native Reserves. General Orders calling the NNC into service were issued on 11 December 1878. The NNC was organised into three regiments, the first regiment consisting of three battalions, and the other two regiments of two battalions each. There were ten companies to each battalion, and the nominal establishment of each battalion was 33 white officers, 62 white NCOs and 1,011 African men. Each of the African levies was paid £1 a month (purchasing power today of about £154) which was better than the usual pay for *isibhalo* labour.

44 Sand Spruit, between Greyton and Helpmekaar, about 85 miles north of Pietermaritzburg, and close to the present village of Pomeroy, was the isolated seat of the Resident Magistrate of the Umsinga Division, Henry Francis Fynn, Jnr.* His newly built magistracy was on the slopes above the stream where the NNC were encamped.

45 Ninth Cape Frontier War, 1877–8.

This was a stroke of luck such as I had not counted on; no doubt my being able to speak Zulu had helped me into it.

I put up at the Plough Hotel, which in former days had been the Officers' Mess, and was within a stone's throw of the Major's old house.[46] The members of the Maritzburg Club also very kindly made all of us "Specials" honorary members.[47] When my name appeared in General Orders next day, I was in a position to make final preparations for the Front. I set to work to draw my pony and carbine,[48] which the Government allowed and which, if still in existence at the end of the campaign, had to be returned; visited the Pay Office to present my last pay certificate and get some money; arranged for my baggage to be sent on as soon as it arrived from Durban; got a few items of saddlery from my old friend Williams, the saddler;[49] and, as one pony would not suffice for my work, bought another, a sturdy little grey which afterwards saved the life of a Corporal of the Contingent,[50] who escaped on it from Isandhlwana *[Isandlwana]*,[51] but died from over-exertion in getting over such terrible ground as they traversed.

46 The singled-storeyed, verandaed Plough Hotel (now demolished) was in Longmarket (now Langalibalele) Street overlooking Market Square, the commercial hub of Pietermaritzburg, teeming with wagons and draught-oxen. It was close by the house Major Erskine had lived in when Colonial Secretary of Natal.

47 The Victoria Club on Longmarket (now Langalibalele) Street in Pietermaritzburg was founded in 1859. Its members (initially limited to 60 gentlemen) always made officers from the garrison at Fort Napier and visiting officers welcome. The club closed its doors in 1996, its demise a symptom of changing social patterns and a symbol of the lamentable degradation of the city's once architecturally renowned late-Victorian core.

48 This would most likely have been a Swinburn-Henry .45 breech-loading carbine, the standard issue to colonial units, since Martini-Henry Mark II carbines were not shipped to South Africa until late February 1879.

49 Untraced.

50 Untraced.

51 Battle of Isandlwana, 22 January 1879.

In a couple of days I was able to start. Riding one pony and leading the other, which carried all my requirements till the wagons arrived at Sand Spruit with the heavier baggage—which was a little over a month—I travelled to Greytown the first day,[52] about forty-five miles. As there were several nasty crossings and spruits, as well as an uncommonly rough road from there on to Sand Spruit, as well as the distance being a little greater, I stopped the next day at a little wattle-and-daub store, known as Sand Spruit Store, a little more than half way. This enabled me to get into Camp the following day before it got dark. Luckily, the weather was splendid, otherwise I should have had a bad time of it as after heavy thunderstorms and rain many of the spruits as well as the river crossings are impassable for a considerable time. Arrived at my journey's end, I found my tent ready pitched for me; and my ponies, which were the first consideration, were soon unsaddled, divested of their traps and taken off to be well groomed and fed. Commandant Lonsdale was away, having gone on a visit to Mr Fynn* for ten days, to consult about some Kaffirs as he was magistrate of the Umsinga district *[Division]* and could afford a great deal of assistance.

Large batches of Kaffirs from all parts poured into Camp daily, in charge of their respective indunas,[53] and the work of organisation went on rapidly.[54] The European officers and N.C.O.'s had all

52 The township of Greytown, named after the Governor of the Cape, Sir George Grey (Natal was then a District of Cape Colony), was laid out in 1850 as the administrative centre of Umvoti County bordering the Thukela River. In 1879 it was a thriving village of 1,500 white inhabitants. A stone laager protected the magistrate's courthouse.

53 *Induna; izinduna* (plural): headman.

54 The majority of the levies making up the 3rd NNC were raised in Weenen County of Natal. Three companies of iziGqoza, four companies of abaThembu and one company of amaBhele formed part of the 1st Battalion, and six companies of amaChunu the 2nd Battalion. To make up the remaining companies of ten in each battalion, men were raised in the Klip River Division of Klip River County from six small chiefdoms.

arrived, and Lonsdale had already told them off to their Battalions …[55] Commandant Hamilton-Browne,* "Maori" Browne, as he was called, had the 1st Battalion and Commandant Cooper* the 2nd … All were adventurers, and all the very best of fellows, ready to do anything and go anywhere.[56] The strength of each Battalion was laid down to be 1000 men, but before we crossed into the Zulu country this number had been considerably increased and we found it impossible to get rid of these additional men, as the Government ration of meat proved too attractive.[57]

All natives on the strength were served out with a blanket, and a red cloth headband as a distinguishing mark. A hundred in each battalion were armed with rifles and the remainder with billhooks, but undoubtedly they put much more faith in their own assegais and shields.[58] Drilling went on throughout the day, and kept everyone hard at work. By the time Lonsdale returned everything was in working order and discipline and drill were the

55 The ellipses are in Child's transcription of Harford's holograph, now missing, and it is not certain whether they indicate she has left words out, or whether they were indecipherable.

56 There were to be three officers and six NCOs to each of the 20 companies in the 3rd NNC. Accordingly, in November 1878 Lonsdale had enrolled some 60 officers and 120 NCOs in King William's Town in the Cape Colony. They arrived in Durban by sea, and on 10 December they left Pietermaritzburg, where they were equipped with firearms and uniforms, for Sand Spruit. Some spoke isiXhosa, which was just intelligible to isiZulu speakers, but others knew no African language at all. Orders were therefore often not comprehended, and when the men complained they did not understand, they were flogged for being impertinent and disobedient.

57 The 3rd NNC was ultimately overstrength by about 300 men.

58 About 300 breech-loading Martini-Henry rifles (either Mark I or Mark II), the standard British infantry weapon, were issued to the 3rd NNC, most of them being distributed to the 2nd Battalion. In addition, 205 obsolete percussion-cap, muzzle-loading Enfield rifles (introduced in 1853) were divided equally between the two battalions. There seems to have been little, if any, practice in these firearms, with the result that they were ineffectually handled in combat.

main points to be attended to. Our camp lay at the foot of the high range of hills at Helpmekaar,[59] on the Rorke's Drift road,[60] and a more stony or rocky position could not well have been selected. On several occasions we were nearly washed away during heavy thunderstorms, owing to the tentpegs not holding, while lighting fires for meals was out of the question.[61]

It was a day or two before one of these terrific storms that Norris-Newman,* the Special Correspondent for the London Standard and Cape Standard and Mail arrived, accompanied by our Medical Officer, Dr Beresford,[62] about a week before Christmas, and quietly plumped himself down on us, and without any by or with your leave announced his intention of attaching himself to the Contingent. This was quite an unlooked-for surprise, more especially as none of us had ever seen or heard of him before. Nevertheless, we made him very welcome, and he turned out to be an excellent and garrulous companion in our Mess. Lonsdale at once dubbed him "Noggs", and by this name he was subsequently known throughout the 3rd Column.[63] At the end of the Campaign he wrote a book entitled,

59 In early December 1878 the main depot for No. 3 Column was established at Helpmekaar on the rolling escarpment that overlooks both the plain around the Umsinga magistracy and Sand Spruit to the south, and the valley of the Mzinyathi (Buffalo) River to the north. Three galvanised iron sheds and large huts were erected to hold the accumulating stores for the imperial and colonial troops concentrating there in late December 1878 and early January 1879.

60 At Rorke's Drift the road north from Greytown and Helpmekaar crossed the Mzinyathi River into Zululand.

61 It was only on 2 January 1879 that the 3rd NNC moved forward from Sand Spruit to a position on Knostrope farm halfway down the escarpment from Helpmekaar to Rorke's Drift.

62 Dr W.H. Beresford, a Civilian Surgeon with the Army Medical Department, served with the 3rd NNC.

63 Newman Noggs was Nicholas Nickleby's quirky, alcoholic but essentially sympathetic and long-suffering confidential clerk in Charles Dickens's novel of 1839, *Nicholas Nickleby*. Dickens described Noggs as 'a tall man of middle

In Zululand With the British Throughout the War of 1879,[64] and in it he describes his first experience of Sand Spruit when he was drowned out of his tent and had to go to bed supperless, an item not at all in keeping with his taste.

Accompanying the Contingent, by permission of the Authorities, as lookers-on or Native Staff, we had two of Cetewayo's brothers, Umkungu *[Mkhungo]* and Isikota *[Sikhotha]*, and a witchdoctor named Ingabangi *[Gabangaye]*.* The two brothers had escaped with their mother from Zululand some time before, at the time of the massacre of Umbelazi *[Mbuyazi]* and his followers.[65] Isikota *[Sikhotha]* was a very fine specimen, and very like his father [King Mpande] in features.[66]

---

age, with two goggle eyes whereof one was a fixture, a rubicund nose, a cadaverous face, and a suit of clothes … much the worse for wear'.

64 Charles L. Norris-Newman, *In Zululand with the British throughout the War of 1879*, London: W.H. Allen, 1880; reprinted London: Greenhill Books: California: Presidio Books, 1990.

65 Mkhungo, Sikhotha and Mbuyazi were sons of King Mpande and were full brothers. Their half-brother Cetshwayo was Mpande's heir-presumptive, but Mpande favoured Mbuyazi to succeed him. Mbuyazi's supporters were known as the iziGqoza and Cetshwayo's rival faction as the uSuthu. The succession struggle was decided in 1856 at the battle of Ndondakusuka when Mbuyazi was defeated and killed. Mkhungo and Sikhotha took refuge in Natal with their surviving followers, the iziGqoza. The two brothers were educated at Bishop Colenso's school for the sons of chiefs. In 1879 the two Zulu princes, who represented a dynastic threat to Cetshwayo, were living in Weenen County, Natal. The iziGqoza, who were anxious to avenge themselves against King Cetshwayo, contributed 273 men to the 1/3rd NNC, making up three companies led by Sikhotha. They held themselves aloof from the other African levies. Mkhungo did not accompany the iziGqoza to war and was represented by his son. Sikhotha was present at the battle of Isandlwana. He escaped, but 54 of his men perished. He returned home when the 3rd NNC was disbanded in late January 1879. In April, when the Weenen Contingent was formed from men of the disbanded 3rd NNC, many of the iziGqoza under Sikhotha joined up but saw no further action because the new formation remained on the defensive in Natal.

66 King Mpande kaSenzangakhona, r. 1840–72.

Ingabangi was rather a wizened-up old man, but an eloquent speaker, and looked upon with great respect by the natives.

The surroundings of my tent were looked upon as the "Indaba" ground;[67] and all who had complaints to make, or who wished to ask questions, found their way there early in the morning, and squatted patiently and silently in rows or semicircles until I made my appearance.[68] It need hardly be said that the chief topic of conversation was grub, and especially as to who were going to get the heads of the cattle killed for consumption that particular day. One morning I had a really wonderful, and at the same time very pleasant, surprise sprung on me. During the indaba a man suddenly stood up in the middle of the assembly and, putting his hand to his chin, exclaimed, "Waugh! Ow!! Wenu Charlie!!!"[69] So I called him up and found that he had worked on our farm at Pinetown.[70] More than eight years had passed since he had last seen or heard of me, and I might have been in Kamchatka for all he knew.[71] Although, perhaps, as a young man I had not changed

67 *Indaba*; *izindaba* (plural): isiZulu for a matter for discussion; a conference.

68 Because there was no official battalion interpreter in the 3rd NNC, and no one else besides Samuel Grant, Lonsdale's Political Assistant, who spoke isiZulu fluently, Harford regularly found himself as the principal conduit between the men of the NNC and their white officers. Harford wrote to his mother on 14 January 1879: 'the European officers and NCO are a thousand percent worse than the natives, no one hardly speaks a word of Kafir [isiZulu] and the Zulu interpreter can't always be present so it is a lucky thing I have not forgotten mine and am picking up a good deal more.' (Payne et al., *Harford*, p. 118.)

69 By hailing Harford as '*Wenu* Charlie', Jim was greeting him familiarly in Zulu fashion as a friend and contemporary from the place where they both belonged. Jim probably never did so again as their relationship could no longer be the easy companionable one it had been when they were both youngsters on Harford's father's farm.

70 The Pinetown farm was called Stapleton Grove. See the Introduction for further details.

71 The volcanic Kamchatka Peninsula is in the Russian Far East, a Victorian byword for somewhere utterly remote.

very much in features, yet under the circumstances the quickness with which he recognised me showed the retentive memory and powers of observation that he possessed. I took him on at once as my personal servant, and stuck to his old name of "Jim".* More will be said of him later on.[72]

It was now nearing the 11th January, the date fixed for the troops to move across the border.[73] Lord Chelmsford had arrived at Rorke's Drift and Lonsdale rode over to have an interview with him but received no definite orders with regard to the movements of the Contingent.[74] However, one morning I had occasion to go to Rorke's Drift myself,[75] to see the Adjutant-General *[Principal Staff Officer to Colonel Glyn in command of No. 3 Column]*, Major Clery,*

72 Yet, when Harford wrote to his mother on 14 January 1879 and told her that he had 'got one of our old Kaffirs as a servant', he informed her that he was 'Jacob by name' and not Jim, and that he was not the cook also called Jacob, but 'a smaller man'. Harford added that although he 'took him over', he was 'awfully lazy'. Not mentioned in the memoir but in the same letter was 'old Allen, Uncle Harry's groom', who was 'now looking after' his horses. (Payne et al., *Harford*, p. 120.) 'Uncle Harry' was Harford's father's eldest brother, Henry Charles, who had preceded him to South Africa and had served with the Cape Mounted Rifles before joining him in Natal. His next brother, Frederick Kill (1836–1906), was an Anglican clergyman, and his third brother, Samuel Henry (1833–1904), served first as an officer in the army and then in the Consular Service.

73 The British ultimatum delivered on 11 December 1878 to King Cetshwayo's representatives expired unanswered on 11 January 1879.

74 Lord Chelmsford had ridden down to Rorke's Drift on 4 January, and the following day all the troops of No. 3 Column encamped in the vicinity of Helpmekaar, including the 3rd NNC, began to move down to Rorke's Drift except for two companies of the 1/24th that remained there to defend the depot. By 9 January all of No. 3 Column (except for the Helpmekaar garrison) were concentrated at Rorke's Drift for the invasion of Zululand on 11 January when the ultimatum expired.

75 The date was 9 January, the day Lord Chelmsford had fixed to inspect and address the 3rd NNC on the standards of 'civilised' warfare he expected them to adhere to in the coming campaign.

(afterwards, *[Major-]*General Sir Francis Clery).[76] Luckily, arriving at a very early hour, and having completed my work with him, I was on the point of mounting my pony to ride back to camp, when Major Clery said, "You will have everything ready, Harford, won't you, for the General today?" "Good Heavens, Major", I said, "This is the first I've heard about his coming!" "You don't mean to say that Lonsdale never told you about it?", he replied, "He is going to inspect you at twelve o'clock. The General gave Lonsdale his orders days ago."

Well, I rode off as hard as I could go, to Camp. I found Lonsdale sitting in his tent, looking over his Masonic orders and paraphernalia, and, on my breaking the news to him as quickly as I could, he said, "Good God! I forgot all about it. Shout for my pony, like a good chap."

I also got a change of ponies. Kaffirs were sent out in all directions to call in the men who were drilling, many of them miles away. As soon as the ponies were ready, we jumped on, Lonsdale saying, "You take that way; I'll take this", and we went off at a gallop. We had scarcely parted company when Lonsdale's pony shied at something and threw him off. I saw the fall. He appeared to have struck his head and then, rolling over on his back, lay quite still with one of his arms projecting in the air at right angles to his body. I got off at once and ran to his assistance, only to find that he was unconscious, and rigidly stiff. I shouted for the Doctor,[77] and as soon as he had come up with some Natives and a stretcher, I galloped off again to collect the men. Eventually, after a real race for it, everybody was got in; but Hamilton-Browne and Cooper

76 Francis Clery was promoted Major-General in 1894. He was made KCB in 1899 and KCMG in 1900. He retired from the army in February 1901. This reference is an indicator that Harford did not compose these memoirs until the late 1890s at earliest.

77 Frank William Buée, Assistant Surgeon to the 1/3rd NNC. He was killed at Isandlwana.

were still getting their Battalions formed up on parade when the General and staff made their appearance.

I had, of course, to ride out and tell the General what had happened. So we first went to Lonsdale's tent, and finding that he was still unconscious, orders were given for his removal to Helpmekaar hospital. It was found afterwards that he had received concussion of the brain. (He rejoined the Contingent the day we went into camp at Isandhlwana, being received with a loud "Bayete" *[Bayede]*.)[78] Through his interpreter, he [Chelmsford] expressed his pleasure at what he had seen, and gave some sound advice on matters of discipline, especially behaviour towards women and children and prisoners.)

On the following day we moved to Rorke's Drift,[79] where Major Black,* of the 2nd Battalion, 24th Regiment was given temporary command until Lonsdale returned. Before crossing into Zululand, the Battalion Commanders[80] devised an excellent plan for keeping their various Companies intact, and for recognising them in the field should they become separated or lose themselves, viz: by having small flags made with the number of the Battalion, 1 or 2, and some special device for each Company painted on them. These devices represented, as nearly as possible, the soubriquets the Natives had imposed upon themselves, such as the ingulube (pigs),[81] izinkunzana (young bulls), and so forth. This caused great delight, and gave rise to endless chaff and amusement on all occasions.

When the general advance took place, a few of our Natives under a corporal named Schiess were left at Rorke's Drift as part

78 The term *bayede*, meaning 'Hail Your Majesty!' is strictly applicable only to the reigning Zulu monarch, but in colonial circumstances was given as a greeting to leading white personages.

79 10 January 1879.

80 Commandant Hamilton-Browne of the 1st Battalion and Commandant Cooper of the 2nd Battalion.

81 *Ingulube* means a pig in the singular. The plural would be *inzingulube*.

of the Garrison of the Fort under Lieutenant Bromhead,* of the 2nd Battalion, 24th Regiment, and Lieutenant Chard,* of the Royal Engineers.[82] Schiess was subsequently awarded the Victoria Cross for very conspicuous bravery. Some of the men of the 24th Regiment told me that he fought like a tiger and at one time, when some Zulus actually managed to clutch hold of his bayonet, he got it out of their hands and, springing over the parapet, bayonetted some six or seven of them straight away.[83]

---

82 The small garrison left to guard the depot consisted of B Company, 2/24th Regiment under Lieutenant Bromhead, a company of the 2/3rd NNC under Captain William Stephenson and various detached personnel and invalids in the hospital. Lieutenant Chard, RE, was the senior officer present.

83 In a later note to his memoir, Harford added that he remembered Schiess, whom he thought erroneously to be 'of Swedish nationality', to have been 'wearing earrings'. He added that Schiess 'was a very small man and had the cut of a seafaring man', which he expected 'was his real calling'. (Payne et al., *Harford*, p. 113.) In fact, Christian Ferdinand Schiess (1856–84) was born in Canton Berne, Switzerland, and he sailed to the Cape in 1877 as part of a government-sponsored scheme to recruit Swiss artisans and farmers. He apparently served in the Ninth Cape Frontier War as an irregular. He then joined the 3rd NNC as a corporal. He was present at the skirmish at kwaSogekle on 12 January 1879 but was soon thereafter admitted to the field hospital at Rorke's Drift with acute blisters. He took part in the defence of the post on 22–23 January and was wounded by a musket-ball in the ankle. His exemplary gallantry was mentioned by several participants and he was subsequently awarded the VC. After the 3rd NNC was disbanded in 24 January and he had recovered from his wound, he joined Lonsdale's Horse as a corporal and apparently served in that unit with the 1st Division throughout the final stages of the war.

CHAPTER 2

Isandhlwana

On the 11th January the 3rd Column crossed the Buffalo into Zululand,[1] the troops making their way over at different points. The Artillery and the 24th Regiment went over by degrees in the pontoon,[2] a little above the main Drift, known as Rorke's Drift after the Dutchman Jim Rorke, whose house and farm buildings were occupied by us as a Fort, after being entrenched.[3] I was ordered

1 No. 3 Column of 4,709 men was made up of N Battery, 5th Brigade, RA, the 5th (Field) Company, RE, the 1/24th Regiment, the 2/24th Regiment, Nos 1 and 2 Squadrons, Mounted Infantry, the NMP, units of the Natal Mounted Volunteer Corps, the 1/3rd NNC, the 2/3rd NNC and the NNPC.

2 More properly a 'pont' in South African usage, a flat-bottomed ferry worked on cables attached to both banks of the river.

3 James (Jim) Alfred Rorke was the son of an Irishman from County Galway, Ireland, who emigrated to the Cape Colony. In 1849 he acquired a farm in Natal on the middle Mzinyathi River abutting a ford that came to be known as Rorke's Drift. There he built a dwelling house and store and played a leading part in the local settler community as a lieutenant in the Buffalo Border Guard and as the local Border Agent for the Natal government. He died in 1875 and his widow sold the farm to John Surtees who, in turn, sold it in January 1878 to the Lutheran missionary Otto Witt (1840–1923), who bought it on behalf of the Church of Sweden. In January 1879 Witt rented the mission station to the military, and No. 3 Column converted the church into a commissariat store and Witt's 11-room house into a hospital. Most contemporary reports state that when No. 3 Column advanced into Zululand, the depot was not fortified or entrenched, and that

to find a crossing for the 2nd/3rd Natal Native Contingent, higher up the river. The fog was so dense one could barely see anything a yard in front, but at last, after hugging the bank very closely for about half a mile or more, we came to a spot that looked worth a trial. So I put my pony at it and got across all right, the bed of the river being nice and hard; but the water came up to the saddle flaps, and there was a nasty bank to scramble up on the opposite side. However, that did not matter, it was good enough.

Then followed a truly unforgettable scene, first of the Natives crossing over and then of the impressive ceremony when the Regiment had formed up again on the other side and were addressed by old Ingabangi, the witch-doctor. In order to scare away any crocodiles that might be lurking in the vicinity, the leading Company formed a double chain right across the River, leaving a pathway between for the remainder to pass through. The men forming the chain clasped hands, and the moment they entered the water they started to hum a kind of war-chant, which was taken up by every Company as they passed over. The sound that this produced was like a gigantic swarm of bees buzzing about us, and sufficient to scare crocodiles or anything else, away. Altogether, it was both a curious and grand sight.

All being safely over, the men were formed up in quarter-column on the hillside, and one or two Officers on their ponies were sent out in different directions to try and find out in the dense fog where any

---

the troops of the garrison were encamped nearby. However, a sprinkling of accounts suggests that there were defences of some sort before 22 January, and Harford seems to endorse that in his phrasing here. Yet on p. 89 he states that 'Mr James Dalton … devised all the rapid arrangements for the defence' of the post 'when warning was received of the nearness of the Zulus.' That accords with the generally accepted view that improvised defences were thrown up around the post just before the Zulu attack, and it was only after the battle, on 29 January, that half the 5th Company, RE, began the construction of a proper, stone-walled fortification, known as Fort Bromhead.

of the other troops were, and what was going on. While this was in progress, old Ingabangi asked permission to address the men. Never shall I forget his extraordinary elocutionary power, and the splendid oration he delivered. The old fellow got to the head of the Column and then started off at a trot, going backwards and forwards at this pace for nearly an hour. He would have gone on much longer, had we not received orders to move. Without stopping to take breath, he recounted the history of the Zulu nation, which was frequently applauded by a loud "Gee!"[4] and rattling of assegais on shields from the whole Contingent. It was a wonderfully impressive scene, and one which will always remain fresh in my memory. The drift at which we crossed was subsequently known as Harford's Drift, but I don't suppose it has been used since.

Our scouts eventually got in touch with the 24th Regiment, and as we moved up to support them the fog gradually lifted. Then a very pretty sight presented itself as the troops were dotted about over the rolling hills in "Receive Cavalry" squares formation, their red coats showing up distinctly in the clear atmosphere. No further advance was made that day, owing to the difficulties of getting the Transport across. So we camped where we were.

During the day, Major Dartnell* with a few Mounted Police were out on a reconnaissance,[5] and took me with him as Staff Officer. On our way up the Bashee *[Batshe River]* valley towards Sirayo's *[Sihayo's]** kraal *[umuzi]* we heard a war-song being sung,[6] evidently by a large body of Natives; but where they were, or what became of them, we were unable to find out. However, as this was the ground

4 A Zulu general exclamation of approbation.

5 The NMP was a permanent force created in 1874 to provide mobile defence for Natal, and was organised along military lines. On 2 November 1879 it was put under military command for the invasion of Zululand. On campaign the NMP's black corduroy uniforms faded to dark grey.

6 KwaSogekle in the Batshe River valley was the *umuzi* ('kraal' was the colonial term for a Zulu homestead) of Sihayo kaXongo.

over which we were going to attack the next day, it looked as if it were certain that we should meet with some opposition. Other parties had also been out in various directions, and had captured a considerable number of cattle.[7]

Reveille sounded very early, about 3 a.m. the next morning,[8] and we marched to attack Sirayo's kraal, up the Bashee valley, through thick bush.[9] It was most unpleasant going, for above us, on

---

7 Lord Chelmsford, as he reported to Sir Bartle Frere on 12 January 1879, decided to attack kwaSogekle in the first action of the war in the hope that 'the news of the storming of Sirayo's stronghold ... may have a salutary effect in Zululand & either bring down a large force to attack us [Chelmsford was hoping to entice the amaZulu into a pitched battle which he was certain of winning] or else produce a revolution in the country' that would overthrow King Cetshwayo and lead to the Zulu surrender. (Laband (ed.), *Chelmsford's Zululand Campaign*, p. 61.)

8 12 January 1879.

9 Chelmsford, in his letter of 12 January to Frere, described the skirmish as follows. 'I ordered Colonel Glyn with 4 Companies of 1/24th & 1/3d Native Contingent to work up under the Kraantz [rocky ridge; cliff] where some of Sirayo's strongholds were said to be in skirmishing order – On the approach of this force near the Kraantz, fire was opened upon them out of the caves [at 8.30 a.m.] for half an hour & ended in our obtaining possession of all the caves ... Colonel Degacher* who had been sent for from Camp when we found that the Kraantz was occupied by the enemy came up towards the end of the affair with ½ battn. 2/24th and about 400 2/3rd Native Contingent – This force went forward to Sirayo's own Kraal which is situated under a very steep Kraantz which is filled with caves – The British soldiers & natives skirmished and entered all the caves which were found empty – I ordered Sirayo's Kraal to be burnt but none of the other huts were touched – The Native Contingent behaved very well & not a native touched a woman or child or killed a wounded man – On our side two natives were killed & one mortally wounded – One N.C. officer Native Contingent slightly wounded.' (Laband (ed.), *Chelmsford's Zululand Campaign*, pp. 60–1.) He was Corporal Meyor who, in fact, had a severe spear wound in the thigh. In addition, Lieutenant J. Purvis of the 1/3rd NNC had been shot in the arm. Twelve of the NNC African levies were also wounded.

During the skirmish in which Harford was engaged, Chelmsford ordered Major Russell* and the mounted men of No. 3 Column to swing around in

our right, were hills with the usual cavernous rocks encircling them a little below their crests. It was evident that the warriors we had heard singing their war-chant the day before were ensconced in these caves, for the instant the troops got within range a continuous popping went on from these places. The crack, crack, crack of their guns and rifles echoed and re-echoed among the hills in the still morning air and made it impossible to detect exactly where the shots were coming from. Now and again a Zulu was seen in the open, and on one such occasion I saw the man taking deliberate aim at Colonel Glyn* who was standing in an open patch above me. Shouting as loud as I could, I told him to get out of the way before the shot was fired.

Colonel Glyn was in command of the troops, and Lord Chelmsford took up a position with his staff on the opposite side of the valley, to watch operations. Colonel Degacher* commanded the 2nd Battalion, 24th Regiment, and Major Black our Contingent, as Lonsdale was still in hospital. We started skirmishing through the bush, Major Black leading the 1st Battalion N.N.C. under Commandant Hamilton-Browne, and I following in support with the 2nd Battalion under Commandant Cooper. Before many minutes, bullets were whizzing about in all directions, and one of our Natives, who was close by my side, got a bullet in the thigh, breaking the bone. A short distance further on, seeing two N.C.O.'s sheltering behind a rock instead of leading their men, I went to drive them on;[10] and had just got them away when "ping" came a

---

support to the high ground to the north above kwaSogekle. As they neared the top, they were fired on by about 60 of Sihayo's men from about 100 yards away. The Mounted Infantry and NMP dismounted and commenced a frontal attack, while the Natal Mounted Volunteers moved out to the right to attack the Zulu left flank and eventually drove the amaZulu back over the side of the mountain. Chelmsford estimated that during the day's fighting the amaZulu lost about 30 men.

10 Harford was more explicit in his letter of 14 January to his mother: 'The Native Force wanted a deal of urging on I had to threaten several men's

bullet and cut away a branch just at the spot where my head was a second before. This was luck![11]

As we got further into the bush all sorts of obstacles, such as rocky ground, ravines, and especially thick masses of creepers, prevented any sort of formation being properly kept, in consequence of which the firing line and supports soon got mingled together. Nevertheless, the men were kept well in hand. Before very long I could hear Major Black's shrill voice in broad Scotch urging his men on, and, making my way up to him with supports, I found that he and Commandant Hamilton-Browne were in a hot corner close to some caves, with hand-to-hand fighting going on. When I was within about twenty or thirty yards of the place, one of their men fell almost at my feet with a terrible assegai wound, which had nearly cut him in half, right down the back. The poor fellow was not dead, and although I could see it was only a matter of minutes my feelings almost led me to try to put him out of his misery with my revolver. But I abstained. I went on to the ridge of the spur of the hill in front of me as fast as I could, with some men, to see what was on the other side and to assist on Major Black's flank.

Eventually, on reaching the foot of a ledge of rocks, where they curved in a horse-shoe bend overhanging a deep valley, a somewhat grim sight presented itself. Confronting me across the bend was a large, open-mouthed cave, apparently capable of holding a good number of men, and hanging below it were several dead Zulus, caught in the monkey-rope creepers and bits of bush. They had evidently been shot and had either fallen out, or been thrown out, by their comrades when killed. Later on, I learned that a Company of the 24th Regiment had been firing at this particular cave for some time, and had been ordered to cease firing on it when our

---

lives before getting them to budge, they were in such a fright hearing the bullets go past.' (Payne et al., *Harford*, p. 118.)

11 Harford was less insouciant at the time, telling his mother, 'I was very nearly killed twice.' (Payne et al., *Harford*, p. 118.)

men came up. It was an uncommonly awkward place to get at, as it meant climbing over nothing but huge rocks and in many places having to work one's way like a crab, besides which a loss of foothold might have landed one in the valley below. However, there was not much time to think, and I determined to make an attempt, so, sending some men to work round below, I took a European N.C.O. who was close at hand, and told him to follow me.[12] Clambering at once over a big piece of rock, I got rather a rude shock on finding a Zulu sitting in a squatting position behind another rock, almost at my elbow. His head showed above the rock, and his wide-open eyes glared at me; but I soon discovered that he was dead.

Scarcely had I left this apparition behind than a live Zulu … suddenly jumped up from his hiding place and, putting the muzzle of his rifle within a couple of feet of my face, pulled the trigger. But the cap snapped,[13] whereupon he dropped his rifle and made off over the rocks for the cave, as hard as he could go. Providence had again come to my aid, and away I went after him, emptying my revolver at him as we scrambled up.[14] Out of my six shots only one hit him, but not mortally. I stopped for a second to reload, but finding the wretched thing stuck I threw it down into the valley below, at the same time turning round and shouting to the N.C.O.,

---

12 Again, Harford was more explicit in his letter to his mother immediately after the event, telling her that 'there had been a great many shots fired from a certain cave and the occupant doing a lot of damage – no nigger [sic] would go up and it was a long time before I could get a soul to come up. So as we could drive certain parties who were hidden out before we got to it, at last a fellow volunteered and up we went of course, then a lot followed.' (Payne et al., *Harford*, p. 118.)

13 The percussion cap of the muzzle-loading rifle failed to flash when struck by the hammer released by the trigger, and consequently did not ignite the charge in the barrel.

14 Officers carried personally owned double-action revolvers, usually either the Mark II Adams model of 1872 or the Webley Royal Irish Constabulary model of 1867 using .450-calibre, centre-fire ammunition. They were not accurate at more than 25 yards.

who I thought was following me, to let me have his revolver. But he remained behind, where I had left him at the start, and all he did was to call out, as loud as he could, "Captain Harford is killed!" However, I soon put this right by shouting down, "No, he is not, he is very much alive!"[15]

---

15 Perhaps the one thing that people remember about Harford is the story – perpetuated by Donald R. Morris in *The Washing of the Spears*, p. 325, and initially aired by Hamilton-Browne in his unreliable and highly coloured memoirs, *A Lost Legionary in South Africa*, p. 108 – that Harford had suddenly dropped to the ground to transfer a rare beetle he had spotted to a receptacle, thus leading lookers-on to believe he had been shot. It is worth quoting Hamilton-Browne's account in full because it incidentally reveals the impression Harford had made among his fellow officers. Harford, wrote Hamilton-Browne, 'was a charming companion ... but he was a crazy bug and beetle hunter, and would run about on the hottest day with a landing-net to catch butterflies and other insects. He moreover collected and treasured snakes, scorpions and loathsome beasts of all kinds. He had never been under fire before and had ... expressed hopes he would be cool and good ... Well we were in a rather hot corner and he was standing to my right rear when I heard an exclamation, and turning round saw him lying on the ground having dropped his sword and revolver. "Good God, Harford," I said, "you are hit!" "No sir," he replied, "not hit but I have caught such a beauty." And there the lunatic, in his first action, and under heavy fire, his qualms of nervousness all forgotten, had captured some infernal microbe or other, and was blowing its wings out, as unconscious of the bullets striking the rocks all around him as if he had been in his garden at home.' On Hamilton-Browne then ordering Harford up to the right flanking company 'to hurry them up ... he looked at me with sorrow, put his prize into a tin box and was off like a shot.'

Now, while there is no doubting that Harford was a keen naturalist, he had clearly reined himself in while on campaign. In his letter to his mother, he wrote, 'I have collected a few things on the road but nothing very much although I've seen heaps of good things but have nowhere to put them.' (Payne et al., *Harford*, p. 120.) It would seem that, in order to spin a good yarn, Hamiliton-Browne was combining Harford's collecting mania (which he and some of the other officers evidently found a trifle absurd) with Harford's own admission that he had thrown his jammed revolver away and that (as we shall see) he had earlier lost his cumbersome sword in the thick bush as well.

All this was a matter of seconds, and after pronouncing my blessings pretty freely on the Corporal, followed up my quarry, who by this time was standing in the mouth of the cave. Speaking to him in Kaffir, I called upon him to surrender, explaining that I had no intention to harm him in any way and would see to it that he was not ill-treated by anyone. He then squatted down in submission. Before getting up into the cave myself, not caring to run my head into a noose thoughtlessly, I demanded to know if there was anyone else inside and was assured that there was no-one, and as all was quiet, although I must say I had some slight misgivings, I clambered in.

Close to the entrance lay a wounded man with his feet towards me. Although unable to rise, he clutched hold of an assegai that was by his side, but I told him at once to drop it, that I was going to do him no harm, and questioned him as to who was with him in the cave. He stoutly denied that there were any others there. By this time I was getting accustomed to the darkness, and saw several likely-looking boltholes and kept on repeating that I knew there were others somewhere in hiding and that they were telling me lies. At the same time adding, in a tone loud enough to be heard by anyone near the place, that if they would come out I would promise on oath that no harm should be done to them and that I would accompany them myself to the General … who would see that they were well treated.

In a short time this had the desired effect, and presently a head appeared from a hole, and as the object crept out I kept careful watch for any sort of weapon that might emerge with it; another and then another crawled out from the same spot. All were unarmed, and squatted down close to me. I then wanted to know where the others were, but they swore that there was no-one else. As this seemed to be the case, I moved off with my four prisoners, leaving the badly-wounded man in the cave.[16] We soon made out way down

16 Norris-Newman later wrote admiringly in his eye-witness account of the war (repeating word for word his newspaper account written on 13 January 1879): 'Lieutenant Harford of the 99th Regiment, attached as Staff Officer,

the valley to where the General and his staff were, and I was met by Major Clery, the Adjutant-General, who greeted me with, "Well, Harford, I congratulate you on your capture, the General and I have been watching your gallantry for some time."[17]

Then he told me that a section of the 24th Regiment had been firing into the cave half the morning, owing to the sniping that had been going on from it, and when Lonsdale's men were seen to be approaching, orders had been sent to them to cease fire. Having handed over my prisoners and telling the Adjutant-General the promise I had made them,[18] and after seeing the man that I had

performed a most plucky action in advancing to the mouth of a cave out of which many men had been shot, and succeeded in inducing four men to come out, deliver up their arms, and give themselves up as prisoners. His revolver had been emptied at the time, and he might easily have been shot by any of them, as they came out one by one.' (Norris-Newman, *In Zululand with the British*, p. 40.)

Harford confided in his mother that 'I then pulled 4 more out, so I got the whole five, two were badly wounded and 2 died just outside the mouth of the cave. I know you would like to know all so I tell you.' He added that as booty he 'took a couple of guns and heaps of assegais and which I should like to keep of course but can get no-one to carry the things'. (Payne et al., *Harford*, p. 120.)

17 Harford proudly informed his mother that 'The Colonel and the Chief of his Staff [presumably Colonel Glyn and Major Clery] who saw the whole proceeding complimented me very much on my success and the manner in which I got up to the cave so I hope it may do me good. My commandant [Hamilton-Browne] especially mentioned me in his report to the General so I dare say I may have been mentioned in despatches.' (Payne et al., *Harford*, p. 120.)

Disappointingly for Harford, he was not mentioned. However, the name of another officer of the 1/3rd NNC did appear in Column Orders on 13 January. He was Captain P.W. Hayes who, during the crossing of the Mzinyathi on 11 January, had jumped into the swollen river and rescued a trooper of the Mounted Infantry who had been swept off his horse.

18 By Adjutant-General, Harford probably again meant Major Clery, but he could equally have been referring to Colonel Bellairs, the actual DAG on Chelmsford's Headquarters Staff.

myself wounded was placed in the ambulance wagon for conveyance to hospital, I went off again.[19]

On getting back to the Contingent, one of the men walked up to me and with the usual salutation of "Inkosi" gravely handed me my sword,[20] spurs and courier bag, all of which had been torn off me in walking through the bush, as well as the discarded revolver. Never was I more thankful than to get these things back, especially the courier bag which had been a parting gift from my Captain, Captain Moir,* when I left Chatham and contained my field glasses, knife, fork and spoon, as well as other valuable odds and ends. It would have been almost impossible to have found them again, even if a search party had been sent out, but luckily this Good Samaritan had followed carefully in my tracks and picked up the things as they were dropped. Curious to say, in the excitement of the moment I never felt anything going.

Now that the Cavalry, Mounted Police and 24th Regiment had gone on to Sirayo's kraal, one or two companies of the Contingent were sent off to capture some cattle,[21] and after a short rest and a meal the whole force returned to camp, drenched to the skin in a thunderstorm. After a day's rest to clean arms and dry clothing, camp was moved forward to the Bashee Valley, not far from the scene of our operations two days before,[22] and here we remained for the next

19 Chelmsford abided by Harford's promise to the wounded amaZulu. He reported to Frere on 12 January: 'I have visited two wounded Zulus who are in our hospital & and have seen that they are well looked after.' Chelmsford's concern was not entirely altruistic, however. He added: 'Directly they are well enough I shall let them go, so that they may tell their friends how [effectively] the British make war.' (Laband (ed.), *Chelmsford's Zululand Campaign*, p. 61.)

20 This would have been the 1822-pattern infantry sword with a gilt half-basket guard and with a 'Wilkinson' blade in a steel scabbard introduced in 1866.

21 About 500 cattle were captured.

22 On 14 January four companies of the 2/24th, the 1/3rd NNC and some NNPC encamped in the Batshe valley and stayed in there until 19 January.

four or five days, the 24th and ourselves working hard at making and repairing roads for our advance to Isandhlwana on the 20th.[23]

In the meantime representatives from all the units of the Force went out with Major Clery … to select positions within the encampment …. At the conclusion of our work we … saw a remarkable instance of how a Pauw—the African Bustard—will squat if he has been unobserved or thinks so.[24] Having ridden all over the ground to be occupied … Major Clery drew rein and we all, some eight or ten of us, formed up in a semicircle round him to receive his final orders. While he was talking I spotted a Pauw lying as flat as he could make himself, with his head stretched straight on the ground like a snake, just between his horse and mine, almost being trodden upon, and called attention to it. Everyone of course took a quiet peep at it, and when the Adjutant-General *[Major Clery]* had finished his discourse we rode gently away without disturbing it. For a considerable time afterwards we rode about the ground and kept an eye on the spot, but the bird never stirred while we were there.

Commandant Lonsdale rejoined us before the move to Isandhlwana, quite recovered from his accident, and Monday, the 20th January, saw us on the road to that now historic campaign ground, and a stiff day's work it was, large working-parties both from the 24th and ourselves having to be sent forward to render the road passable for the wagons.[25] If it hadn't been for the services of two

23 A camping-site at the foot of Isandlwana mountain had been selected as the next staging-post on No. 3 Column's advance towards oNdini. Isandlwana was nearly ten miles by rudimentary wagon-track from Rorke's Drift.

24 The grey and brown kori bustard (*Ardeotis kori*), or pauw, is the largest flying bird native to Africa, with a length of up to four feet and a wingspan of over seven feet. It is a ground-dwelling bird that avoids flying on account of its weight, which can be as much as 40 lbs, and at the first sign of danger its response is to run or crouch.

25 The troops marching from the camping-site at the Mzinyathi River were preceded by those who had been encamped in the Batshe valley and were accompanied by about 100 wagons for regimental transport.

of our officers, Captain Krohn and Lieutenant Vane *[Vaines]*,[26] who were expert wagon-drivers and did nearly the whole of the driving themselves at the bad places, many would have broken down and the Column would have been delayed for weeks.[27] As it was, we got in in time to get the tents pitched during the afternoon. Our camp was on the extreme left, close to the main road and just below Isandhlwana hill itself, with our wagons parked at the base of it immediately in our rear. Plenty of wood being close at hand behind the hill, the Natives soon set to work to run up shelters for themselves on the other side of the road, clear of our camp. A queer-looking place they made of it, being packed like sardines, the space allotted to them being limited.[28]

Late in the evening Lonsdale was sent for by the General. I was sitting in Pope's tent (one of the young fellows of the 24th Regiment)

---

26 Captain Robert Krohn, No. 6 Company, 1/3rd NNC, who would be killed at Isandlwana, and Lieutenant Thomas Vaines (not Vane), 1/3rd NNC.

27 About a third of the wagons had to halt for the night about a mile short of Isandlwana, guarded by a wing of the 2/24th.

28 The camp extended along a line parallel to Isandlwana, some 200 yards from the base of the mountain and 200–300 yards from a donga which ran off to the south-east in front. The camp consisted of a series of smaller camps with the infantry battalions, the artillery battery and the mounted force each having their own. Ordinarily, the NNC camp would have been placed 'downstream' at the southern end of the line because of what the British considered their incurably insanitary habits. But that was where the track back to Rorke's Drift crossed a low rise of ground, the 'saddle', or 'neck' between Isandlwana and a stony knoll to its south. Since the line of communication had to be secured, the camp of the 1/24th was pitched there, and it was believed that the northern end of the camp where the NNC were placed was less likely to be attacked. The men of the NNC began building shelters for themselves from wood found nearby. Despite standing field regulations, the camp was secured neither by a laager of wagons nor by a shelter trench because Chelmsford and his over-confident staff did not think that necessary since they intended to resume the advance at once, and the camp was only a temporary one.

at the time,[29] looking at some of his sketches and he at mine, and presently he came to tell me that the 3rd N.N.C. were to start at daybreak the next morning and reconnoitre the ground over the Malakata *[Malakatha]* Hills, together with some Mounted Police under Major Dartnell, who were to work round on our left.[30] Two companies of the Contingent from each Battalion were to be left in camp to furnish outposts and a camp guard, and food taken out for the day. Very stupidly, however, very few of us took out anything but a few biscuits, thinking that we should be back in camp again before nightfall, but our experience on this occasion taught us a lesson that I don't suppose any of us have forgotten, as it was some fifty-six hours, or a little over two days, before we got any more food of any sort, though there was splendid water to drink everywhere. As soon as Lonsdale had given me his instructions, the necessary orders were issued and I went off to see the officers of the four companies detailed to remain in Camp,[31] as all for outpost duty would have to parade at once and accompany me to their positions.

One or two of them were terribly disappointed at the thought of being left behind in Camp and lose the chance of a fight, and

29 Lieutenant Charles D'Aguilar Pope (1849–79), 2/24th Regiment, served in the Ninth Cape Frontier War from February to August 1878 and was present at kwaSogekle on 12 January. He commanded G Company at Isandlwana, and was killed in the battle.

30 The NMP and half the Natal Mounted Volunteers (150 men) under Dartnell were to move out ahead of Lonsdale and 16 companies of the 3rd NNC (1,600 men) at 4.30 a.m. on the morning of 21 January. Their mission was a reconnaissance-in-force to the south-east where Lord Chelmsford had been led to believe by his scouts that Matshana kaMondisa* was gathering a force in the region of the Qudeni bush and Mangeni River to interrupt No. 3 Column's line of supply once it advanced further into Zululand.

31 The four companies were No. 6 Company (Captain Robert Krohn) and No. 9 Company (Captain James Faunce Lonsdale, Jnr), 1/3rd NNC; and No. 4 Company (Captain Edward Erskine) and No. 5 Company (Captain A.J. Barry), 2/3rd NNC. Of the four officers, only Captain Barry survived the battle of Isandlwana.

begged hard to be allowed to find substitutes, and as these were forthcoming, matters were satisfactorily arranged. Little did any of us conjecture what a momentous difference these exchanges were going to make in the course of some twenty-four hours, and many messages have I received since the campaign ended, and particularly from a Lieutenant *[Sergeant?]* Thompson,* who now lives in London (having married a very rich wife), declaring that I saved their lives.

To any who watched our departure as dawn broke[32] we must have afforded some considerable amusement going off as we did like a swarm of bees in a sort of "Devil take the hindermost" fashion. The Natives, who had been cooking and eating most of the night, still had pots full of smoking hot porridge which they brought on to parade with them, determined to leave nothing in the shape of food behind, and as it would never have done to take any notice of this irregularity we let them travel at their own pace and get well ahead so as to snatch time to finish their meal. A real cheery lot they all were—full of buoyant spirits and chaff, excellent fellows to work with … but, as was found out too late in the campaign, quite useless as fighters.

As the sun rose that morning there was a very wonderful sky scene. Overhanging Isandhlwana and the camps was a long, tortuous, more or less low-lying dark cloud, based on the horizon, much in the same form as a trail of smoke from the funnel of a steamer and ending immediately above Isandhlwana hill, which as the sun got higher was first tinted almost blood red, then passing into ashybrown with broad golden edges, assumed a marvellous variety of tints with the rise of the sun. And there it hung for the best part of the morning, frowning, as it were, over the fated Camp. I have never forgotten it. After several hours we arrived at a beautiful spot where a stream that ran through the valley above us dropped over

32 On 21 January 1879.

a precipice in a most picturesque waterfall, and on getting up into the valley, which was a dense mass of mimosa bush with precipitous krantzes and kloofs on either side, and Zulu kraals and mealie fields dotted about down below,[33] the Battalions separated, Lonsdale with the 1st Battalion, 3rd N.N.C. taking the left of the stream and I with the 2nd Battalion the right. As we worked our way along, the 1st Battalion managed to capture a considerable number of cattle, but we saw none. All the kraals that we came across were empty, and no Zulus were seen by anyone.

About midday a halt was made for a frugal meal and a rest, as most of us, and especially the Europeans who were on foot, were very nearly dead beat.[34] At the head of the valley the two Battalions got together again, somewhere between 4 and 5 p.m. and went on to the Isipezi *[Siphezi]* hill,[35] Lonsdale riding off to see Major Dartnell, who was with the Mounted Police a mile or so to our left.[36]

The sun was full setting as we reached the top of the Isipezi,[37] and as we got to the ridge the Natives, with their sharp eyes, at

---

33 The Ndweni River has its source on the high ground which rises abruptly on the east to the flat-topped Malakatha mountain, and less steeply on the west to Hlazakazi mountain.

34 Harford's account elides events. The two battalions advanced in skirmishing order up the valley and swung to their right up Malakatha. The 1/3rd NNC moved along the top of the mountain while the 2/3rd NNC advanced in parallel along the difficult terrain of Malakatha's northern, western and southern slopes. When they joined up again to the east of Malakatha to rest and eat, they sent several hundred captured cattle back to the camp at Isandlwana, escorted by one company under Captain Orlando E. Murray, 2/3rd NNC who thus had the misfortune to be caught in the battle the next day and killed.

35 After their midday meal, the two battalions continued their sweep of Malakatha and then proceeded east up Hlazakazi (and not Siphezi, which is nearly ten miles to its north-east), reaching its eastern end by late afternoon.

36 The Natal Mounted Volunteers also constituted part of Dartnell's force alongside the NMP.

37 The NNC encamped on Hlazakazi, and not on Siphezi.

once spotted a lot of Zulus on the opposite hill,[38] across a very steep and rugged valley about 800 or 900 yards off in a straight line.[39] The men were ordered to keep well out of sight below the hill, and from behind some rocks Hamilton-Browne, Cooper and I watched the Zulus stealthily moving about, their outline being well defined against the clear evening sky. Before long Major Dartnell joined us with his mounted men; they also had seen the enemy and had found them to be occupying a very strong position, and as it was still daylight he called for volunteers to go over and try to draw the Zulus out in order to see what sort of force confronted us.

Instantly a number of men jumped on their horses and were off, with orders on no account to engage the enemy but simply draw him out and then gallop back. The manoeuvre was most successful; scarcely had our men crossed the valley and got up to within some 800 yards of their position than a regular swarm of Zulus, that we estimated to be over 1000 men, swept down upon them in their horn formation and tried to surround them. Our men got back as hard as they could; no shots were fired and the Zulus returned back over their hill again.[40] A council of war was now held, and Major Dartnell decided that the troops should bivouac on the spot,[41] a message being sent to the General at once by Lieutenant Walsh*

38 Magogo mountain.

39 This was the valley of the Mangeni River.

40 The 3rd NNC was supposed to rendezvous with Dartnell's mounted force at the eastern end of Hlazakazi before returning to the camp at Isandlwana. During the afternoon some 2,000 amaZulu under Matshana had skilfully retired eastwards before them, and by evening were massed on the Magogo heights. When Dartnell attempted to approach them from the Mangeni valley below, the amaZulu proficiently deployed into two horns in skirmishing order, and the mounted men had to withdraw to avoid being enveloped.

41 Darkness was falling, and to forestall an advance by Matshana's force towards Isandlwana, Dartnell and Lonsdale decided to bivouac in a hollow square for the night on the eastern eminence of the Hlazakazi heights, westwards across the valley from Magogo and the Zulu watch-fires.

(Somerset Light Infantry), with his three mounted infantrymen to explain our position and asking for reinforcements and food. It was very evident that we were opposite a very large impi, if not the whole Zulu army.[42]

Walsh's was a very perilous journey with a fifteen-mile ride in the dark over very stiff country, hills, valleys, bush, krantzes, dongas, etc., all quite unknown to him. An occasional Kaffir path, perhaps, leading to goodness knows where, and with every chance of being attacked by a lurking body of Zulus. However, he managed to reach the camp at Isandhlwana safely, and in time for the reinforcements we asked for reaching us by daybreak the next morning, as on the receipt of Major Dartnell's message the General himself started off without a moment's delay, marching through the night with a squadron of Mounted Infantry, seven companies of the 2nd Battalion, 24th Regiment, and four guns[43] under Colonel Harness,* R.A.[44]

---

42 An 'impi' means a military force. In fact, the main Zulu army was bivouacked at Siphezi mountain some nine miles to the north-east from the NNC bivouac, and was beginning to move surreptitiously in small units north-west across the British front to the Ngwebeni valley north-east of the Isandlwana camp nine miles away.

43 These were 7-pounder rifled muzzle-loader Mark IV steel mountain guns on low-slung wheeled carriages, each drawn by three mules.

44 Major Clery received Dartnell's note carried by Lieutenant Walsh at 1.30 a.m. and woke Chelmsford up. The General believed that Dartnell's message confirmed that the main Zulu army was pushing down the Mangeni valley and threatened to invade Natal downstream of Rorke's Drift. He swiftly decided that he would move out immediately with half the force still encamped at Isandlwana, not simply to reinforce Dartnell as requested, but to intercept the Zulu army and force on the decisive battle he had always sought, and which he was confident he would win. He accordingly ordered Colonel Glyn to be ready to march out at daybreak at 4.30 a.m. with a flying column accompanied by no wagons, consisting of about half the force encamped at Isandlwana: four out of the six 7-pounder guns of N/5 Battery, RA, six (not seven) companies of the 2/24th Regiment in light marching order, a detachment of No. 1 Squadron Mounted Infantry and men of No. 1

There was some grumbling among the officers of the Native Contingent, who were tired out, at having to bivouac without food, forage or blankets (the Natives all carried their blankets on their persons), and two young officers, Lieutenants Avery and Holcroft, went off without leave, evidently to ride back to camp, but were never seen or heard of again.[45] We bivouacked that night in a hollow square, the Contingent forming the front, right and rear faces, two-company [sic] deep and the mounted men on the left. Where the mounted men tethered their horses I don't know, but our animals were all ringed together in a clump in the centre with saddles off, except mine as I should have to be constantly on the move all night while Lonsdale was superintending the formation of the bivouac. I went off to post the outposts. It was now getting dark,

---

Company, NNPC. Chelmsford and his staff were to accompany the flying column.

That left the camp with its stores, oxen and wagons under the protection of a reduced garrison consisting of a division of two 7-pounder guns, five companies of the 1/24th Regiment and one of the 2/24th, the balance of the mounted troops not already deployed, two companies each from the 1/3rd NNC and the 2/3rd NNC and small details from other units. Chelmsford put Lieutenant-Colonel Henry Burmeister Pulleine (1839–79), 24th Regiment, who had seen service in the Ninth Cape Frontier War, in command of the defence of the camp.

Conscious that Pulleine's depleted garrison ought to be augmented against what he nevertheless considered an unlikely Zulu attack, Chelmsford summoned Colonel Anthony William Durnford (1830–79), RE – who had served disastrously during the Langalibalele Rebellion of 1873 and was now commander of No. 2 Column and anxious to retrieve his reputation – to bring up what troops he had available at Rorke's Drift to reinforce the camp. These comprised a detachment of 11/7th Brigade, RA (a rocket battery of three 9-pounder Hale's rockets), five troops of the Natal Native Mounted Contingent, and two companies of the 1/1st NNC. When Durnford arrived at Isandlwana with his reinforcements at about 10.30 a.m. on 22 January, this brought the garrison up to 67 officers and 1,707 men, of whom approximately half were African.

45 Samuel Avery and Frank Holcroft were both Lieutenants in the 1/3rd NNC, and both perished at Isandlwana.

and a rare business it was. The Natives showed unmistakable signs of being in a mortal funk, and all wanted to clump together in one spot. At last, however, we strung them out like a thread of beads, each man squatting and touching his neighbour, and behind each section a European N.C.O. and a superior Native were ordered to keep up a continual patrol to see that they kept awake and didn't stir from their position. The captains and other company officers then exercised further control over their own men. In this manner more than a mile of outposts were strung out, almost encircling the bivouac.[46] By this time the Zulus had lighted fires all along their position and kept them going throughout the night,[47] and from this fact we felt pretty certain that we would be attacked in the morning. There was very little fear of a real attack during the night, as night fighting was not the Zulu method.

Having satisfied myself that the outposts were working, and after taking special note of different features, such as bushes, rocks, etc. to guide me on my visits during the night, I got back to the bivouac. Then, hitching my pony on to the others, went to report to Lonsdale whom I found sitting chatting with some of the officers and "Newman Noggs". I think the subject of this conversation was food, everyone was hungry and from my holster I produced a solitary biscuit that had been husbanded all day, which we all shared, each of us getting a piece about the size of a shilling which was better than nothing.

Intending to make a round of the outposts again in about an hour's time, I plumped myself down to snatch a rest and a short sleep, but had scarcely closed my eyes when bang went a shot from somewhere

46 Harford, as Lonsdale's Adjutant, oversaw the posting of four companies of the NNC as outposts surrounding the bivouac, while Lonsdale and Cooper formed the remainder of the NNC along three sides of the square.

47 The Zulu bivouac was on Magogo, directly east of the British bivouac about 700 or 800 yards away across the deep Mangeni valley.

in the outpost line,[48] and in a second the whole square rose up.[49] Hearing the noise the men were making, rattling their shields and fumbling about for their things, I rushed up and speaking to them in their own language ordered them to keep quiet and lie down. Their own company officers, too, did all they could to establish calm, but it was of no avail. The whole lot made a clean bolt of it and came bounding over us like frightened animals, making their way down the hillside behind us.[50] In this terrific stampede of some 4000 men the wretched ponies were swept along in a solid mass, kicking and struggling ... with several Europeans hanging on to try and stop them.[51] As these passed me, on looking round I caught a glimpse of both Lonsdale and "Noggs" turning a somersault as a lot of Natives bounded over them. Poor "Noggs", who highly resented such treatment, spent the rest of the night with the Mounted Police, having, as he afterwards told me, "had enough of the Contingent".[52]

48 The shot was fired some two hours before dawn, at about 2.30 a.m.

49 Norris-Newman reported that it was No. 1 Company, 1/3rd NNC, at one of the corners of the square, that first gave way and fled, initiating the stampede.

50 Dartnell's mounted men did not join the stampede, but maintained their discipline and lay down in line with bayonets fixed, awaiting further orders from their officers.

51 The NNC bivouacked on Hlazakazi would have numbered 1,500 at the most, and not 4,000.

52 Norris-Newman's own vainglorious account of the incident, which first appearing in his report of 26 January 1879 for the *Times of Natal*, and again in his *In Zululand with the British*, p. 52, is amusingly at variance with what Harford later called 'his fright in the square'. Norris-Newman wrote: 'I was trying to sleep, in the centre, near the Commandant [Lonsdale] ... when the first thing I remember was being trod upon by horses ... and several dusky forms, naked and with brandished weapons, ran over me, at which, waxing wroth, and very naturally imagining the Zulus were come, I "up with" my rifle and clubbed the man down, and then went to try and find my horse ... I was coming back with revolver in hand prepared for anything, when I recognised the red strip on some of the men's heads, and then knew they belonged to the Contingent.'

Amid all this confusion, someone managed to get my pony free and brought him to me, for which I was more than thankful as the situation was serious and I was now able to go in pursuit of the runaways who, at the pace they were going and the rate at which Kaffirs can travel, might soon be out of reach. Luckily, however, I found them almost at the foot of the hill, squatting in various-sized clumps, and addressing them in anything but Parliamentary language, hounded them back to the bivouac. In the darkness of the night it was impossible to say whether everyone had been rounded up, but there was no time for further search as I had to get out to the outpost line as quickly as I could.

Leaving the company officers to get their men together again, and having learnt that no reports had come in from the outposts, I went off to see what had happened, making as straight as I could for the nearest company on the extreme left of the line. On arriving at the spot where they had been posted, not a soul was to be seen, but only a very short distance from me a dark mass of something that I had no recollection of having seen when posting the men loomed up largely to my front. "Zulus!", I said to myself, and rather a shiver went down my back. Everything was dead silence, and I sat on my pony for some minutes, watching it, but as no movement took place, and feeling certain that I was mistaken, rode up to it and found that it was nothing but a mass of rock cropping out of the ground, which had not caught my eye by daylight but in the darkness showed up considerably. The company, however, had vanished.

Further on, I was more successful and found Lieutenant Thompson with his company intact, and as we met I asked him what on earth had happened at the outpost, and told him all that had taken place at the bivouac. He solved the problem by telling me that an N.C.O. of one of his sections, who should have been patrolling in company with a Native, had sat down and fallen asleep, then suddenly waking up and seeing, as he thought, a Zulu coming towards him, fired at him.[53] He said, "It's no use your going any further, as directly the shot was fired the remainder of the outpost went. There is no-one now on my front."

However, I thought it best to go and see for myself, but only found that he was quite right. Everyone but his company had vanished. A nice state of things, had we been really attacked! By the time I had completed my rounds, dawn had broken, and just as I was getting to the top of the hill near the bivouac I saw the General and his staff coming up below me, so went down to meet them.[54] Numerous questions were asked, as to where the bivouac was, what we had seen of the enemy, etc., and I was able to point out a few Zulus still hanging about on the opposite hill-top, as well as some of their fires which were still smoking.[55] After which I conducted them to where Major Dartnell and Lonsdale were,[56] when plans were thought out.[57]

53 In an additional memorandum on the incident, Harford noted, 'it appears that the European NCO with Thompson, had sat down on a rock for a second, being dogged tired, and went to sleep. Then waking suddenly, and seeing a native coming towards him, thinking it was a Zulu, fired at him, luckily, he missed the man, who turned out to be a native NCO patrolling to rear of his section.' (Payne et al., *Harford*, p. 124.)

54 Chelmsford and the flying column reached Hlazakazi at about 6.30 a.m., bringing the number of troops in the vicinity up to about 2,500.

55 The amaZulu on Magogo had broken away by then, some withdrawing south-east onto the Phindo heights where Matshana had his stronghold, and others north to Silutshana mountain. Their strategic intention is still a matter of debate, but it seems both groups planned to pull back to Siphezi mountain, where the main Zulu army had bivouacked before advancing piecemeal to the Ngwebeni valley. They appear to have calculated that they would draw the British forces on Hlazakazi after them, away from the camp at Isandlwana which the main Zulu army was going to attack.

56 Harford added in a later memorandum that he 'carefully said nothing of our little escapade' – the panic of the previous night – to Chelmsford and his staff, and that once he had brought them to Londsdale and Dartnell to confer, he immediately 'went on my way'. (Payne et al., *Harford*, p. 124.)

57 Chelmsford took Matshana's bait, and his forces in the field were dissipated during 22 January as they were drawn further eastwards. He ordered the 3rd NNC to advance in skirmishing order north-east from Hlazakazi to

Heavy mists hung over the tops of all the hills till the sun appeared and cleared the atmosphere, when our Force advanced to attack, supported by the troops the General had brought out with him and which were now in the valley below us. The Contingent were ordered to sweep over the Isilulwane *[Silulwane]* hill, where the Zulus had kept their fires burning during the night, and then work on to Matyana's *[Matshana's]** stronghold a little to the right of it.[58] Not a Zulu was to be seen when we got over the rise, and as we afterwards found out, their fires were only a blind to mislead us as to their intentions, and the few men that we had seen exposing themselves and moving about had only been left there to make us imagine that the place was occupied by a large force. On finding no enemy we swung round, descending the other side of the hill, and

---

take Silulwane hill to the west of Magogo while Dartnell's mounted men advanced up the Mangeni valley towards the Phindo ridge with its dense bush and cliffside caves. There Dartnell became involved in a heavy skirmish with Matshana's men, and the 2/3rd NNC moved forward in support with Harford conducting operations while Lonsdale and the 1/3rd NNC under Hamilton-Browne's command remained on Silulwane. Meanwhile, Glyn and his flying column were ordered to clear the area around Silutshana where some Zulu forces had withdrawn north from Magogo, and then to wheel south to the rear of Dartnell's operations, sweeping along the Nondweni River valley between Magogo and the Phindo heights. At about 10.30 a.m., concluding that he would not bring on a major engagement in the vicinity of the Phindo heights, Chelmsford sent word to Pulleine at Isandlwana to remain in the camp, but to send forward tents and supplies of food. Chelmsford then ordered Hamilton-Browne and the 1/3rd NNC on Silulwane to march back to Isandlwana to assist in bringing up the camp equipage and supplies. Having given these orders, Chelmsford rode off with his staff and a small escort to scout for a suitable campsite when the whole of No. 3 Column moved forward from Isandlwana. He selected level ground just east of Hlazakazi on the Mangeni river above its spectacular horseshoe falls, and in the early afternoon ordered all the troops operating in the vicinity to concentrate there. Meanwhile, Chelmsford's unpredictable whereabouts while he scouted made it extremely difficult for reports of the increasingly desperate situation at Isandlwana to reach him.

58 Matshana's stronghold was at the southern end of the Phindo heights.

crossed the valley on to Matyana's stronghold, a hill with nothing but a mass of huge rocks with numerous caves. Here we met with a rather warm reception, bullets began to rain down upon us from all directions, and a few men were hit. It became quite clear that a systematic attack would have to be made on the position, so the two battalions were closed in and formed up in as sheltered a position as we could find, for the companies to be told off for specific work on the front and flanks. While this was being done, both Lonsdale and Hamilton-Browne went off in pursuit of some mounted Zulus, evidently Chiefs, who had been seen somewhere on our right, and we never saw them again till late in the afternoon,[59] when they brought in the news of the terrible disaster that had overtaken the camp at Isandhlwana.

In Lonsdale's absence I sent the companies off on their different ways, and continued to conduct the operations myself. Being day instead of night, our men showed nothing of the fear they had exhibited at the bivouac, and under the leadership of the officers did uncommonly well, tackling several very nasty situations. At one spot alone, thirteen men were shot down one after another, and others were quite game to make further attempts had I not gone up myself and put a stop to an impossible undertaking. Nothing but some high explosive like dynamite could have effected an entrance to the cave, which was evidently cut well into the hillside, and the only way to get into it was by a hole underneath a massive overhanging rock, above rather a deep donga. A widish crack through the rock enabled those inside to fire straight down the donga, and made it certain death to attempt to cross it, and above again an extension of the crack provided another place to fire through, making any attempt to get at anyone inside the cave from there impossible, so I ordered the men to leave it alone and get on.

59 In the late morning, Lonsdale, Hamilton-Browne and the 1/3rd NNC had marched back towards Isandlwana on Chelmsford's orders to assist in bringing up the camp equipage and supplies.

Somebody, however, later on, had a lot of brushwood brought up and thrown into the donga with the idea of smoking the Zulus out, but this was put a stop to. At another place where several of us were being held up by snipers, I spotted a man at the entrance hole of a mass of large rock some twenty or thirty yards off taking a deliberate aim at me, and … I quickly shot at him. I then went after him, and, crawling on all fours, found him badly wounded, with a dead Zulu lying close to him. It was a curious little den, quite lighted up through the aperture in the rocks, with space enough for four or five men, and on one side a natural shelf of flat rock much like a bunk on board ship, broad enough for a man to lie on.[60]

Having got the man out and sent him back to the Doctor,[61] we continued the fight, which went on till about midday when Major Clery rode up and ordered me to take the 3rd N.N.C. back a few miles to the Amange *[Mangeni]* Gorge and let them fall out, as the General had sent into camp for provisions and intended to camp there that night.[62] On reaching Amange, and after warning the men not to get out of reach of bugle call, they were told to fall out, and in less than five minutes there was not a vestige to be seen of something like 4000 [sic] men; being hungry, they bounded off like a herd of scared deer in all directions in search of kraals and mealie fields, and were soon out of sight.

60 Norris-Newman, who was a witness to these operations on Phindo, wrote admiringly of the incident in *In Zululand with the British*, p. 55 (slightly amended from his report of 26 January 1879 in the *Times of Natal*): 'Lieutenant Harford, 99th Regiment, staff officer to Commandant Lonsdale, again distinguished himself by going in alone under a nasty crevice in some stones, shooting two men and capturing another. This officer did the same thing at the attack on Sirayo's strongholds, and would seem to have a charmed life. "May he long keep it!" – was our wish at the time.'

61 Presumably Dr Beresford, the Civilian Surgeon since Dr Buée, the Assistant Surgeon, had remained in the camp at Isandlwana.

62 At the same time, at about 12.30 p.m., Chelmsford ordered the flying column under Glyn to concentrate at the Mangeni campsite.

Not very long after the men had dispersed, and somewhere about 2 p.m., the Headquarters' bugle sounded and I at once rode off to where the General and his staff were located, and received orders to get the Contingent together at once and bring them up. This took some little doing, as many of the men were miles off, however we eventually arrived at the general rendezvous. Here, the first person I came across was Major Black, 2nd Battalion, 24th Regiment, who, like other officers, was scanning the ground towards Isandhlwana with his field-glasses and was evidently in a great state of anxiety. I said to him, "What's happening, Major?", and he replied, "The camp has been attacked and something very serious has occurred", adding, as he turned to ride away, in his peculiarly delightful Scotch accent, "E-h, Harford, keep your d…d black fellows well out of the way!"

While our men were being formed up, I proceeded to have a look at Isandhlwana and the camp myself, with my glasses, and could only see two tents standing not far from the "neck",[63] and these looked partially black as scorched by fire, but was unable to see a living creature of any sort.

News now began to leak out, and our movements made more clear. While we were fighting at Matyana's the General had received reports from the mounted men that the camp at Isandhlwana was being attacked, hence the reason for the order for the Contingent to retire to Amange. Then, after our men had all been let loose, further and more serious reports had come in,[64] and finally we were assembled preparatory to an advance on the Camp, when

63 The *nek* (a mountain pass in Afrikaans) meaning in this context the saddle between Isandlwana mountain and the stony knoll to its south where the camp of the 1/24th had been pitched.

64 Throughout the course of the morning and early afternoon, increasingly urgent messages were sent to Chelmsford that the camp at Isandlwana was under serious attack, but they either failed to find him or were discounted by the General and his staff who were utterly over-confident after their successes in the Ninth Cape Frontier War and, most recently, at kwaSogekle.

Lonsdale's message to the General, written on a scrap of paper, "For God's sake, come. The camp has been taken", was brought in by Hamilton-Browne.[65]

Both Lonsdale and Hamilton-Browne, as I have already said, left us at Matyana's … and both apparently found their way to the camp at Isandhlwana, but Lonsdale evidently got their [sic] first.[66] In a fit of absentmindedness he rode straight into the Camp and, as he told me afterwards, got up to where his tent was pitched when he suddenly discovered nothing but Zulus looting and dressed in soldiers' coats, whereupon he turned round and rode away. Apparently the apparition of a live white man in their midst, when they felt certain that they had killed everyone, so alarmed them that they let him go unheeded—a marvellous adventure!!! When well clear, of course he rode for dear life to bring the terrible news to the General, but before he could reach Headquarters his pony, Dot, became exhausted, and by a piece of luck Hamilton-Browne (who on approaching the camp had found his way barred by Zulus

65 In fact, the message was a verbal one, so it is inevitable that variations were recorded. But its essence was as Harford reported, and it was Hamilton-Browne from his position with the 1/3rd NNC four miles from Isandlwana (see note below) who at about 1.30 p.m. ordered Captain R. Develin to ride in Chelmsford's direction and deliver it to every officer he met. Develin relayed it to Lieutenant-Colonel Harness, who was slowly moving towards the Mangeni campsite with his four 7-pounder guns and an escort of the 2/24th. Harness immediately turned back towards Isandlwana. He had covered two or three miles when Chelmsford, who was not yet convinced the camp was under Zulu attack, ordered him to turn around again and join Glyn and the flying column at the Mangeni campsite.

66 In the late morning, Lonsdale and the 1/3rd NNC under Hamilton-Browne had marched back towards Isandlwana (see pp. 64–5 n. 57 above). At about midday they halted about four miles away from the camp on receiving intelligence that it was under attack. It was not until 1.30 p.m., and after Lonsdale had ridden forward to Isandlwana, that Hamilton-Browne realised that the amaZulu had overrun the camp. He then withdrew the 1/3rd NNC for about a mile and halted at a defensible rocky position, ordered each company to form a defensive circle, and waited on developments.

and was returning with the news) met him, and as his pony was fairly fresh Lonsdale sent on his chit to the General by him and then came slowly on, leading his pony.[67]

By the time the Scouts and reconnoitring parties who had been recalled, and other units, had assembled at the rendezvous it was nearly four o'clock,[68] and before being formed up for attack the General briefly addressed the troops, telling them that the Camp had been taken and saying that he relied on us to re-take it.[69] We then marched off in the following order:

The four guns, Royal Artillery, in the centre, with companies of the 2nd Battalion, 24th Regiment on either flank. On either side of them again, a little to the rear, our Contingent, Lonsdale with

67 Lonsdale had insouciantly ridden into the Isandlwana camp at about 2 p.m. to arrange for supplies to be brought up to the forces in the field, and barely escaped the triumphant amaZulu who were in possession. It was at about 3.30 p.m. that Lonsdale reached Hamilton-Browne and the 1/3rd NNC halted about five miles away. He was able to make his report to the incredulous and appalled Chelmsford who at 2.45 p.m. had at last decided to return to Isandlwana with his staff and a mounted escort to investigate, and had reached Hamilton-Browne's position at about 3.15 p.m.

68 From his position with Hamilton-Browne, Chelmsford sent Major Matthew Gossett (1839–1909), 54th Regiment, a member of his personal staff, galloping back to the Mangeni camp five or six miles in his rear. He reached Glyn at 4.05 p.m. and ordered him to concentrate his troops and march immediately to join the General. Chelmsford, meanwhile, advanced another mile or so towards Isandlwana with the 1/3rd NNC deployed in three ranks with the white officers and NCOs and those levies with firearms to the fore, and with the Natal Mounted Volunteers and Mounted Infantry on either flank. Glyn finally came up at 6.10 p.m. with the men of the flying column, and with the apprehensive men of the 2/3rd NNC led by Harford making up the rear.

69 Chelmsford's words, as reported by Major Clery were: 'Men, the enemy has taken our camp. Many of our friends must have lost their lives defending it. There is nothing left for us now but to fight our way through – and mind, we must fight hard, for we will have to fight for our lives. I know you, and I know I can depend on you.' (Clery to Harman, 17 February 1879, in Clarke, *Invasion of Zululand*, p. 85.)

the 1st Battalion, 3rd N.N.C. on the left and myself with the 2nd Battalion on the right. Beyond us again on either flank were the Mounted troops.[70] When getting within about a mile of the camp a large body of Zulus were seen disappearing over a hill to the right of it, looking like an enormous mass of ants or swarm of bees, so we were halted for a few minutes to let the artillery send a few shells into them.[71] We saw every shell burst right in the middle of them, but the mass was so dense that whatever gaps were caused by the shot were instantly filled up and it was impossible to see what damage had been done. Anyone who has handled a swarm of bees would see the simile.

---

70 This was a regulation fighting formation. The guns in the centre were in column with room to form line for action. There were three companies of British infantry on either flank of them, a battalion of the NNC to each flank of the regulars, and the mounted troops rode on the flanks of the NNC and in advance of them. Skirmishers were thrown out in front and a small guard looked after the wagons and ambulances in the rear. Shortly after 6.15 p.m. in the gathering darkness of a moonless night, this force began its cautious advance on Isandlwana.

71 Chelmsford's force neared the stricken camp at about 8 p.m. At about a quarter of a mile from the 'neck', Harness fired about a dozen shells in the dark, and the British infantry on the left went forward to take the stony knoll on the southern side of the camp. They met no resistance since (except for a few stragglers) the victorious amaZulu had retired, and the rest of the force then went forward and reoccupied the camp at about 8.30. p.m.

CHAPTER 3

Rorke's Drift

It was quite dark when the Force reached the now devastated camp.[1] On the right, where I was with the 2nd Battalion, 3rd N.N.C., the grass on the undulating ground over which we advanced had been trampled quite flat and smooth by the Zulu army, but no dead were lying about, so without doubt they must have carried off their own casualties. On the left, towards the "neck" where the 24th and others of our men made their stand, the dead lay thick, and it was a ghastly sight. Had it not been for the seriousness of the situation, the manner in which my lot of the N.N.C. had to be driven along would have been amusing. A two-deep line formation was not at all to their liking, all were in a most mortal funk, nothing on earth could make those who were armed with rifles keep their place in the front rank, and all the curses showered on them by their officers could not prevent them from closing in and mixing up in clumps. I had an awful time of it, too, directly it got dusk, doing nothing but ride from one end of the line to the other, hustling them on to prevent lagging. How Lonsdale and his lot got on I don't know, but no doubt had the same trouble having got into the camp and meeting with no resistance.

---

1 British casualties along the firing line at Isandlwana, in the camp and along the line of flight down to Sothondose's or Fugitives' Drift across the Mzinyathi comprised 52 white officers, 739 white troops and 67 white NCOs of the 3rd NNC. 471 black troops (including noncombatants) were recorded as killed, although the number was probably closer to 500.

The Troops were ordered to bivouac on the ground, and a large hollow square was formed on the "neck" across the main road, a deep valley running down between us and the opposite hill behind which Dabulamanzi* with a considerable impi lay hidden.[2] The greater portion of the Zulu army which had taken part in the massacre in the camp, we learnt afterwards, had gone straight off to Kambula, sixty miles away, that night, to attack Colonel Evelyn Wood's* column the next morning.[3] To the 2nd Battalion, 3rd N.N.C. was assigned the rifle face of the square which rested at the foot of the slope running down from Isandhlwana hill itself, and the men kept in mass formation in quarter column. The night was pitch dark, and the stench, which was mostly from the smashed-up contents of the Royal Army Medical Corps[4] wagon containing all manner of chemicals, within a few yards of us, was truly awful. As soon as the bivouac had settled down—and by this time the Zulus had begun to light fires and could be seen moving about on the ridge just across the valley, barring our line of retreat to Rorke's Drift[5]—Lord Chelmsford himself took a look round to see how

2 In fact, Dabulamanzi and the Zulu reserve were fully committed that night in attacking the post at Rorke's Drift on the further side of the Mzinyathi.

3 This is mistaken. When the amaZulu looting the camp saw Chelmsford returning in battle order, they precipitately retired with their plunder to their bivouac at the Ngwebeni River, leaving their wounded on the field. The army then dispersed home to undergo the ritual purification that followed combat. Probably, no fewer than 1,000 amaZulu perished in the battle. The Zulu veterans of Isandlwana did not reassemble until late March, when Cetshwayo despatched them to attack Colonel Wood's No. 4 Column. The Zulu army defeated part of Wood's force on Hlobane mountain on 28 March, but were routed in the pitched battle at Khambula the following day – a battle that was the decisive turning-point in the war.

4 Harford means the Army Hospital Corps, formed in 1873. The Royal Army Medical Corps was not formed until 1898.

5 These must have been Zulu watch-fires, or the bivouacs of their dispersing army, because the only Zulu force still operating in the field was that under Dabulamanzi attacking Rorke's Drift.

things were going. On coming across to us he had many questions to ask concerning the Contingent, and stayed talking for some time, among other things asking me what I thought the Zulus would do, whether they would attack us or not, and I told him that I felt pretty certain that they would as soon as it was daylight.

Later on during the night he paid us another visit, just after a nice escapade by our terrorised Natives. What happened was this. At a quiet moment, when I saw my way to getting away for a few minutes, I hurriedly stole out into the camp to the spot where my tent had rested, to see if I could find any of my belongings lying about, and on returning to the bivouac found that nearly the whole of our Natives had disappeared as by magic. Curiously, no-one had noticed them as they squatted, gently and gradually sliding down the hill into the valley like a huge landslide, notwithstanding the inky darkness of the night and the fact that the moving mass consisted of some 800 men or more. It was an uncommonly serious state of affairs, and might have given rise to a false alarm at any moment, so after sending some of our own officers off to give immediate warning of what had taken place to the troops near us, I bolted down the hill as quickly as I could. Inky dark as it was, I managed by degrees to stumble on clumps of men here and there, and many of the dark figures I ran up against, who were not squatting, I feel certain were Zulus and not our men. Anyway, I was never interfered with.

After a good deal of trouble I rounded up at all events the majority of the men, and literally drove them back to the square. Scarcely had they been got into position again than the General paid us another visit, and I had to tell him what had taken place. He was very angry, and said, "I will give you two men of the 24th Regiment", and sending for them at once placed them himself as sentries, with orders to bayonet the first Native that attempted to move from his position, and directing me in his presence to explain this to the men. After this there was no further trouble.

The visit to my tent proved a blank, everything had gone, and the same with Lonsdale's tent, which was next to it, but between our tents lay the bodies of two artillery men, disembowelled and terribly mutilated.[6]

Within a few yards of where our wagon had been drawn up I found the dead bodies of our two drivers, with their faces blackened, and it struck me at the time that they must have done this themselves in the hope of being able to escape. On passing the hospital wagon from whence all the abominable stench came, I came across the body of Surgeon-Major Shepherd, the P.M.O., who in years gone by had been Assistant-Surgeon in the 99th Regiment. He was lying face downwards, and had been stabbed in the neck, but his body had not been mutilated.[7]

Several times during the night Major Clery, the Adjutant-General, came over and had a talk, and on one of these occasions

---

6 The British were appalled to discover their dead partially stripped of their clothes and with their bellies ripped open and their bowels hanging out. They did not understand that both these actions were Zulu religious rituals for the removal of supernational evil influence, or *mnyama*, that followed on the shedding of human blood. Disembowelment ensured that *mnyama* did not cause the killer to swell up like the dead; while it was necessary to exchange some of his clothing, ritually contaminated by his victim's blood, for his own, and to wear it until ritually cleansed on his return home.

7 Surgeon-Major Peter Shepherd (1841–79), MB. A graduate of the University of Aberdeen, in 1863 he joined the 99th Regiment in South Africa as Assistant Surgeon. After the regiment returned to England in 1869, he held appointments in India and England. Promoted Surgeon-Major, he returned to South Africa in November 1878 attached to the 24th Regiment. He took part in the advance of No. 3 Column, and was in the camp at Isandlwana when the Zulu attacked. A report by Trooper Muirhead of the Natal Carbineers asserted that when Shepherd was galloping down the Fugitives' Trail, he dismounted to assist a wounded trooper and was speared before he could remount. This does not accord with Harford's description of Shepherd lying within a few yards of the ambulance wagon close to the 'neck' where Harford was posted on the night of 22 January. Since Harford knew Shepherd personally, his account is to be preferred.

we were strolling out on the "neck" when we came across a large tarpaulin rolled up, and being a comfortable-looking seat both of us at once sat down but silently rose up again somewhat horrified on feeling that we had sat on something soft and undoubtedly a dead body. Why we neither of us thought of unrolling the tarpaulin to ascertain whose body it was I don't know, except that under the circumstances of the moment, with dead all around one, we had no stomach for curiosity.

During the night one or two officers of the different Corps were permitted to go off for a short time in search of food, but as the Zulus had turned out the contents of the Commissariat wagon, stabbing or smashing up all the tinned articles and apparently carried off all the biscuits, little or nothing was found. One officer, however, Lieutenant Newnham Davis, of the "Buffs",[8] who was with the Mounted Infantry, managed to get a two-pound tin of corned beef, almost whole, and as we tramped in together to Rorke's Drift the following morning demolished the lot, never offering me or anyone else even a mouthful. I don't think another officer, N.C.O. or Private, in the whole column, would have been guilty of such selfish gluttony.

Of course we never saw anything more of the four companies of the N.N.C. that had been left in the Camp, with the exception of the Captain, who had escaped on my little grey pony.[9] Every other European had undoubtedly been killed, but a good many of the Natives from all accounts got away, though they never rejoined us again. Throughout the night we could see the intermittent flashes

8 Lieutenant Nathaniel Newnham-Davis, 2/3rd Regiment, served with No. 1 Squadron, Mounted Infantry throughout the war. He was absent with Chelmsford's reconnaissance-in-force during Isandlwana. Subsequently, No. 1 Squadron remained in garrison at Helpmekaar until it joined Wood's No. 4 Column in mid-March and fought at Hlobane and Khambula. It advanced with Wood's Flying Column and was present at Ulundi. It then joined Baker Russell's Column in pacification operations.

9 Captain A.J. Barry. See p. 55 n. 31 above.

of light from the firing at the Rorke's Drift post, which was only some three or four miles off in a straight line, though twelve miles by road. Everyone felt very anxious for the fate of the little garrison after what had happened in the Camp, and longed for daylight to march to their relief.[10]

At last the day dawned and the troops began to move off. The Contingent formed the rearguard and were the last to quit the ground, in broad daylight, and it was my business to see the last man away.[11] Contrary to all expectations, Dabulamanzi with his impi made no attempt whatever to interfere with the Column, though some hundreds of his warriors sat and stood within a few yards of us on the right of the road, simply gazing at us like sightseers at a review. I and … many others … were absolutely dumbfounded at this extraordinary spectacle, and could scarcely believe our eyes. Personally, I felt very suspicious about it all and thought a trap was

---

10 Dabulamanzi led the reserve that had not been engaged with the rest of the Zulu army at Isandlwana – a force of between 3,000 and 4,000 – against the post at Rorke's Drift, where the defenders – who numbered eight officers, and 131 men, 35 of whom were sick in the hospital – hastily threw up improvised defences. The Zulu attack commenced at about 4.30 p.m. and reached its crescendo after 6 p.m. Daunted by the desperate defence, the amaZulu launched no more attacks after about 9 p.m. and ceased their desultory fire at about 4 a.m. on 23 January. Most retired at daybreak, the last melting away after 7 a.m. The defenders lost 17 men killed, and one officer and seven men wounded. An estimated minimum of 600 amaZulu died in the attack.

11 Chelmsford gave the order at 4 a.m. to march back to Rorke's Drift hoping in the pre-dawn light to spare as many of his men as possible the grisly sigh of the sacked camp and the mutilated dead. In his haste to be gone, Chelmsford left the British dead unburied, a decision that raised a storm of indignation in Natal and Britain. The 2/3rd NNC at the head of the column, marching four abreast, indeed saw little of the devastation, but the 1/3rd NNC, with Harford chivvying them along, were the last foot soldiers to quit the ground. By then the sun was up, and they saw it all, as did the Mounted Infantry, NMP and Natal Mounted Volunteers who formed the column's rearguard and flankers.

being laid, especially as a few hundreds [sic] yards below on our left, just above the Buffalo River, great masses of Zulus were coming away from Rorke's Drift who could easily have swept up the hills, joined Dabulamanzi's men, and come down like an avalanche from the rear on our straggling Column.

As we were hurrying along at a great pace, I thought that perhaps the masses of Zulus in the valley below us had escaped the notice of the head of the Column, so rode on as fast as I could, to report. But I found that the General was aware of their presence, and that unless they attacked, the Column was to push on with all haste to Rorke's Drift. Luckily, we got in unmolested.[12] As we approached the Drift and reached the hill overlooking the river and the Post, the excitement became intense, all eyes were strained and field-glasses raised, to see if there was any sign of life in the Fort. Then, as we drew nearer, a man was seen on the bared roof of one of the buildings, signalling with a flag, which was hailed with a tremendous cheer from the whole Column as we knew then that the garrison had not been wiped out.[13]

The General and his staff galloped off at once to the Fort and the troops got in by degrees,[14] the selecting of their camping grounds taking some little time. We were the last to get in, and for some

12 When the retreating British column had crossed the Manzimnyama stream and were within three miles of Rorke's Drift, they came in sight of the amaZulu as described by Harford. The two forces passed by each other close enough for some provocative verbal exchanges, but the British were almost out of ammunition, and both they and the amaZulu were exhausted, hungry and demoralised. Consequently, neither side fired a shot and continued on their separate ways. See Harford's explanation for this extraordinary event on pp. 96–7 below.

13 Chelmsford's relief column came in sight of Rorke's Drift at about 8 a.m. on 23 January.

14 To call the depot and its rudimentary defences a 'Fort' is misleading. The British only began to turn the post into a real fort with stone walls after the battle, (see pp. 84–5 n. 27 below), and in late March work began on Fort Melvill nearby, which was built overlooking the pont at the drift (see p. 92 n. 44 below).

time it was quite impossible to keep the men in hand. They were all round the surroundings of the Fort in a second, crowding about the Zulu dead who were lying thick everywhere, partly, no doubt, from curiosity but I dare say some may have been looking out to identify friends or relations as many of the Natal Kaffirs are refugees from Zululand.

Commandant Lonsdale having gone to interview the General and to get something to eat, I also strolled into the Fort and helped myself bountifully to some biscuits, several boxes of which the thoughtful Commissariat Officers, Dunne[15] and Dalton,* had hauled out and opened for us hungry souls. What a Godsend it was, as it was over two days and two nights since most of us had had a mouthful of food. Hunger, however, luckily does not affect one like thirst, and one could have gone on much longer as there was plenty of good water.

As I ate biscuits I wandered about the Fort, looking at the wreckage which gave the appearance and feeling of devastation after a hurricane, with the dead bodies thrown in, the only thing that remained whole being a circular miniature fortress constructed of bags of mealies in the centre. Several of our dead lay just where they had fallen, and one of them—a youngster in the Natal Mounted Police—a very fine specimen of humanity, struck me particularly. Having given our natives ample time to exhaust their curiosity, they were got together and marched off to the position allotted to us at the back of the Fort, behind the Itchiane hill *[Shiyane hill; also known as the Oskarsberg]* to guard the valley up which the Zulus had made

15 Deputy Assistant Commissary-General Walter Alphonsus Dunne (1853–1908), Commissariat and Transport Department, served throughout the Ninth Cape Frontier War and in the First Anglo-Pedi War, 1877–8. He then joined No. 3 Column as the Senior Commissariat Officer and was stationed at Rorke's Drift. He played an active and critical part in the defence of the post. He subsequently served with Wood's Flying Column as Commissary of Supplies and was present at Ulundi.

their attacks, well hidden until the last moment. Outposts were at once posted and Mounted Patrols sent out, and the remainder of the troops not thus occupied were told off to clear the surroundings of the Fort and renovate the defences. As many of our men as could be supplied with picks and shovels were set to work to dig pits and bury the dead Zulus,[16] and the remainder brought in stones for reconstructing and strengthening the barricades.[17] Altogether, it was a stiff day, and officers and men worked alike.

The General left very shortly for Helpmekaar, en route for Pietermaritzburg, leaving Colonel Glyn in command with Major Clery as Chief Staff Officer, and Colonel Degacher then took over the command of the 24th Regiment.[18] Before leaving, the General issued orders for the disbandment of the Natives of the Contingent,[19] and leave was granted to Commandant Lonsdale to

---

16 The British ultimately buried 351 amaZulu who had been killed close to the post. A further 200 Zulu bodies were reported to have been found further off from those buried at the post. Many of these 'dead' were Zulu wounded whom British patrols, conserving their ammunition, systematically finished off with bayonet, rifle butt and spear. For months after, the garrison at Rorke's Drift kept coming across further bodies of the wounded who had crept away to die. The British took only three wounded amaZulu prisoner.

17 Not knowing Zulu intentions and fearing another attack, on the morning of 23 January Rorke's Drift was prepared for defence. The barricades were rebuilt and strengthened and the four 7-pounder guns of the N/5th RA were mounted at the corners of the post. The half-burnt thatch was pulled off the roof of the storehouse (previously the mission church) and the brush and trees cleared away all around the perimeter.

18 At 9 a.m. on 24 January Chelmsford and his staff with a small escort of NMP set off for Helpmekaar. They were followed by the artillery and the rest of the mounted men, leaving at Rorke's Drift the company of the 1/24th that had defended the post and the six companies of the 2/24th that had not been engaged at Isandlwana.

19 Before leaving for Helpmekaar, Chelmsford ordered Lonsdale to find out which men of the 3rd NNC were willing to re-enter Zululand when he resumed the offensive, and to disband those who were not. Lonsdale addressed the regiment and concluded that only the iziGqoza were

proceed to Cape Town for the purpose of raising a Mounted Corps (but I don't think this was carried out),[20] and he left us. The orders regarding myself were, that I was to remain for duty in charge of the European Officers and N.C.O.'s of the Contingent until they had all been drafted off to other columns,[21] after which I was to rejoin my

---

prepared to fight on, and that the rest were hopelessly demoralised. He thereupon took the decision to disband the entire regiment (although he subsequently gave Chelmsford the impression that they had deserted). The white officers and NCOs took in the men's firearms along with the red puggarees that identified them as members of the NNC. At the whim of their officers, some companies were allowed to take their flags home. Not all the men understood what was happening, and had to be driven out of camp. The iziGqoza companies left in good military order, but other levies simply bolted for home in small groups, sowing panic wherever they went through northern Natal. In April, some of the former members of the 3rd NNC were reassembled as the Weenen Contingent to assist in the defence of the northern border of Natal. It was mustered in traditional African fashion and no longer organised along British military lines as the NNC had been, but its morale was poor.

20 Harford's uncertainty about this is puzzling. Lonsdale raised four troops of white irregular cavalry, known as Lonsdale's Horse (Mounted Rifles), three of which joined the 1st Division. Two of them under Captain Lumley went on to serve with Clarke's Column in the final stages of the war. Since Harford was himself a staff officer with Clarke's Column, he surely must have been aware of their presence.

21 In February the remaining two NNC regiments were reorganised into five battalions, and their officers and those of the disbanded 3rd NNC were reassigned. However, many of the under-utilised or redundant white NCOs volunteered to form a new unit of irregular cavalry named the Natal Horse. It consisted of three troops totalling about 150 men wearing their old NNC uniforms. No. 2 Troop (Cooke's Horse) joined the Eshowe Relief Column and fought at Gingindlovu. It subsequently joined the 1st Division. No. 3 Troop (Bettington's Horse) joined the 2nd Division and fought at Ulundi. No. 1 Troop (de Burgh's Horse), recruited from NCOs from Harford's old regiment, the 3rd NNC, joined the 1st Division in late April. Harford later served alongside them when they formed part of Clarke's Column conducting pacification operations.

Regiment with No. 1 Column *[the 1st Division]* on the Coast.[22] The matter of collecting arms and equipment from our men was taken in hand at once, and took some little time. They were all, of course, allowed to retain their blankets,[23] much to their joy—and with as much beef as they could stuff themselves with the night before being set free, all were in the highest spirits. I shall never forget the scene at their departure, we started them off soon after sunrise, and the whole mass of some 3000 bounded gaily off, laughing and joking and performing all sorts of antics, then presently dividing into separate parties, making bee-lines for their homes, very soon presented the appearance of swarms of ants covering the hillsides.

A considerable number went via Helpmekaar, and here a most amusing, though at the same time rather an alarming, situation was created. There being no telegraphic communication between Helpmekaar and Rorke's Drift, and the staff at Rorke's Drift having

22 Harford wrote to his mother on 14 January that he was 'awfully annoyed' when he learned the 99th Regiment was 'coming out' to South Africa since that made all his efforts to be sent out on Special Service unnecessary. (Payne et al., *Harford*, p. 120.) He had already sailed for the Cape when in late November the 99th received its orders to embark for active service in Zululand. The regiment landed in Durban in early January 1879 and joined Colonel Charles Knight Pearson's (1834–1909) No. 1 Column, leaving three companies behind on garrison duty at Durban, Stanger and Fort Tenedos. Two companies of the 99th were present at the battle of Nyezane. Three companies and the headquarters (which, if he had been present, would have included Harford as Adjutant) were holed up in Fort Eshowe during the Zulu investment. Five companies formed part of Chelmsford's Eshowe Relief Column and fought at Gingindlovu. After the relief of Eshowe on 3 April, the regiment was stationed at the Lower Thukela and formed part of the 1st Brigade of the 1st Division that advanced up the Zulu coast in June. It is then that Harford rejoined his regiment.

23 Other reports state that the blankets were taken in. As with the company flags, this was probably a matter left to the discretion of individual company commanders.

quite forgotten to send a messenger to let the O.C. Helpmekaar[24] know that the Contingent were being disbanded—their outpost took our men to be a Zulu impi advancing, and sent in reports to that effect. This of course caused the Helpmekaar garrison to man their defences and prepare for a fight. Several shots, I believe, were fired at our men by the outposts, but luckily no-one was hit. Someone, however, before the outposts retired, discovered in some way that the supposed enemy were men of the Contingent, but the Helpmekaar garrison had had a good fright.[25]

With the disbandment of our men,[26] the officers and N.C.O.'s of the Contingent were brought into the Fort and given the N.E.

24 Colone Fairfax Charles Hassard (1822–1900), RE, CB, saw service in the Crimean War and in the Ninth Cape Frontier War. In 1879 he joined Chelmsford's Headquarters Staff as Officer Commanding RE in South Africa and the Field. In the aftermath of Isandlwana, he dug in at Helpmekaar and built a proper fort. He then suffered a nervous breakdown and on 29 January surrendered his command to Colonel Edward William Bray, 2/4th Regiment, and proceeded to Cape Town.

25 The dispersing 3rd NNC were not the only African levies on 24 January to alarm the jittery garrison at Helpmekaar, which consisted of about 180 officers and men, including 30 who had escaped from Isandlwana. On 19 January, Chelmsford had ordered the 2/1st NNC, which formed part of Colonel Durnford's No. 2 Column under the command of the Special Service office, Brevet Major Bengough,* to take up position downstream from Rorke's Drift at the Mazongweni (KwaMahamba) Drift, six miles south-west of Malakatha mountain. They were to be ready in three days' time to cross the Mzinyathi and support Chelmsford's right flank when he advanced. This disposition left the 2/1st NNC uselessly stranded during the battles of Isandlwana and Rorke's Drift. On the following day they hurriedly moved up from the river to Helpmekaar. They were shaken by the news of Isandlwana and were already starting to desert, encouraged by the men of the disbanded 3rd NNC. On the evening of 24 January Bengough marched them back south towards the Umsinga magistracy, where they began constructing Fort Bengough.

26 Harford does not mention it in his reminiscences, but since Lonsdale had left for the Cape, he was now technically the Officer Commanding the 3rd NNC, disbanded though it was. In that capacity, on 31 January 1879 he

corner of it to hold, and a very tight fit it was for everyone as the place was overcrowded with the number of men in occupation.[27]

---

wrote officially to Colonel Glyn, the Officer Commanding the Troops at Rorke's Drift:

'I have the honour to state that the two officers viz Captain Stephenson & Lieutenant Higginson lately reported as missing after the fight at Isandhlwana, & supposed to have escaped to P.M Burg, have rejoined their Corps, & having been placed under arrest in accordance with orders from Commandant Lonsdale, for absenting themselves since the 22nd inst from their Corps without cause, and permission.

'I have the honour to request in the absence of Cmt Lonsdale, that I may be informed what steps to take in the matter.' (Payne et al., *Harford*, p. 133.)

Captain William Stephenson was in command of a company of the 2/3rd NNC stationed at Rorke's Drift. On the afternoon of 22 January, when it was learned that the amaZulu were advancing on the post, his poorly trained and demoralised company of the NNC abandoned the garrison and fled towards Helpmekaar. Unable to prevent them, Stephenson galloped off after his men instead of staying to fight. W.C.R. Higginson, who had been a Lieutenant of the Dublin City Militia, was Lieutenant and Adjutant of the 1/3rd NNC. He was present at Isandlwana but escaped down the Fugitives' Trail on a horse seized from one of his own men. To make matters worse, even though he assisted Lieutenants Coghill* and Melvill* in crossing the Mzinyathi at Fugitives' Drift (see below pp. 105–6 and pp. 107–8 n. 26) (he had been thrown from his horse in the river), on reaching the Natal bank he cravenly abandoned the exhausted pair to die and made his escape on foot to the top of the hill, and then by holding on to the tail of the horse of one of four men of Hlubi's Troop (Mounted Basutos) passing by. Higginson, in a letter to Sir Joscelyn Coghill, Bart, (Lieutenant Coghill's father) disingenuously explained that when the two lieutenants stopped and he carried on, none of them 'imagined at this time there was anyone following us'. (Higginson to Sir J. Coghill, n.d., cited in Verbeeck, 'Saving the Queen's Colour', p. 51). Because both Stephenson and Higginson were colonial – not imperial – officers, it transpired that they could not be court-martialled for desertion. Instead, on 19 February 1879 they were officially informed that their services were dispensed with, being no longer required.

27 The garrison consisted of six companies of the 2/24th and one of the 1/24th (B Company that had defended the post) under Major Wilsone Black, a detachment of RE, ten NMP and the officers and NCOs of the defunct 3rd NNC. In early April, Lieutenant-Colonel Degacher took three companies of the 2/24th to the camp of the 2nd Division, South African Field Force

To make matters worse we had a lot of rain, and the interior of the Fort became a simple quagmire from the tramping of so many feet. Fatigue parties were employed for the best part of the day in carrying liquid mud away and emptying the slush outside. In this state of filth we lived and ate and slept for more than two months, no-one being in possession of anything more than a blanket and the clothes that he stood up in.[28] An exception was made, however, with B Company, 2nd battalion [sic] 24th Regiment, who had made such a gallant defence, and they were housed in the attic of Rorke's house[29] with a tarpaulin thrown over the rafters (from which the thatch had been removed) to shelter them from the wet, a well-deserved honour. However, even they had their troubles in trying to keep dry, as the tarpaulin often bagged in between the rafters with a collection of water which had to be ejected, and I shall not easily forget one particular night when Dr. Reynolds,* who got the V.C., and I met in the dark having been literally washed out of our sleeping place, and mooched about, endeavouring to find a more sheltered spot. Suddenly we hit upon the idea of lying down under the eaves of B. Company's roof, so coiled ourselves up in our soaking wet blankets, thanking our stars that at all events there would be no river running under us, when presently swish came about half a ton of water clean on top of us—B. Company were emptying their tarpaulin! It was useless moving, as we could

---

at Dundee, a tiny hamlet that had sprung up near the coal deposits on the farms Dundee and Coalfields 25 miles north-north-west of Helpmekaar. By the second week of February the temporary fortifications at Rorke's Drift had been replaced by a strong stone wall and was loopholed all round, sometimes referred to as Fort Bromhead. The sector facing Shiyane was two storeys high with a firing platform made of planks.

28 Norris-Newman noted that the officers and NCOs of the 3rd NNC 'had lost all their baggage and effects at Isandhlwana; and the stores for their re-equipment, by some mischance, had never reached Rorke's Drift'. (Norris-Newman, *In Zululand*, p. 118.)

29 The commissariat store, previously the mission church.

not better ourselves, and wet as we were, thanks to the temperature of the atmosphere and the heat from our bodies, were comfortably warm as long as we lay still.

This terrible state of things, living in such slush, caused a lot of sickness from fever and dysentery which carried off a large number of men and one or two of the officers.[30] Notwithstanding this, and the knowledge that the Fort was overcrowded, Colonel Glyn declined to have any tents pitched outside to relieve matters, being afraid that the Zulus might sweep down on the place again; and so conscientiously did he believe that this would happen that no-one but the officers and N.C.O.'s of the Contingent were allowed outside the Fort.[31] The officers of the Contingent being all mounted, it fell

30 When Norris-Newman visited Rorke's Drift on 10 February, Harford 'was the first to welcome' him and the evening was spent 'yarning' about recent events. He found 'over fifty men in hospital, and forty sick, while eight had died'. (Norris-Newman, *In Zululand*, pp. 116, 117.)

31 Colonel Glyn was not being unduly cautious. In the wake of Isandlwana, a great panic swept over Natal and it was supposed that the victorious Zulu army would invade the colony. We now know that Cetshwayo had no such intention and was committed to fighting a defensive war on his own territory, but the military and colonial authorities presumed otherwise. The soldiers held fast in their forts, and the settlers took shelter in their town and country laagers, or trekked over the Drakensberg to take safety in the Orange Free State. Larger towns like Pietermaritzburg and Durban were prepared for defence with improvised fortifications.

The mood among colonists was expressed in a letter written on 27 January 1879 by Robert Jameson* in Durban to Harford's mother:

'Thank God, Charlies is safe – he was not in the camp at the time of the massacre.

'I have felt absolutely sick with fear since we learnt it was his column which was cut up – , and the suspense of waiting for the list of killed is something dreadful – , if so to me, what must it be to his Mother?

'Many of my best friends have perished in the massacre, and I feel altogether unmanned by the sudden and awful Calamity.

'We are in a sad state here, never knowing what a night may bring us. Every man in the Town is drilling and all are armed and determined to make a good stand up fight for our wives and bairns if these brutes should come.

to our lot to perform all the reconnoitring and patrolling work,[32] and at dawn every morning while the garrison stood to their arms we issued out to scour the surrounding country for a mile or two, closely examining the ground everywhere, which was not altogether a pleasant undertaking at that hour of the day.[33] Then, returning to get something to eat and feed the horses, we again saddled up, and dividing into two parties started to patrol and reconnoitre the river, one lot going up towards Helpmekaar and the other down towards the "Fugitives' Drift"—so-called from being the crossing by which all who escaped from Isandhlwana made their way.

The distance that each patrol covered was from eight to ten miles, and on returning, verbal reports were made to Major Clery, the Chief of the Staff. Some 300 or 400 yards behind the Fort, and overlooking it, was Itchiane [Shiyane] hill from the summit of which a splendid panorama of the country for a great many miles round could be obtained, and where, after the arrival of the relief column a heliograph station was established.[34] On the morning of

'Our natives are all running away from Town, everyone looks worn & sad and troubled and the place is most doleful, so many people have lost relatives & friends, it is a sad time for women & children.

'We feel something of the "Meerut" – revenge spirit [during the Indian Mutiny] which will result in bad things for the Zulus.

'Enclosed is a line from Charlie to enclose which must be my excuse for troubling you.

'Your boy does you every credit and you may well be proud of him.' (Payne et al., *Harford*, pp. 146–7.)

32 When the 3rd NNC was disbanded, the African hospital bearers and NNPC deserted, leaving the British garrison without any black auxiliaries for outpost duty or other more menial military tasks.

33 Colonel Glyn placed Commandant Hamilton-Browne in command of the mounted troop of former officers and NCOs of the disbanded 3rd NNC.

34 The Mance-pattern heliograph sent its signals by reflecting sunlight towards the recipient with a mirror mounted on a tripod, the flash being keyed on and off with a shutter or tilting mirror, transmitting Morse code at the rate of up to 12 words a minute. Under good conditions a flash could be seen from 30 miles away with the naked eye and up to 50 miles away with a telescope.

the Isandhlwana fight, the Rev. George Smith* went up there to see what was going on, as he had heard the guns in the distance, and a day or so after we got in he took me up to explain to me what he had seen. On the "neck" just below Isandhlwana hill he saw the artillery firing, and presently a large body of Natives moving round the hill towards them. Thinking it was our Contingent, he said to himself, "Well done, Lonsdale!", as they were moving with such precision. Then shortly after, he noticed a number of horsemen galloping for their lives, away on his right, making towards the Drift, which made him think that Lord Chelmsford's column were being driven back, and almost at the same time large numbers of Natives appeared away to his left front, coming up from the river very leisurely and massing in the valley. After taking a look at these, and seeing that none of them wore the red head-band of Lonsdale's men, his first impulse was to go down and parley with them, but noticing that their numbers were considerably increasing he hastened down the hill again to inform Chard and Bromhead who, however, had already received warning that a Zulu impi was advancing on the Fort.[35] The horsemen he had seen were fugitives from the Camp and had passed the Post before he got down, and be it to their everlasting shame and dishonour, galloped on as hard as they could, refusing to stop a moment to assist the garrison, and merely shouted out that the Zulus were close on them. How far their flight took them, I don't think was ever ascertained.[36]

---

35 The approaching Zulu *impi* consisted of those *amabutho* that had been held in reserve during the battle of Isandlwana, but had led the pursuit of those fleeing from the camp towards Natal. The young men of the iNdluyengwe crossed the Mzinyathi just above Fugitives' Drift and proceeded up the Natal bank of the river towards Shiyane. There they joined up with the older men of the uThulwana, iNdlondlo and uDloko who had crossed the Mzinyathi close to its confluence with the Batshe. Dabulamanzi led this force of between 3,000 and 4,000 men.

36 Harford is not being entirely fair, although he was echoing the sentiments of those who had defended Rorke's Drift and had not escaped to

The part which the Rev. Mr. Smith played in the defence, and the splendid example he set throughout that terrible night, ought to have earned for him the V.C. The same with the Acting Commissariat Officer, Mr. James Dalton, who in the absence of Lieutenant Chard, R.E., (who was down at the river ... superintending Pontoon work at the moment when warning was received of the nearness of the Zulus), devised all the rapid arrangements for the defence as well as working like a Trojan himself with the men at the barricades and did much gallant work during the night. All this was gratefully acknowledged by Lieutenant Chard in his report to the Commander-in-Chief after the fight, but neither Dalton nor Smith received any further distinction than promotion.[37] Mr Thomas Atkins is the best judge of gallant deeds,[38] and when he applauds you may be certain that he is right and does so with good reason, and I noticed that directly Mr Smith or Mr Dalton showed

---

Helpmekaar. The Natal Native Mounted Contingent of No. 2 Column, comprising Nos 1, 2 and 3 Troops, Sikali's Horse, the Edendale Troop and Hlubi's Troop, had all fought at Isandlwana. The men of Sikali's Horse and the Edendale Troop had become scattered in the flight from the battlefield, although enough of them were rallied to give support to fugitives crossing the river. They then made their way to Helpmekaar. Hlubi's Troop under Lieutenant A.F. Henderson and other mounted fugitives reached Rorke's Drift at about 3 p.m. They and their horses were exhausted, and they were demoralised and short of ammunition. Nevertheless, they took up temporary position watching the pont and other crossing places. At about 4.20 p.m. when the Zulu approached, they reported back to the post, fired a few shots at the enemy and rode off to Helpmekaar. Considering the catastrophic defeat they had already experienced that day, it is understandable they did not stay to help defend Rorke's Drift.

37 Harford is partially mistaken. Dalton was awarded the VC, albeit he was not among those first recommended for the award, probably because he was a Commissariat officer. After considerable lobbying, his VC was finally gazetted on 18 November 1879.

38 Thomas (or Tommy) Atkins is slang, well-established by the nineteenth century, for a private soldier in the British Army.

themselves they received an ovation from the men, which was unmistakable.

Among the six or seven young soldiers of the 24th who garrisoned the hospital and received the V.C. for defending it against such tremendous odds, and removing most of the sick while absolutely surrounded by Zulus,[39] was one named Hook,[40] who was taken on as servant by Major Black, whose shrill voice with its Scotch accent could be heard above the Fort calling for "H-o-o-k!" many times a day. So the men had their little joke, and whenever Hook was called for they themselves shouted for Hook and then yelled out, "I think he's hooked it, sir!", which always caused great merriment.[41]

The following astounding incident of Colonel Harness's servant's escape from the hands of the Zulus was told me by one of the garrison; Colonel Harness, C.R.A. of the 3rd Column, had been obliged to leave his servant behind sick at Rorke's Drift when the Column crossed into Zululand, and on the night of the attack on the Fort he happened to be outside the barricades at the moment when the Zulus made their sudden rush on the hospital. As he would to a certainty have been shot down by the fire of our own men had he attempted in the darkness to run in and clamber back again, he quickly bolted under a small hand-cart that had accidentally been left propped up outside against the back of the hospital wall and which (luckily for him, but unfortunately for the garrison), was in such a

39 There were six soldiers of B Company, 2/24th, who were awarded the VC for their defence of Rorke's Drift: Corporal W. Allen and privates Frederick Hitch, Alfred Henry Hook, Robert Jones, William Jones and John Williams (b. John Fielding).

40 Alfred Henry Hook (1850–1905), Private, B Company, 2/24th Regiment, saw service in 1878 in the Ninth Cape Frontier War. During the advance of No. 3 Column in 1879, his company was detached to guard the depot at Rorke's Drift. He received a scalp wound in the battle and was awarded the VC. For the remainder of the war, he and his company were stationed in the vicinity of Rorke's Drift.

41 To 'hook it' means to run away.

position as to be completely out of the line of fire. Here he remained throughout the night, wrapped up in his blanket, with the Zulus swarming all round him—many of them actually jumping on to the cart to try and get on to the roof of the hospital, which some of them succeeded in doing and setting fire to it. But none of them, curiously enough, made any attempt to move the cart, in which case he would have been done for. In the morning, however, when the Zulus had decamped and all firing had ceased, to the great astonishment of the garrison he walked in safe and sound, after about as terrifying an experience as any man could have gone through.[42]

By another lucky coincidence, too, the whole garrison had escaped a terrible catastrophe as only a very short distance away at the back of the Fort, between it and the Itchiane hill, a large hay rick had been left standing, there being no time to clear it away before the Zulus commenced their attack, which if they had fired it would have smoked everyone out and rendered the Fort enterable; but luckily, in their eagerness to wipe out the garrison with the assegai, it was left untouched.

42 Lieutenant-Colonel Harness's servant was Gunner Arthur Howard, whom he had left behind in the hospital at Rorke's Drift suffering from diarrhoea. Contrary to Harford's second-hand account, Howard was not 'outside the barricades' when the amaZulu stormed the hospital, but, according to his own statement, he helped defend one of the hospital's rooms with his rifle. However, Howard made no mention of his eventual escape from the hospital. The details (rather different from those recorded by Harford) were supplied by Lieutenant Chard in the report he wrote in January 1880 at Queen Victoria's request. Chard stated: 'Gunner Howard R.A. ran out of the burning hospital, through the enemy, and lay down on the upper side of the wall in front of our N. Parapet – The bodies of several horses that were killed early in the evening were lying here, and concealed by these, by Zulu bodies & the long grass and bushes, he remained unseen with the Zulu all around him, until they left in the morning.' (Laband and Knight (eds) *Archives of Zululand*, vol. 2, p. 182.) That Howard's Royal Artillery uniform was dark blue probably helped make him less conspicuous than if he had been wearing an infantryman's scarlet tunic.

After some little time, Colonel Glyn left and the command devolved on Colonel Degacher, Major Black taking over command of the 2nd Battalion, 24th Regiment.[43] A completely new regime was now established; everyone was cleared out of the Fort, tents were pitched, and an encampment formed outside. No more living in mud and slush, and a marked decrease of sickness was the result.[44]

Now no sooner had the whole place been thoroughly cleaned up than a plague of flies set upon us, which was truly awful, and bad as it was for us human beings it was ten thousand times worse for the wretched ponies and mules, for whom we kept smoky fires going all day to try and keep the scourges off them as much as possible, but it was of very little avail. From sheer worry, the poor beasts lost flesh to such an extent that their bones protruded as if they had been starved.

For us, too, it was a terrible state of things, the brutes were everywhere and got into our pots and pans even while the food was being cooked. To get a cup of tea or coffee one had to cover the tea-cup with one's hand, leaving only enough room for the spout of the kettle while someone else poured the tea in, and even then they got in. But the worst part of all this was that in nine cases out of ten food was ejected almost as soon as it was swallowed. Unfortunately, there was not a sufficient supply of disinfectant to cope with matters, so nothing could be done. Naturally, towards evening the flies all went off to sheltered spots for the night, and many millions got inside the

43 With the creation on 13 April of the 2nd Division of the South African Field Force, Colonel Glyn left Rorke's Drift to take up his appointment as the Brigadier of its 1st Brigade concentrating at Dundee.

44 Since Harford left Rorke's Drift for Helpmekaar on 18 April (see p. 115, n. 1 below), it is not altogether surprising that he fails to make mention of Fort Melvill begun at the beginning of March on the high ground overlooking the pont at the drift across the Mzinyathi. The garrison stationed at the old fort assisted in the construction of the oblong structure of masonry and dry-stone with two flanking towers surrounded by a broad ditch, but only moved in towards the end of April, after Harford had gone.

tent, only to get a very warm reception. One mode of procedure was to get rid of them thus: after peeping into the tent and seeing a black mass covering the top to about three feet or more, three or four of us would enter quietly, close up the tent and each with a torch made of paper, grass or anything that would give a flame, light these and then quickly, altogether, rush them. In this way we slew many thousands every evening.[45]

45 Commandant Hamilton-Browne never seems to have got over that Harford, whom he considered 'a splendid companion', was nevertheless 'a mad naturalist'. In a lengthy anecdote he relates how, after procuring with great effort 'the only bottle of gin or any other drop of decent drink within 100 miles' of Rorke's Drift, he discovered to his anguish that Harford had used it to 'preserve his infernal microbes'. He adds that Harford 'was such a good fellow that he was soon forgiven', but doubted that 'the dear fellow ever quite understood … what a wicked waste of liquor he had perpetrated'. (Hamilton-Browne, *Lost Legionary*, pp. 162–4.)

CHAPTER 4

Recovery of the Queen's Colour

Very soon after the relief column got to Rorke's Drift, rumours got abroad—how, I don't know—that Lieutenants Melvill* and Coghill,* of the 1st Battalion, 24th Regiment had been seen escaping from the camp at Isandhlwana with the Colours.[1] One

1 Every British battalion of infantry (excluding Rifle regiments) carried two Colours (or identifying flags) embodying the regiment's individuality and traditions. The Sovereign's (King's or Queen's) Colour was a gold-and-red fringed Union Flag with the crowned regimental numeral in the centre. The Regimental Colour was in the colour of the regimental facings (green for the 24th Regiment), and the first quarter bore the Union Flag. In the centre was a red circle bearing the regimental number surrounded by a scroll with the regimental title. Above the central device was the royal crown and surrounding it was a Union wreath of roses, thistles and shamrocks. The regimental device (a sphinx in the case of the 24th Regiment) might be added below. On either side of the central device were scrolls bearing the battle honours awarded by the sovereign. The Colours were made of silk, measuring 3 feet 9 inches by 3 feet, and were attached to a pike (or Colour pole) 8 feet, 7 inches long, topped by a crown surmounted by a lion. The Colours were carried furled in a brass-capped black leather case on the march, and were kept in a guard-tent in camp. When the Centre Column advanced into Zululand, the 1/24th Regiment carried the Queen's Colour with it, but left its Regimental Colour with its 12 battle honours with the two companies of the 1/24th garrisoning the camp at Helpmekaar. The 2/24th carried both its Queen's Colour and Regimental Colour into Zululand. To lose a Colour to the enemy was considered a deep disgrace, and it was expected that every effort would be made to prevent that happening.

rumour said that the Colours were on their staffs, and another that they had wrapped the Colours under their uniforms, round their bodies. This gave special interest to our patrol work in the direction of Fugitives' Drift, and I made it my business to accompany any patrol every day and keep an eye on the state of the river, which kept in flood for a long time at that time of the year from heavy thunderstorms up-country.

Those of us who were not on patrol duty assisted in renovating and adding to the defences of the Fort and putting up enclosures for the animals, and as soon as an opportunity offered, a Prize Committee of Officers and N.C.O.'s of the Contingent was ordered to assemble to assess the value of the captured cattle, sheep and goats. These were all bought by a Mr Button, a butcher and trader from Maritzburg,[2] for £3000,[3] and we heard a short time afterwards that before he had returned to Maritzburg he had sold the cattle alone for £40000.[4] A nice little fortune. What became of the £3000 none of us ever heard, anyhow none of us ever received any Prize money.[5]

I forget now what brought Captain Jones,* R.E. to Rorke's Drift, but while he was with us he managed to obtain through the General's interpreter[6] a very interesting account of how it was that the Zulus did not attack us at Isipezi, and also how it was that

---

2 This was probably Mr J.T. Button, a butcher and town councillor of Pietermaritzburg.

3 Purchasing power today of about £462,000.

4 Purchasing power today of about £6,160,000. At the going average price in 1879 of £15 a head for cattle (purchasing power today of about £2,310), this would have put the number Mr Button sold at about 2,600 head.

5 Nor should they have. Prize money refers to naval warfare and was shared among the crew that had captured an enemy vessel in accordance with the regulations of British prize law. The Crown could grant booty or the spoils of war and specify its distribution to land forces, but only by special proclamation.

6 Henry Francis Fynn, Jnr.

no attempt was made to interfere with Lord Chelmsford's march to the relief of Rorke's Drift—from a Zulu prisoner. The man said that the Zulu impi which confronted us at Isipezi had been ordered by Cetewayo to wipe out all the "redcoats" of Lord Chelmsford's column, and were on their way to attack the camp at Isandhlwana when we came across them. They saw that we were not "redcoats", but only Police Volunteers and Natives, so they left us alone, intending to come back and wipe us out after they had finished with the Camp. So this is how we escaped disaster at Isipezi.[7]

Now for the reason why Lord Chelmsford, with the remnants of his Column, was not interfered with on the march in to the relief of Rorke's Drift. After the massacre at the Camp, messengers had been at once sent back to Cetewayo to say that the whole camp had been wiped out, and not a "redcoat" left alive, but when late in the afternoon we, with the seven companies of the 24th and some artillery, were seen advancing on the camp the Zulus became thoroughly alarmed and said, "Didn't we kill every 'redcoat' in the Camp, and haven't we sent word to Cetewayo to say so, then how is it that these 'redcoats' we see are still alive? They must have come to life again!"

So, during the night Dabulamanzi held a council of war, at which all the younger men were for attacking us in the morning but the older warriors agreed that it would be quite useless to fight men who could rise again from the dead, so it was decided that we were

7 The status of the Zulu prisoner in the Zulu military hierarchy whom Captain Jones interviewed is unknown, but his testimony as reported by Harford suggests he was one of the rank and file with no clear idea of what the Zulu commanders were intending. Thus, when referring to fighting at Siphezi mountain, the prisoner apparently meant the skirmishes at Magogo and Phindo on 21–22 January. It was Matshana's men who confronted the British forces operating in the area, and not the main Zulu army.

not to be interfered with.[8] Hence the extraordinary spectacle that we had witnessed, of a Zulu impi actually at war with us standing by the roadside, quietly watching us on the march without raising a finger. Lord Chelmsford's night march to our assistance at Isipezi had completely baffled them; having under cover of darkness left the camp and made his way along the plains, nothing had been seen of his movements. They themselves, in their eagerness to completely surprise the camp, had made a tremendous detour throughout the night, hidden behind a far range of hills without throwing out any feeler towards the lower ground. Consequently, they knew nothing of any troops having left the Camp, and imagined that on their attack on the camp they had killed every "redcoat" belonging to the Column.[9]

Our daily occupation of patrolling the river kept us in excellent health and spirits, and was most interesting. The landscape all round was simply magnificent, and the scent from the different flowering shrubs and grasses, especially the tambooti grass,[10] in the warm atmosphere was too delicious for anything. I used to long for my gun when a buck jumped up, but alas, my two beautiful weapons—a twelve and an eleven bore from George Gibbs, of

8 The night of 22–23 January is apparently being referred to when Dabulamanzi and the Zulu reserve were fully committed to attacking Rorke's Drift. The decision not to attack Chelmsford's relieving column the next morning was the result of their demoralisation after being repulsed with heavy casualties.

9 The *impi* bivouacked at Siphezi mountain stealthily moved westwards to the Ngwebeni valley north of Isandlwana most likely because the Zulu commanders, far from being unapprised (as the prisoner claimed) of British troops leaving their camp, were aware that Chelmsford had fatally divided his forces and were determined to exploit the situation.

10 Tambookie (tamboekie or tambootie) grass (*Hyparrhenia hirta*), a tall, tufty grass commonly used for thatching.

Bristol[11]—together with every other of my belongings, had been lost in the Camp.

Isandhlwana hill and the "neck" on which we had slept on the night of the disaster was always in sight, together with the hospital wagon which showed up clearly against the skyline and which, for some reason or another, the Zulus had left alone and had never made any attempt to remove. A sharp eye was kept on all the ground in that direction, and for the first week or so small parties of Zulus could be seen clearly through our glasses, wandering about, searching the place all over, no doubt, for either full or empty cartridges. Several were dressed in white shirts, some of which were undoubtedly my property, as I had a dozen new ones in my portmanteau.

Notwithstanding the fact that some of the enemy were still hanging about in the vicinity, the whole of the men of the garrison were eager to march back to Isandhlwana and bury the dead, but the authorities considered that too great a risk would be run, so, much to the regret of all, the dead were left where they lay.[12]

---

11 George Gibbs Ltd has been a West Country gunmaking business since 1840. Harford's two prized and expensive shotguns were a 12-bore (barrel diameter of 0.727 inches) and a slightly bigger 11-bore (barrel diameter of 0.751 inches). They both would have been breech-loading, break-action double-barrelled shotguns.

12 From his further silence on the matter, it seems Harford (who, from his narrative below, was apparently out on patrol elsewhere that day) did not accompany Major Black on 14 March when, at the head of a force of volunteers consisting of three officers and a sergeant of the 2/24th, Commandant Cooper and 12 other officers of the disbanded 3rd NNC and ten NMP under Major Dartnell, he led a reconnaissance to inspect the Isandlwana battlefield. The unburied dead were found to be in an horrific state of putrefaction, and Black's report persuaded Chelmsford, who was under intense government and public pressure to inter the British dead, not to attempt to do so until the process of decomposition was more advanced and he could deploy a large enough burial party to undertake the gruesome task in safety. On 21 May a large detachment from the advancing 2nd Division began the burials, but Colonel Glyn insisted that the corpses of

Traps were often set for our Patrols by the Zulus, in the hope of catching us tripping. Cattle were driven up into enticing places in the hope that we might try and capture them, seeing that there was no-one with them. This was their favourite ruse, but occasionally they lodged their women and children, partially concealed in the bush, from whence a rush could have been made had we been such idiots as to go anywhere near them. But on only one occasion during the whole of our patrolling did we have a scare, which luckily ended without any unpleasant incident. We happened to drop on a mealie garden which we had not come across before, with the stalks still standing, and thinking that we might with luck find a cob or two and perhaps a stray vegetable of some sort, we got off our ponies, which we left outside to graze as they were all reliable shooting ponies, and went into the field, which was situated on the side of a little hollow just above a deep krantz overlooking the river. I suppose we must have been searching about for a quarter of an hour, when suddenly within about thirty yards or so of me I saw a Native crop up out of the krantz and stand with his shield raised above his head, scanning the ground all round. I thought to myself, "Now we are in a nice mess!", so I lay flat on my stomach. Young Wainwright,* one of my officers, was not far from me, and I beckoned to him to get down and come up to me, pointing at the same time towards the Native. As soon as he had crawled up we had a short consultation, and in the meanwhile some four or five more Natives had come up and it looked very much as if we had been spotted and were being surrounded.

Having quickly arranged our plans, we rose up and quietly walked out of the field towards our ponies as if we had seen nothing, and called to the remainder of our party that we were going off, and

---

both battalions of the 24th Regiment should be left undisturbed until their comrades could bury them. That process began on 20 June and continued for many months, not being officially completed until March 1880.

to come in at once. Then catching our ponies, we got on and rode very quietly up the hill, waiting for the others to mount. When we had put a good hundred yards between the Natives and ourselves I ordered a halt, and sent two of our party to scout a little distance back, along the krantz, to see if an attempt was being made to cut off our retreat, everything looking so suspicious and the group at the edge of the krantz having made no attempt to move. Scarcely had we halted than several other Natives joined the group, one of them carrying a large green flag. This was most puzzling, as Zulus carry no standards, but we thought it was only a further blind to trap us, and I'm ashamed to say that at this juncture one of the officers of my patrol turned tail and went back to Rorke's Drift as hard as his pony could carry him.

Seeing the peculiar behaviour of the Natives, I decided to call on them to surrender and told them to come up to us with their flag, but for some time they made no answer or any attempt to move. At last I called down to them that if they didn't come up and surrender at once we should fire on them, whereupon the man carrying the flag, escorted by two or three of the others of the group, advanced towards us and halted when within a few yards of us. We now learnt that they belonged to Major Bengough's* Contingent and had been sent on ahead to scout towards Rorke's Drift, as the Contingent were marching up in that direction.[13] So, after telling them that no-one had received any intimation of Major Bengough's coming, and that they had had a precious narrow squeak from being shot, we went our several ways. It

13 This incident must have occurred just before or on 14 March because these two companies of the 2/1st NNC (on 18 March reconstituted as the 2nd Battalion, NNC) stationed at Fort Bengough (see p. 83 n. 25 above) had been ordered up to support Major Black in his reconnaissance patrol to Isandlwana on that day. The two companies stayed on at Rorke's Drift to help in the construction of Fort Melvill (see p. 78 n. 14 and p. 92 n. 44 above).

was an adventure, and but for the disgraceful act of one solitary individual,[14] we had got out of the mess all right.

Occasionally I rode out by myself to take a look round, and one afternoon about a mile from the Fort came across a portmanteau torn in half and empty, but lying by the side of it was a Bible, and a few feet further on a silver watch, which I restored to their rightful owner, the Rev. Mr Smith, when I got back, and very pleased he was to have them in his possession again. The portmanteau itself was far too damaged to be of any further use, so was left where it was.

The same day, I think it was, I came across the body of a very fine specimen of a Zulu in the skeleton stage, which I took Surgeon Reynolds out to have a look at. He too was impressed with the stature and splendid proportions, and brought away one or two bones of Scientific interest, and the soles of the feet which had become detached and were just like solid pieces of horn.[15] I also took one of the collar bones and the lesser bones of one of the arms, which I intended some day to give to the Durban Museum.[16]

In the year of grace 1879, subaltern officers were of very small account, and in my position of Staff Officer to a Native Contingent, (with the honorary rank of Captain while so employed), and consequently an outsider, one did not expect very much from anyone, but the kindness and hospitality extended to me by the

14 Presumably, he had galloped off to safety.

15 Zulu *amabutho* went barefoot, so the soles of their feet became extremely hardened.

16 The collection of body parts from indigenous peoples for supposedly 'scientific' anthropological study was common in the Victorian era, a practice now deplored. The Durban Natural Science Museum was founded in 1887. When the original building became too small, it was moved in 1910 to the imposing neo-baroque Durban City Hall designed by Stanley Hudson, where it is still located. On 7 May 1914 the Durban Town Council presented an illuminated address to Harford 'to place upon record its appreciation of the many interesting and valuable donations' to the museum of specimens he had collected over many years 'whilst serving in various parts of His Majesty's Dominions'. (Payne et al., *Harford*, p. 287.)

24th Regiment very soon made me feel almost as one of them, and many lasting friendships was the result. I remember Lieutenants Smylie *[Smyly]*, Phipps and Geoghegan joining us at Rorke's Drift,[17] the latter becoming a Captain within a month or two, through death vacancies. Major Black became an especially intimate friend of mine, and I could always go to him for advice and to talk over matters. Besides being a splendid soldier he was a most amusing companion, and his fondness for bringing in lines of poetry to suit the occasion was a treat to listen to, with his Gaelic accent.

The necessity of keeping our clothes (which were none other than what we stood up in), as clean as we could, without such luxury as soap, we often went down to the river together, washed our things and swam about … till they were dry—which was not a long process on warm rocks with a nice hot sun in addition. But the swimming part came to an end rather abruptly when one day an alligator showed himself some yards above us,[18] with his head just out of the water, and made us skedaddle at our best swimming pace. Though, as John Dunn* taught me, when bathing with him at the Lower Tugela where the river was literally swarming with them, they will never come near you as long as you keep up a tremendous amount of splashing.

In front of the Fort and some 600 or 700 yards down the slope of the hill, a scaffold had been put up by the Commissariat

17 Lieutenant Arthur Barré Phipps, 2/24th Regiment, was transferred to the 1/24th after Isandlwana. He acted as Orderly Officer to Colonel Glyn during the advance of the 2nd Division, and was severely wounded at the battle of Ulundi. Lieutenant Frederic Philip Smyly (not Smylie) of the 2/24th served throughout the campaign. The only Geoghegan in the *Army List* is not an infantry officer. He is Surgeon-Major William Geoghegan, MB, of the Army Medical Department who was stationed at the Cape of Good Hope. It is quite possible (although unconfirmed) that he was deployed to the Rorke's Drift garrison.

18 Harford means a crocodile since alligators are native only to the United States of America and China.

Department on which the carcasses of the cattle were hung up previous to issue, and one morning Major Black and I were sitting outside, warming ourselves in the sun and chatting, when we saw a most extraordinary-looking object suspended on the scaffold, and wondered what on earth it could be. Presently, a Private of the 24th came up from that direction, and Black asked him what the thing was, and he said that it was a Kaffir spy that had been hanged. "Good Heavens!", said Black, "By whose orders was he hung?" "Captain Harford, sir", was the reply, so we went down at once to look into the matter. The poor wretch, who was an old, wizened-up, grey-headed Native, had apparently been dead for some hours, and must have been hung some time during the night, but by whom it was never discovered. Every possible enquiry was made, but not a soul knew anything about it and nothing was known of the Native or where he could have come from.[19]

19 Hamilton-Browne apparently knew all about the incident (see Hamilton-Browne, *Lost Legionary*, pp. 168–72), but his bombastic and self-exculpatory memoir is at suspicious odds with Harford's account. He records that he and two officers formerly of the 1/3rd NNC, Captains R. Devlin and R. Duncombe, captured an elderly Zulu 'spy' wearing 'a turkey-red cloth bound around his head'. This was the uniform of the NNC, and the Zulu captive apparently admitted he was wearing it 'to deceive the red soldiers if he chanced to meet any'. Hamilton-Browne, according to his account, handed him over to the main guard, who used a wagon outside the fort for a guardroom. He then (so he claims) reported to Colonel Glyn for instructions, and was ordered to interrogate the 'spy' further. Hamilton-Browne got nothing more out of him and, he asserts, when irritably turning round in frustration he struck his shin which he had badly bruised a few days before. The 'pain was atrocious', writes Hamilton-Browne, and when the Sergeant-Major, a huge Irishman in charge of the guard, asked what to do with the spy, Hamilton-Browne, who was rubbing his aching shin and cursing spies, wagons and everything else, rapped out, 'Oh hang the bally spy.' He meant only to curse him, but (or so he unconvincingly maintains) the Sergeant-Major took him at his word and strung the unfortunate old Zulu 'spy' up on the scaffold where Harford and Black later discovered him. Further embroidering his tale, Hamilton-Browne describes how a drum-head court martial that was being

As time went on the river got lower, and at last became shallow enough to enable our patrols almost to count with the naked eye articles of debris of every description with which the now bare shingle was strewn at the Fugitives' Crossing—saddles, bridles, stirrups, helmets, clothing, boots and numbers of other things could be seen, but no sign of the 24th Regiment's lost Colours. It was now clear that measures should be taken in hand at once to search for them, and I reported this to Major Clery. Colonel Glyn, however, for some reason of his own, declined to allow a search party to be organised by the 24th, and I, on the other hand, felt very unwilling to carry out a mission which—subaltern only, as I was—I considered would be anything but creditable to the Regiment, they being actually on the spot. Had I been ambitious for self-advertisement, I should have said no more and simply undertaken the job with my own officers and N.C.O.'s, all of whom were as keen as possible for the outing. So I talked matters over with Major Black, and asked him to use his influence with Colonel Glyn, and see what could be done.

I had returned from patrolling on this particular day early,[20] in order that no time should be lost in arranging about a search party going out the next morning. Major Black's interview, happily, ended in Colonel Glyn giving him permission to go out in command of our Contingent, and his face beamed with delight when he came

---

set up to try the Zulu 'spy' was dumbfounded to discover that the Sergeant-Major had already hanged him. Yet, in Harford's account there is no mention of officers being assembled for a court martial, nor of the Sergeant-Major admitting to having hanged the Zulu prisoner. Moreover, Harford firmly states that nobody could be found who knew anything about the incident. It would seem, therefore, that in his memoir a conscience-stricken Hamiliton-Browne, who felt compelled to write about the hanging but who could not bring himself to admit that he and his two hard-bitten fellow-NNC officers had lynched the old Zulu man during the night, concocted the tale about the dim, literal-minded Sergeant-Major.

20 3 February 1879.

out to tell me the news.[21] As we had all had our frugal meal, and the afternoon was before us, he at once said, "Come along, we'll saddle up and you show me the ground", so he and I went off on a most enjoyable and interesting ride. Having been confined to the vicinity of the Fort for so long, our spirits rose high as we cantered across country, watching the surroundings of Isandhlwana and speculating on the morrow's adventure.

On coming to the spot which overlooked the crossing, we first of all had a good look with our glasses at the mass of debris lying about, and then walked about to examine the ground with a view to finding a good position for a covering-party to be placed while the actual search-party were down in the river bed. Having arranged this, and as there was still sufficient of the afternoon left, Major Black suggested that we should go a little further down, following as well as we could over the stony and precipitous ground, the Kaffir path by which, it was said, the fugitives had made their way. Suddenly, just off the track to the right of us, we saw two bodies, and on going to have a look at them, found that they were those of Lieutenants Melvill and Coghill! Both were clearly recognisable. Melvill was in red, and Coghill in blue, uniform.[22] Both were lying on their backs about a yard from each other, Melvill at right angles to the path and Coghill parallel to it, a little above Melvill and with

---

21 A 'correspondent on the Zulu frontier' (Moodie, *Moodie's Zulu War*, p. 51) details the composition of the patrol. It was led by Major Black accompanied by the Rev. George Smith, Harford, Lieutenant Charles Raw,* James Alexander Brickhill (1836–92), the interpreter to the staff of No. 3 Column who, like Raw, had escaped from Isandlwana, and 19 other mounted volunteers. Another correspondent, published in the *Illustrated London News* of 29 March 1879, refers to the mounted volunteers as consisting of 'about twenty men of the 24th, and about four or five Mounted Natives'.

22 Melvill was in his scarlet serge 'undress frock' and dark-blue trousers with a red welt; while Coghill was wearing a dark-blue patrol jacket and cord breeches (Smith-Dorrien, *Memories*, p. 16).

his head up-hill. Both had been assegaied,[23] but otherwise their bodies had been left untouched.[24]

Major Black at once said, "Now we shall see whether they have the Colours on them", and proceeded to unbutton Melvill's serge, while I opened Coghill's patrol jacket, but there were no Colours. Presently Major Black said, "I wonder if Melvill's watch is on him! He always carried it in the small waist-pocket of his breeches!", and on looking, there was his gold watch, which was subsequently sent to his widow. Nothing was found on Coghill, but his bad knee was still bandaged up.[25] Undoubtedly, Melvill must have stuck to him

23 The identity of the amaZulu who overtook and killed Coghill and Melvill cannot be known for sure. When they enveloped the camp at Isandlwana, the *amabutho* of the right horn, the uDududu, iMbube and iSangqu, embarrassed that they had missed much of the hard fighting, joined the iNgobamakhosi and uVe of the left horn in pursuing the British fugitives down to the Mzinyathi, cutting down those they overtook and firing volleys at those making their way across the rain-swollen river and up the steep bank opposite. They were joined in the pursuit by the adherents of Gamdana kaXongo, the Qungebe *induna*, who lived in the area. Some of the pursuers crossed the river into Natal, but fortunately for the fugitives mostly opted to do so further upstream where the drifts were safer. Unhappily for the fugitives, the adherents of Sothondose kaMalusi, the Nxumalo *inkosi* who in 1843 had taken refuge in Natal when King Mpande had purged those plotting against him, and who lived opposite Fugitives' Drift (also known as Sothondose's Drift), seem to have decided to help intercept the escapees, possibly out of fear that the *amabutho* would take reprisals against them if they did not.

24 Lieutenant H. Hillier of the disbanded 2/3rd NNC, who was a member of the patrol, wrote in a letter published in the *Telegraph and Eastern Province Standard* on 28 February 1879: 'We came across the bodies of poor Lieuts. Melvill and Coghill; they lay behind the bodies of two soldiers where they made their stand.' Evidently, there had been more British soldiers involved in Melvill's and Coghill's final fight than officially suggested, and a small cairn of stones now marks the spot where the two unknown soldiers, who could not have been officers, are buried.

25 Other sources suggest that additional articles were carefully taken charge of by Black, including Coghill's ring and Melvill's spurs.

and helped him along, otherwise he never could have got so far over such terrible ground.[26]

---

26 The true circumstances surrounding Melvill's escape from Isandlwana carrying the Queen's Colour can never be known. Colonel Glyn reported that 'it would appear that when the enemy got into the camp, and when there was no longer any hope of saving it', Melville 'departed from the camp on horseback, carrying the colour with him in hope of being able to save it'. (Colonel R. Glyn to Lieutenant-General Lord Chelmsford, 21 February, 1879, in *Supplement to the London Gazette*, 4 April 1879.) Chelmsford, when questioned by Lieutenant-General Sir Alfred Horsfold, Military Secretary at the Horse Guards, about the circumstances, responded on 14 May 1879: 'I feel sure Melvill left camp with the colours under orders received. He was too good a soldier to have left without.' (Knight, *Zulu Rising*, p. 564). In all likelihood, whether on Colonel Pulleine's orders or on his own initiative, Melvill brought out the Colour to serve as a rallying point for the troops, but the military situation deteriorated so rapidly that he decided instead to save it from the dishonour of falling into the enemy's hands.

What then of Coghill's escape? Lieutenant Smith-Dorrien later wrote that he was passed along the Fugitives' Trail by Coghill and then, when he was half a mile behind Coghill, Melvill overtook him 'with a cased colour across the front of his saddle'. Smith-Dorrien therefore concluded that 'Coghill … and Melvill … did not escape together.' (Smith-Dorrien, *Memories*, p. 16.) Chelmsford, in his reply on 14 May 1879 to Horsfold's query about what Coghill was intending, responded that as Colonel Glyn's Staff Officer, he 'had every right to leave the camp when he realised the fact that nothing could be done to save it'. (Knight, *Zulu Rising*, p. 564). That was not the opinion of General Sir Garnet Wolseley, who noted acerbically in his journal when on 3 August 1879 he visited the graves of Coghill and Melvill: 'I am sorry that both of these officers were not killed with their men at Isandlwana instead of where they were: I don't like the idea of officers escaping on horseback when their men on foot are killed.' (Preston (ed.), *Wolseley's Journal*, p. 70, 3 August 1879.)

What seems to have cemented the heroic reputations of 'two young but courageous officers, who, even in death, had shown their spirit and gallantry', as Norris-Newman reflected when visiting their graves (Norris-Newman, *In Zululand*, p. 117), and which glossed over Coghill's questionable flight from the battlefield, was his selflessly turning back, even though he had reached the apparent safety of the Natal bank, to assist Melvill, who had been unhorsed, had lost the Colour which was swept away by the torrent, and was floundering in the river under Zulu fire. Moreover, Lieutenant

Our search over, we set to work at once to cover the bodies with large stones and bits of rock, for protection till proper interment could take place,[27] after which we rode home, as it

---

Higginson's craven decision to abandon Melvill and Coghill with his crippled knee to struggle along on foot once they reached the Natal side of the river only added to the poignancy of their deaths in a last stand against their Zulu pursuers. In 1882 Major W.J. Elliott summed up this widespread perception when he sentimentally wrote: 'They died the death of noble-minded heroes … Who can doubt that these excellent young men grasped in silence each other's hand as they saw their enemies' approach, and then prepared for an honourable end in their country's service?' (Elliott, *Victoria Cross in South Africa*, pp. 75–6).

That indeed became the official line, forcefully expressed by Colonel Glyn who was determined to protect the honour of his regiment. In his official despatch to Chelmsford on 21 February (printed in the *Supplement to the London Gazette*, 4 April 1879), he ringingly declared that 'both these officers gave up their lives in the truly noble task of endeavouring to save from the enemy's hands the Queen's colour of their regiment; and greatly though their sad end is to be deplored, their deaths could not have been more noble or more full of honour.' The War Office concurred, and in a 'Memorandum' printed in the *Supplement to the London Gazette* of 2 May 1879, in which was listed the names of those upon whom the Victoria Cross was to be conferred, stated that Lieutenant Melvill, 'on account of the gallant efforts made by him to save the Queen's Colour of his Regiment after the disaster at Isandhlwana, and also Lieutenant Coghill … on account of his heroic conduct in endeavouring to save his brother officer's life, would have been recommended to Her Majesty for the Victoria Cross had they survived'. Ultimately, when it was resolved that the Victoria Cross could be awarded posthumously, on 6 February 1907 King Edward VII conferred it on both Melvill and Coghill.

27 The Revd Smith performed the burial service. On 14 April 1879, Colonels Glyn and Lieutenant-Colonel Degacher went down to where Coghill and Melvill were temporarily buried. They had the bodies exhumed, placed in coffins, and reburied a few yards away below in the lee of a huge, conspicuous boulder. Later that year, Sir Bartle Frere had a marble cross erected on top of the boulder bearing the following inscription:

'In memory of Lt. and Adjutant Teignmouth Melvill and Lt. Nevill J.A. Coghill, 1st Batt. 24th Regt., who died on this spot, 22nd Jany., 1879, to save the Queen's Colour of their Regiment.'

was getting dusk. It was a memorable afternoon, and had made it certain that neither Melvill or Coghill had the Colours about their persons. Our news, on getting back, naturally caused a good deal of interest and excitement, and speculation as to the result of tomorrow's expedition.

Soon after sunrise the following morning our little cavalcade of officers and N.C.O.'s of the Contingent,[28] headed by Major Black in command, and myself, moved quietly away. Orders had been given to the signallers stationed on the top of Itchiane hill, who could see almost the whole of our route with their telescope, to keep an eye in our direction and signal down to the Fort anything of importance concerning our movements. Captain *[Lieutenant]* Raw* was the senior of the officers of the Contingent *[Natal Native Mounted Contingent]*, and when we arrived on the ground chosen by Major Black for the covering-party to establish themselves on, a substantial sangar of rocks and stones was soon built up and he was given charge of the party.

Major Black now decided Captain Harber and Lieutenant Wainwright should accompany me to the river bed and carry out the search operations.[29] After a tremendous climb down, and on getting to the bottom of the krantz, we found ourselves at the corner of a delta formed by the river, which was now dry shingle and covered with every imaginary article of equipment discarded by the fugitives as they crossed the swirling stream, as well as other species of debris. Losing no time, I told off Harber to walk downstream close to the river edge, and Wainwright to follow the

---

On the other side is inscribed: 'For Queen and Country – Jesu Mercy'. In 1973 the graves were vandalised and Frere's cross on the boulder severely damaged. The South African War Graves Board refurbished the graves in 1974 and subsequently placed the restored cross as their head.

28 4 February 1879.

29 Captain S. Harber, formerly of the 1/3rd NNC, had been absent on the reconnaissance-in-force during Isandlwana.

curve of the delta, while I moved through the centre. We were thus only a few yards apart, and it was unlikely that anything would escape detection.

Scarcely had we taken a few steps than I stumbled on the Colour case mixed up with a heap of other things, and picking it up I said to Harber, who was closest to me, "Look here, here's the case! The Colours can't be far off!" We all three then had a look at it, put it on a conspicuous boulder, and went on. Then, as Harber was returning to his position, I noticed a straight piece of stick projecting out of the water in the middle of the river, almost in a line with us, and said to him, "Do you see that straight bit of stick sticking up in the water opposite to you? It looks to me uncommonly like a Colour pole." He waded straight in, up to his middle, and got hold of it. On lifting it out he brought up the Colour still adhering to it, and on getting out of the water handed the standard to me, and as he did so the gold-embroidered centre scroll dropped out, the silk having more or less rotted from the long immersion in the water.[30] Our cheers very soon brought Major Black tearing down the krantz as fast as precipitous rocks, boulders and thorn bush would allow him, and in the meanwhile we continued our search in the hope of dropping across the other Colour, as two had been lost,

30 The 'Records of Service of the 1/24th for 1879' in the Royal Regiment of Wales Museum, Brecon (BRCRM R1950.41) has a somewhat different account from Harford's, in which only his presence at the recovery of the Colour is noted. While Captain Harber is credited (as in Harford's account) with finding the Colour itself, it is stated that Lieutenant Hillier recovered the Colour case, while Lieutenant J. Trow, 2/3rd NNC, retrieved the crest of the Colour which must have come loose from the standard. In his official report of 21 February, Colonel Glyn wrote that he had sent Major Black back to 'prosecute' the search for the Colour which, 'with the ornaments, case &c., belonging to it, were found, though in different places, in the river bed'. Note Glyn's use of the passive voice that avoided having to name the 'colonial' officers of the defunct 3rd Regiment NNC who had retrieved the Colour, leaving the impression that the honour fell on Major Black of the 1/24th.

but without any further luck.[31] Major Black having got down to us, I handed him the Colour amid ringing cheers in which he joined, and after having congratulated and thanked us, and shaken us well by the hand, we proceeded to climb back to the covering party, he carrying the Colour.

It was a real business getting up, but he gave us such an entertaining time of it in our scramble that little heed was taken of the difficulties of the situation. On getting up to them, Captain Raw and his party drew up, and after saluting the Colour gave three times three for Her Majesty, the Queen, and ourselves. The ponies were now got together and saddled up, and we returned back to the Fort in the following formation: Major Black leading, carrying the cased Colour erect, the butt of the Standard resting on the right stirrup, so that the signallers on Itchiane hill could make no mistake. Harber and Wainwright and I followed at some twenty yards' interval, and the rest of the party about the same distance in rear of us.

We knew that the sight of the Colour would cause some excitement at the Fort, but I don't think any of us expected the little surprise reception that awaited us there. A Guard of Honour was stationed outside at the entrance, and the whole garrison turned out to give us an ovation. It certainly was a triumphal return, but I suppose with the exception of Major Black none of us thought of the significance of the occasion. Speaking for myself personally, I felt that we had had a most enjoyable and exciting day, and the luck in recovering the Colour gave one the same feelings of pleasure as one experiences in capturing a new or rare butterfly or having got up to an almost inaccessible nest and brought the egg safely down.

31 The Regimental Colour of the 1/24th was at Helpmekaar, so Harford must be referring to the two Colours of the 2/24th that had been in the camp at Isandlwana, and were never recovered.

Captain Symons made a sketch of the scene on our arrival,[32] which appeared in one of the illustrated papers.[33] The sketches that I made of the recovering of the Colour, and the burial of the bodies of Melvill and Coghill, and Otto de Witt's *[Witt's]* house at Rorke's Drift,[34] all of which were considerably altered by the engraver, appeared in the Illustrated London News in the issue dated 12th April, 1879. I really sent these sketches to dear old Jameson,* never thinking of publication, but he sent them on to the Publishers.[35]

After a day or two,[36] an escort consisting of Major Black and myself, with a Sergeant of the 24th to carry it, were detailed in orders to convey the Colour to Helpmekaar for the purpose of restoring it to the Battalion, which was quartered there,[37] and for me this ride

---

32 Captain William Penn Symons (1843–99), 2/24th Regiment, had seen action in the Ninth Cape Frontier War but was absent with Chelmsford's reconnaissance-in-force during Isandlwana. Subsequently, he was in garrison with his battalion at Rorke's Drift until June, when he was sent to the Cape Colony to purchase horses for the government.

33 Harford evidently has in mind the sketch by Lieutenant William Whitelock Lloyd (1856–97), 1/24th Regiment, which appeared in the *Illustrated London News* of 29 March 1879 and was captioned 'The Zulu War: Recovery of the Lost Colours of the 24th Regiment. A Scene in the Fort at Helpmekaar'. His confusion about the authorship of the sketch is understandable since in the same edition of the *Illustrated London News* a sketch was published of the 'Retreat of Fugitives from Isandhlwana across the Buffalo River' and was accredited to both Penn Symons and Lloyd.

34 The missionary Otto Witt's (not de Witt's) house at Rorke's Drift had been converted into the hospital by No. 3 Column (see p. 42 n. 3 above).

35 On 23 September 1907 the editor of the *Illustrated London News*, responding to Harford's request for 'a proof' of the sketches and the accompanying published description, could send him only 'a typewritten account' taken from the files since the issue of 12 April 1879 was out of print (Payne et al., *Harford*, pp. 282–4).

36 On 5 February 1879.

37 Two companies of the 1/24th were stationed at Helpmekaar. A third company was in garrison at Port St John's in the Transkei and never took part in the Zulu campaign. The remaining five companies of the battalion had perished at Isandlwana.

was to be an ever-memorable event. From the Fort to Helpmekaar was about eleven miles, and after having covered some two or three of them Major Black stopped for a moment and, after making me a delightful little speech referring to my share in the undertaking, took the Colour from the Sergeant and handed it to me to carry for the rest of the journey, saying, "It is nothing but your right." It was the proudest moment of my life, and I shall ever consider it so. I very much doubt whether such another case has ever occurred that an officer on duty and belonging to another Regiment has been given the honour of carrying its Queen's Colour. This same Colour when the 24th Regiment returned to England, was crowned by Her Majesty, Queen Victoria, with a wreath of silver laurels and sanctioned by her to be carried on Parade as a Third Colour.[38]

At Helpmekaar the Regiment was drawn up in line to receive us on the heights, and as we rode on to the ground Major Black took the Colour and advanced with it towards the centre. The officer detailed to receive it then came forward,[39] and having received it faced the Line, when the Regiment "presented arms".[40] The

38 The Queen's Colour was brought home to England in October 1879, and on 28 July 1880 a Colour-party from the battalion presented it, at her request, to Queen Victoria at Osborne House on the Isle of Wight. The Queen had learned that while the Colour was awaiting transport back to England, a group of Durban ladies had bound a wreath of flowers around its finial. The wreath had long since decomposed, and the sentimental Queen replaced it with a wreath of Immortelles. She then commanded the Adjutant-General of the Army that in future a silver wreath should be borne on the peak of the staff of the Sovereign's Colour 'to commemorate the devotion displayed by Lieutenants Melvill and Coghill in their heroic endeavour to save the Colour'. (Atkinson, *24th Foot*, p. 358.) The tattered Colour itself was carried on parade until 1933, when it was laid up in Brecon Cathedral in Wales.

39 This officer was Lieutenant Wilfred Heaton, D Company, 1/24th Regiment. His company later formed part of the 2nd Division, and was part of the garrison holding the camp at the White Mfolozi during the battle of Ulundi.

40 This was the moment portrayed in the *Illustrated London News* of 29 March 1879, based on a sketch ascribed to Lieutenant William Whitelock Lloyd, 1/24th Regiment (who, like Heaton, was one of those in the camp at the White

officers and Colour having joined the ranks, Major Black proceeded to address the Regiment in a remarkably eloquent speech which must have stirred the feelings of every officer and man who had the privilege of listening to it. This concluded the ceremony, and thus was concluded a truly memorable and historical event.[41]

Mfolozi during the battle of Ulundi). Note the Regimental Colour, which had been kept safe at Helpmekaar, being paraded by the guard of honour.

41 Lieutenant-Colonel Harness, writing to his sister Co on 19 February about the ceremony (Clarke, *Invasion of Zululand*, pp. 96–70), reported that 'Poor Glyn, in speaking to the two companies under Major Upcher,* fairly broke down. He said that fourteen years before, he and Upcher were then the officers to receive that colour and they were again receiving it being almost the only officers left with the regiment. He paid a compliment to Black and his volunteer followers. Major Black made a capital speech – very short but excellent.'

Yet, there was more to it than that. Norris-Newman, who also witnessed the ceremony, has Glyn emphasising to the soldiers 'that through the gallant and most praise-worthy efforts of Major Black, 2-24th Regiment, the colours of the 1-24th had been found' and that the bodies of Coghill and Melvill had been recovered and respectfully buried. The men responded by giving Black three cheers (Norris-Newman, *In Zululand*, p. 116). No mention, or at least not enough of one also to elicit three cheers, was made by Glyn of the critical role played by Harford and the officers of the disbanded 3rd NNC and Natal Native Mounted Contingent. In his mind, all the honour was to go to the 24th Regiment. But Major Black, who was a fair and honest man, would not leave it there. Speaking 'very feelingly', according to Norris-Newman in his report to the *Times of Natal* of 13 February 1879, and 'almost overcome with emotion', Black put the record straight. Disclaiming the cheers of the soldiers, he declared that 'they were giving him too much praise; they had not only to thank him, but the officers of the Natal Native Contingent who accompanied him, and who also gave him most valuable assistance in recovering the bodies of his two brother officers, as well as the colours of their own gallant regiment.'

CHAPTER 5

Return to the 99th Regiment

In course of time, when reliefs were about to take place, I was ordered to move to Helpmekaar with what remained of the Contingent, a welcome change to higher ground.[1] We were camped a short distance away from the Laager there,[2] on a treeless plateau; below us, looking down on the Rorke's Drift road and on our first old camping-ground, was a precipitous krantz of huge rocks and thornbush, but all else was miles and miles of green, rolling, grassy hills. I now felt the loss of my guns and material for

1 By April 1879 preparations for the second invasion of Zululand were well under way, with Dundee designated as the main depot for the 2nd Division, South African Field Force. Accordingly, the bulk of supplies at Helpmekaar were transferred there. Colonel Harness's N/5th Battery, RA, and the detachment of the 5th Company, RE, stationed at Helpmekaar left for Dundee on 17 April, and were followed the next day by most of the NMP. To replace the latter, a detachment of the officers and NCOs of the disbanded 3rd NNC, which included Harford, moved up from Rorke's Drift.

2 On the evening of the battle of Isandlwana, the garrison at Helpmekaar made a laager of wagons around the stores, surrounded by an entrenchment. Within a few weeks it was replaced by a strong fort with an earthwork parapet designed by Captain W. Parke Jones. It was rectangular in shape with bastions at the four corners. The surrounding ditch was eight feet deep and revetted with grain and mealie sacks. The entrance was protected by a drawbridge. Conditions within the waterlogged fort were dire, and in the months before Harford's posting there, there were sometimes as many as 40 sick receiving rudimentary medical attention.

collecting, which went in the camp at Isandhlwana, as the rocks were full of rock-rabbits and I saw several Steenbuck[3] and covies of partridge. A herd of some seven or eight Hartebeest,[4] strictly preserved as they are becoming extinct, roamed about undisturbed and occasionally came within sight of the camp. A fine of £100[5] was the penalty for even firing at one.[6]

A few days after my arrival, Major Upcher,* 24th Regiment, commanding the garrison, sent for me and told me that the 4th King's Own Regiment were coming in very soon and that the Commissariat were without any cattle, the contractor having failed to bring any up, which placed him in an awkward fix.[7] He asked me to go off at once with one or two of the Contingent who could speak Dutch, and endeavour to obtain 300 head of cattle from the outlying farms in the district.[8] It was a Sunday, and with

---

3 A steenbuck, steenbok or steinbuck (*Raphicerus campestris*) is a small, slender antelope with long legs and big ears. Only the males have horns.

4 A hartebeest (*Alcelaphus buselaphus*) is a large, gregarious antelope with oddly shaped, backward-bending horns. It is readily hunted for its meat and many of its subspecies are today critically endangered.

5 Purchasing power today of about £15,400.

6 By the 1870s little wild game survived in this part of Natal. As recently as the 1860s the plains had been covered with ostrich, buffalo, hartebeest, zebra, quagga and some elephant on their annual migration down the passes of the Drakensberg. But hunters had exterminated all the larger species except for a few buffalo still haunting inaccessible wooded ravines, and a herd of hartebeest in northern Natal preserved by a large landowner. Some species of smaller antelope, such as the steenbok mentioned by Harford, as well as other game such as guinea fowl and partridge still abounded, but the activities of poachers kept their numbers well in check.

7 Three companies of the 2/4th under Major Augustus Charles Twentyman had formed the garrison at Greytown since the beginning of the war. In mid-May they were to be relieved by two companies of the 94th Regiment that had just arrived from England, and would march north to help garrison the base depots of the 2nd Division at Dundee and environs.

8 This was Klip River County, where two-thirds of the farmers were Boers whose principal concern was stock-farming, with little attention paid to arable agriculture. They were descendants of the Trekkers who had invaded

Stapleton Grove, Pinetown, Colony of Natal, with a distant view of the Indian Ocean. A watercolour of 1869 by Captain H. Townsend, a close family friend of the Harfords. (*David Payne, Emma Payne and Adrian Greaves (eds)*, Henry Charles Harford, *The Ultimatum Tree, 2008, with permission*)

Harford's cover design for his reminiscences of the Anglo-Zulu War. Pencil drawing on tracing paper. (*David Payne, Emma Payne and Adrian Greaves (eds)*, Henry Charles Harford, *The Ultimatum Tree, 2008, with permission*)

The verandaed Plough Hotel on Market Square, the commercial hub of Pietermaritzburg, where Harford put up on his way to join the 3rd Regiment, NNC at Sand Spruit. (*Campbell Collections of the University of KwaZulu-Natal*)

The Sand Spruit store and hotel where Harford stopped on his way to the camp of the 3rd Regiment, NNC. (*Campbell Collections of the University of KwaZulu-Natal*)

'Dinner time at Fort Bengough.' Men of the 2nd Battalion, NNC clustered around their communal pots of food. (*Campbell Collections of the University of KwaZulu-Natal*)

Sikhotha kaMpande, Cetshwayo's half-brother and political refugee in Natal, commanded three companies of iziGqoza in the 1/3rd NNC. (*David Payne, Emma Payne and Adrian Greaves (eds)*, Henry Charles Harford, *The Ultimatum Tree, 2008, with permission*)

The Isandlwana camp before the battle. It extended along a line parallel to Isandlwana mountain, some 200 yards from its base, and consisted of a series of smaller camps with the infantry battalions, the artillery battery, the mounted force and the NNC each having their own. (*Campbell Collections of the University of KwaZulu-Natal*)

A panorama of Isandlwana painted by Lt Lloyd on 21 July 1879, looking south-west from Siphezi mountain with burnt winter grass in the foreground. The Conical hill is in the foreground, Isandlwana mountain looms in the centre, and Shiyane mountain rises above Rorke's Drift to the left. The Helpmekaar heights are in the distance. (*David Rattray*, A Soldier-Artist in Zululand, *Rattray Publications, 2007, with permission*)

Drawing by the soldier-artist, Lt-Col. John North Crealock, 95th Regiment, 'Our return to the camp of Sandhlwana. (22 Jan. 1879).'
(*R.A. Brown (ed.),* The Road to Ulundi, *University of Natal Press, 1969, with permission*)

Trooper N. Nelson of the Natal Mounted Police's eye-witness drawing of the remnants of No. 3 Column marching away from the stricken field of Isandlwana towards Rorke's Drift. (*Campbell Collections of the University of KwaZulu-Natal*)

Harford's 'Rough sketch taken of Natives of the 3rd NNC handing in their equipment preparatory to disbandment at Rorke's Drift. Jany 1879. – Lt. Adendorff with some of his men.' (*David Payne, Emma Payne and Adrian Greaves (eds)*, Henry Charles Harford, *The Ultimatum Tree, 2008, with permission*)

Col. Richard Glyn, 24th Regiment. (*R.A. Brown (ed.)*, The Road to Ulundi, *University of Natal Press, 1969, with permission*)

'"All's well!" Sketch of the fort at Rorke's Drift.' In the days after the battle, the improvised defences were turned into a proper stone-built fort – known as Fort Bromhead. (*Ian Knight Collection*)

Lt Lloyd's watercolour of the stone-built Fort Bromhead. The scaffold from which Commandant Hamilton-Browne's Zulu 'spy' was hanged is in the foreground. (*David Rattray*, A Soldier-Artist in Zululand, *Rattray Publications, 2007, with permission*)

Harford's watercolour of 'Captain F Hart. Principal Staff Officer to Col. Clarke's Column, Zululand.' (*David Payne, Emma Payne and Adrian Greaves (eds)*, Henry Charles Harford, *The Ultimatum Tree, 2008, with permission*)

The carved wooden milk pail (*ithunga*) Harford obtained while out on patrol between 17 and 24 August in search of the fugitive King Cetshwayo. (*David Payne, Emma Payne and Adrian Greaves (eds)*, Henry Charles Harford, *The Ultimatum Tree, 2008, with permission*)

Harford's South Africa Medal with date bar for serving in the Zululand campaign of 1879. (*David Payne, Emma Payne and Adrian Greaves (eds)*, Henry Charles Harford, *The Ultimatum Tree, 2008, with permission*)

The Companion's Breast Badge of the Order of the Bath with which King Edward VII invested Col. Harford at Buckingham Palace on 15 July 1907. (*David Payne, Emma Payne and Adrian Greaves (eds)*, Henry Charles Harford, *The Ultimatum Tree, 2008, with permission*)

Maj. Charlie Harford (31 December 1850–25 March 1937) in his prime when serving in India with the 2nd Battalion, The Duke of Edinburgh's (Wiltshire Regiment). (*David Payne, Emma Payne and Adrian Greaves (eds)*, Henry Charles Harford, *The Ultimatum Tree, 2008, with permission*)

Harford (right) in later life with his ubiquitous butterfly net. (*David Payne, Emma Payne and Adrian Greaves (eds)*, Henry Charles Harford, *The Ultimatum Tree, 2008, with permission*)

Lt-Gen. Lord Chelmsford, the General Officer Commanding Her Majesty's Forces during the invasion of Zululand. (*Campbell Collections of the University of KwaZulu-Natal*)

Rupert LaTrobe Lonsdale, Commandant of the 3rd Regiment NNC with No. 3 Column, Natal Field Force. (*Ron Sheeley Collection*)

George Hamilton-Browne, Commandant of the 1/3rd NNC with No. 3 Column. (*Col. George Hamilton-Browne*, A Lost Legionary in South Africa, *T. Werner Laurie, 1912*)

(*Opposite*) Harford's porpoise-hide field boot, looted by the amaZulu from the Isandlwana camp and returned to him in Pietermaritzburg by a member of the NNC. (*David Payne, Emma Payne and Adrian Greaves (eds)*, Henry Charles Harford, *The Ultimatum Tree, 2008, with permission*)

On 12 January 1879 elements of No. 3 Column stormed kwaSogekle, the stronghold of Sihayo kaXongo in the first armed encounter of the campaign, and also Harford's first experience under fire. *Illustrated London News*, 1 March 1879. (*Campbell Collections of the University of KwaZulu-Natal*)

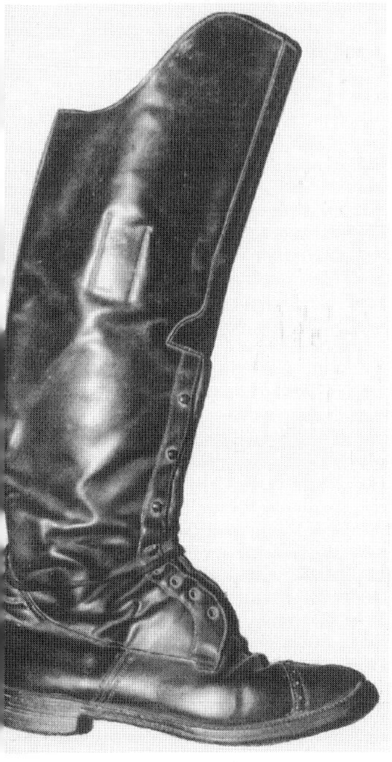

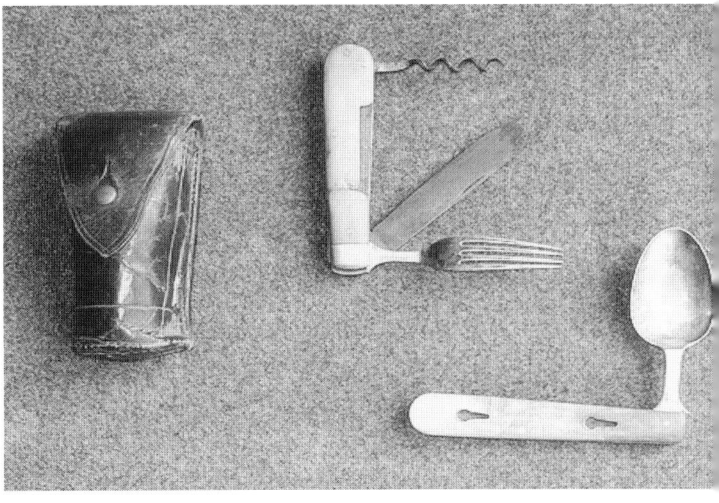

Harford's knife, fork and spoon which had been in the courier bag he dropped during the skirmish at kwaSogekle on 12 January 1879. (*David Payne, Emma Payne and Adrian Greaves (eds)*, Henry Charles Harford, *The Ultimatum Tree, 2008, with permission*)

Lt Nevill Josiah Aylmer Coghill, 1/24th Regiment. (*J.P. Mackinnon and S.H. Shadbolt,* The South African Campaign of 1879, *Sampson Low, Marston, Searle, and Rivington, 1880*)

Lt Teignmouth Melvill, Adjutant of the 1/24th Regiment. (*J.P. Mackinnon and S.H. Shadbolt,* The South African Campaign of 1879, *Sampson Low, Marston, Searle, and Rivington, 1880*)

'The Zulu War: Sketches at Rorke's Drift by Lieutenant H.C. Harford, 99th Regiment. Recovery of the Colors of the 24th. Graves of Lts Melville & Coghill.' Harford's depiction of these two related events, engraved for the *Illustrated London News* of 12 April 1879, was most significant because it was the only eye-witness one made. (*Alamy*)

'The Zulu War: Recovery of the lost Colours of the 24th Regiment. A scene in the fort at Helpmekaar.' Lt Lloyd probably made the sketch on which the engraving in the *Illustrated London News* of 29 March 1879 is based. (*David Rattray*, A Soldier-Artist in Zululand, *Rattray Publications, 2007, with permission*)

'The Dutch population' as portrayed by a somewhat satirical British observer. (*Campbell Collections of the University of KwaZulu-Natal*)

Men of Capt. Geoffrey Barton's 4th Battalion, NNC on parade. Note the number carrying rifles. (*Campbell Collections of the University of KwaZulu-Natal*)

'"The King under guard at Brigadier Clarke's Encampment on the Black Umvolosi." From a sketch by Lieutenant H.C. Harford, 99th Regiment', from the *Illustrated London News*, 18 October 1879. (*Campbell Collections of the University of KwaZulu-Natal*)

King Cetshwayo, dressed in European clothes, while held prisoner in the Castle in Cape Town between September 1879 and February 1881. With him, from left to right are his sympathetic custodian, Captain Joseph Ruscombe Poole, RA, Mkhosana kaZangqana, his adviser, William Longcast, interpreter, and Mdekzana, an attendant. (*Ian Knight Collection*)

Harford in full-dress uniform as Colonel of the Wiltshire Regiment with Sweetie on his lap, proudly wearing the Companion's Breast Badge of the Order of the Bath, the South Africa Medal and the Duke of Edinburgh's Silver Wedding Commemorative Medal. (*David Payne, Emma Payne and Adrian Greaves (eds)*, Henry Charles Harford, *The Ultimatum Tree, 2008, with permission*)

a couple of officers I started off about midday and reached the nearest farm about sundown. Being the Sabbath, the doors were closed against us and all supplies refused,[9] so we had to make the best of it, and after looking to the needs of our ponies coiled ourselves up in our blankets on the verandah of the house and listened to the family at their prayers and singing hymns to the accompaniment of a harmonium.[10]

In the morning, however, they gave us some excellent coffee, milk and bread and butter, these latter items being an immense treat, many months having elapsed since we had tasted such luxuries. No cattle, however, were obtained at this farm, as the owner declared that they had only very recently been inoculated. Altogether, we were away about a fortnight, riding through beautiful scenery and visiting a great many farms before we got the number of cattle we required. Our furthest point came within a few miles of Ladysmith,[11] and nearly everywhere the veld hospitality was extended to us. I had never before had an opportunity of seeing anything of Boer family life, so thoroughly enjoyed our mission.

Before leaving Helpmekaar,[12] Major Upcher never told me (and I and my two officers entirely forgot to ask him), how much he was

---

the Zulu kingdom in 1837. After defeating King Dingane, the Trekkers founded the Republiek Natalia in 1839, but in 1842 they submitted to British authority. Many Boers then trekked out of British Natal onto the highveld, and those who remained were generally antipathetic towards all things British.

9 The Boer farmer and his family would have been strict Calvinists and narrowly observant Sabbatarians.

10 Also called a reed organ, a harmonium is a keyboard instrument that makes a sound like an organ by blowing air from a foot-pumped bellows through reeds tuned to different pitches.

11 The town of Ladysmith, proclaimed in 1850 and named after the wife of the Governor of the Cape, Major-General Sir Harry Smith (Natal was then a District of Cape Colony), is about 65 miles west of Helpmekaar.

12 The two companies of the 1/24th left Helpmekaar in the first week of May for Dundee, the main depot of the 2nd Division. Only a detachment of the

in a position to pay per head for the cattle, but as we all three knew what a fortune the contractor had made out of our captured beasts and that there was no reason except gain for his having left the troops in the lurch,[13] we decided among ourselves to teach him a lesson and make him pay for it. So, whatever the price was that the different farms asked, we agreed, and some went as far as £20 per head.[14] Each farmer was told the date on which his cattle must be at Helpmekaar, and having procured our 300 head we returned and reported our doings to Major Upcher, who was very pleased and quite satisfied with our arrangement.

But now came an awful shock and catastrophe. The very morning on which the Dutchmen were bringing in their cattle, who should appear on the scene, suddenly and unexpectedly, but Major *[Deputy Commissary-General]*[15] Brownrigg,* the Senior Commissariat officer, who had ridden in from his Headquarters at Greytown to look into the matter of the meat supply. He was an uncommonly peppery gentleman and, bursting with rage at the steps that had been taken by us, blackguarded the Dutchmen all round for the price they had asked for the cattle and declined to pay one penny more than £8 a head.[16] Not caring to be mixed up in the row, I went off to my tent and from under the curtain of it watched the proceedings. The Boers, of course, were very angry, and I saw one of them take off his large Dopper hat and fling it

NMP and a few of the officers and NCOs of the disbanded 3rd NNC then remained at Helpmekaar.

13 Harford is referring to Mr Button, the butcher and trader who made a huge profit in Pietermaritzburg from the captured cattle he had purchased from the army at Rorke's Drift (see p. 95 nn. 2 and 4 above).

14 Purchasing power today of about £3,080. The going average price for a beast in 1879 was £15 (purchasing power today of about £2,310), so Harford was over-paying by 25 per cent.

15 A deputy commissary-general ranked with a colonel, not a major.

16 Purchasing power today of about £1,232.

down at Brownrigg's feet,[17] and heard him shouting out and calling him every name under the sun. At last, after a tremendous row, they drove all their cattle away, cursing the "damn Englishman" as they went off. I should have been precious sorry to have gone anywhere out in their direction again, unless I wanted a bullet put through me.

It was a great pity that Major Upcher did not stand firm and take the responsibility on himself of keeping the cattle and making the Contractor pay the bill. All the more so, as it turned out only a few weeks later, when a very junior but smart young Commanding Officer, just out from England, was sent for duty to Greytown and,[18] finding that Major Brownrigg was not only feeding the civil community at the expense of the troops and Government, but allowing their horses to be shod free of charge and generally standing in with the contractors, reported the matter to Headquarters. Whereupon, by some extraordinary coincidence, a fire broke out in Major Brownrigg's office, destroying all his account books in addition to stores, so that no trace was left of his illicit dealings. The end of it was that he was dismissed from the Service.[19]

---

17 *Doppers*, as they were known, were the adherents of a particularly conservative and fundamentalist Calvinist sect that in the 1830s had caught on in Boer frontier communities. They had a principled and uncouth resistance to refinement of manners (as Harford witnessed), and signalled their distinctiveness by adopting a unique manner of dress. Men's jackets were worn extremely short, displaying an expanse of shirt between the hem and unusually wide and sagging trousers held up by drawstrings. And, as Harford observed, they wore broad-brimmed hats on their closely cropped heads.

18 This was Captain George Froom, 94th Regiment, in command of the detachment of two companies of the 94th in garrison in Greytown between mid-May and late August 1879.

19 Harford's account of this affair is puzzling because Brownrigg, far from being dismissed, was in fact promoted in April from Assistant to Deputy Commissary-General of the 2nd Division. He returned to Pietermaritzburg

Transport-riders,[20] one of whom told me that he reckoned to clear £300 on his trip,[21] periodically appeared both at Rorke's Drift and Helpmekaar when the lines of communication were free from any chance of attack, and proved to be both a blessing and a curse as they not only brought every sort of article much needed by us all in the shape of clothing and boots and little accessories, but by far the greater portion of their stores consisted of drink. The regular troops of course were kept in hand and could only make their purchases under supervision, but with the Contingent it was a different matter,[22] and directly these wagons arrived no work could be got out of them and it became impossible to keep any state of discipline; all had plenty of money, and they spent it freely. The prices asked for everything were enormous, boots were from £2 to £5 a pair,[23] beer 2/6d a bottle,[24] brandy £1,[25] whiskey and "Cape Smoke" (called "square-rigger" from the shape of the bottle),[26] 15/- and 10/-. Champagne £3, and so on.[27] Nevertheless, wagons were soon emptied.

---

in November 1879 on account of ill-health and thereafter succeeded Deputy Commissary-General Edward Morris in the South African command of the Commissariat Department.

20 The lucrative Natal Overberg trade over the Drakensberg passes to the interior, especially to the Diamond Fields of the northern Cape, was carried on by transport-riders who, in the main, were farmers supplementing their income. A wagon, drawn by a span of 14 to 16 oxen, carried a load of about 7,000 lbs of goods. Three trips to the interior were usually enough to cover the initial capital outlay.

21 Purchasing power today of about £46,200.

22 Harford is referring to the remaining officers and NCOs of the disbanded 3rd NNC.

23 Purchasing power today, respectively, of about £308 and £770.

24 Purchasing power today of about £19.

25 Purchasing power today of about £154.

26 Cape Smoke was a rough, cheap brandy made of either peaches or grapes. A square rigger is a sailing ship where the four-cornered sails are set at right angles to the length of the ship and are extended on horizontal yards slung to the mast by the middle.

27 Purchasing power today, respectively, of about £115, £77 and £462.

On one particular occasion an N.C.O. of the Contingent, an oldish man who had been a digger at the Witwatersrand[28] gave us an anxious time and a lot of trouble which ended in rather an amusing episode. He had purchased a whole case of brandy—twelve bottles—and disappeared with it somewhere in the bush, unbeknown to anyone. For a whole week search-parties including myself were out searching every nook and corner to discover his whereabouts, but not a trace could be found of him until one afternoon Lieutenant Wainwright walked over to a small hut about half a mile from the camp, which was right out in the open and which several of us including myself had visited before and found perfectly empty with the exception of an iron bedstead with a mattress on it. On going inside, seeing nothing more than that, he had called out, "Corporal, you come out of this, we know you're hiding somewhere about here!" Suddenly the mattress began to move, and out popped a head from the inside of it, which said, "Ah, hah! It's you, my bold pippin, is it? All right, I'll come out." Wainwright brought him back none the worse for his debauch and a week in the jungle without food.

While at Helpmekaar I got a Helio message[29] from Colonel Welman, asking me if I would take over the Adjutancy of the Regiment again as poor Davison, who had taken over the work from me, had died at Etchowi *[Eshowe]*,[30] and saying that the 99th Regiment were now at the Lower Tugela with No. 1 Column.[31] Of

28 The gold was only discovered on the Witwatersrand in 1886, so Harford clearly meant the Kimberley Diamond Fields where digging began in 1871. This is further internal evidence that Harford's reminiscences were written at least a decade after the events they describe.

29 Heliograph message.

30 Davison had died in Fort Eshowe of typhoid fever on 27 March 1879, just a week before the garrison was relieved by Lord Chelmsford and the Eshowe Relief Column.

31 Following the relief of Eshowe on 3 April 1879, on 13 April 1879, No. 1 Column became the 1st Division, South African Field Force under the

course I accepted at once,[32] and in a very few days received orders to hand over what details of the Contingent remained with me to the Senior officer and rejoin my Regiment without delay. Being in want of a charger, and knowing how difficult it would be to get one down country, I bought a very nice animal, and a splendid shooting horse into the bargain, from one of the Contingent. His colour was a little against him, being a flea-bitten red skimmel,[33] but for real worth he couldn't be beaten. With a mate he would follow like a dog, and required no leading.

My way to the Lower Tugela was via Greytown, Maritzburg and Durban, and my faithful Kaffir, Jim, preferred to make a short cut across country and meet me at Verulam.[34] The day of my departure was another memorable occasion in my existence, for just before starting I was presented by the assembled officers and N.C.O.'s of the Contingent with an illuminated Address, which I shall always consider the most precious of all my belongings. After the ceremony I was escorted by all who had mounts for eighteen miles to Sand Spruit store where, of course, I stood them all a

---

command of Major-General Henry Hope Crealock (1831–91), CB. He had served in the Crimean War, the Indian Mutiny and the Third Anglo-Sino War, and had been DQMG in Ireland, 1874–7. On Special Service in 1879, he commanded the 1st Division from its formation in April until it ceased to exist in July, and was made CMG. The 1st Brigade of the 1st Division, comprising the 2/3rd, 88th and 99th Regiments (the latter under Lieutenant-Colonel Welman's command) was encamped at the Lower Thukela, principally on the left (Zululand side) of the river at Fort Tenedos opposite Fort Pearson, which was the main depot for the 1st Division.

32 The date is uncertain, but was probably late May or very early June.

33 A red roan (skimmel) is a horse with a uniform mixture of red (chestnut) and white hairs on the body and a chestnut head and legs. 'Flea-bitten' refers to the sprinkled reddish spots on the lighter background of the horse's roan colouration.

34 Verulam, a village 22 miles north of Durban, was founded in 1850 by a party of Methodist settlers and named after their patron, the Earl of Verulam.

good breakfast. From here I was given a very pleasant send-off, and got into Greytown in the evening where, after looking to my horses' needs and having something to eat myself at the hotel, I called and had a chat with my old friend, Willie Wainwright *[Wheelwright]*, the Magistrate.[35]

The next evening found me in Maritzburg, and here I had to stay three or four days as I had to give in my pony and Government carbine at the Remount depot, get some money as well as other commissions, which all took time, and during spare moments looked up old friends.

After returning my pony and carbine to Captain *[Major]* Russell,* 12th Lancers, the O.C. Remount Depot (who told me that I was the first individual who had returned anything at all), my first visit was to the Command Pay Office, where I called on Mr. White, the Chief Paymaster,[36] and asked him if he could let me have some money as I hadn't a penny to get on with; but as he required a Pay Certificate signed by Commandant Lonsdale, who was some 1000 miles away in the Old Colony,[37] in order to draw my staff pay amounting to some £90,[38] I could not get that. Then I asked about my ordinary Regimental pay.[39] Couldn't he give me something on

35 Harford means William Douglas Wheelwright (1847–1924), a Natal civil servant who had served during the Langalibalele Rebellion in 1873. Since January 1878 he had been the Resident Magistrate of Umvoti County at Greytown. From December 1878 to July 1879, he was Commandant of Colonial Defensive District VII, responsible for the defence of the Natal middle border with Zululand.

36 It would seem that Harford has given the Chief Paymaster the wrong name. The Staff Paymaster was Major W.C. Ball, Army Pay Department. Major Francis Freeman White, who was killed at Isandlwana, had been the Paymaster of the 1/24th Regiment.

37 The pay was for service as Adjutant of the 3rd Regiment, NNC, of which Lonsdale was the commander. Lonsdale was in the Cape raising Lonsdale's Horse (Mounted Rifles).

38 Purchasing power today of about £13,860.

39 Regimental pay with the 99th Regiment.

that account? But there again, our Regimental Paymaster held my last Pay Certificate, so he could give me no Regimental pay and expressed his regret at not being able to give me any assistance. Then, just as I was leaving the office, evidently seeing the plight I was in, he called me back and said, "Have you any money with your Regimental Agents?" "Yes", I said, "£38".[40] "Well", he replied, "If you will write out a cheque on them, I will cash it for you." So there and then I wrote out a cheque for that amount on Messrs Price and Boustead, who only about two or three months after went smash, so but for this Providential coincidence I should never have seen a penny of my £38 again.

On one of the evenings, somebody, I forget now who, gave a dance to which I was invited, and went. Where I raised a dress suit to go in I also forget, but when I walked into the ballroom, which was full of old friends and familiar faces, not a single soul made any attempt to recognise me—as I still wore my beard! I felt rather shy of introducing myself, so only stayed for five or ten minutes and strolled off, but before getting very far I met Arthur Shepstone* and his wife on their way to it,[41] and was hauled back again, this time to dance all night and have a very pleasant time of it.

Being an honorary member of the Maritzburg Club, I went there a few hours after my arrival and was told that a Kaffir had been there daily for weeks past, enquiring for me, not saying what he wanted except that he wished to see me. I left word as to when I should be at the Club again, and when I did, found my friend squatting patiently waiting on the doorstep for my arrival.[42]

40 Purchasing power today of about £5,852.

41 Arthur Jesse Shepstone (1852–1912) was a Natal civil servant, and in 1876 he had been appointed Natal Labour Agent and Superintendent of Labour. He was one of the six sons of Sir Theophilus Shepstone.*

42 There is a critical chronological problem here. Harford would appear to have reported to the 99th Regiment at the Lower Thukela in early June, yet here is his unnamed African 'friend' in Pietermaritzburg presenting him with belongings picked up on the battlefield of Ulundi, an engagement that would

Getting up and greeting me with the usual salutation of Inkosi, and evidently very pleased at having unearthed me at last, judge my surprise when from an old bundle he produced the left boot of my favourite pair of Dean's field boots,[43] in which was stowed away two pocket handkerchiefs with my name on them—relics from the camp at Isandhlwana which he had picked up at Ulundi, on the battlefield not far from Cetewayo's kraal.[44]

He had belonged to our Contingent, and on the disbandment of the Natives he had made his way to No. 1 Column on the Coast, whence he had apparently attached himself to the 2nd Natal Native Contingent (in which, no doubt, he had pals), and came in for the fight there.[45] Isandhlwana was fought on the 22nd

---

only be fought on 4 July, about a month later. Moreover, he had purportedly been waiting for Harford for 'weeks past'. The only way to explain this conundrum is to presume that the incident occurred four months later, after Harford, as a member of Clarke's Column, had returned to Pietermaritzburg in the first week of October (see p. 166 n. 76 below), and that in these reminiscences he mistakenly records the meeting as occurring in June when on his way from Helpmekaar to the Lower Thukela.

43 For a description of the distinctive boots Harford had purchased at Dean's in the Strand, see p. 23 above.

44 oNdini.

45 Harford's account of his NNC 'friend's' military record is opaque, and difficult to disentangle. He had clearly been a member of the 3rd Regiment, NNC, disbanded after Isandlwana. It seems he then made his way to the coast and joined either the 4th or 5th Battalion, NNC, most likely the former. These had been formed in February from the 2nd Regiment, NNC that had been part of No. 1 Column, and had been sent back to Natal on 30 January when Colonel Pearson was blockaded in Fort Eshowe. The fight 'he came in for' was most likely the battle of Gingindlovu on 2 April, in which both these battalions fought as part of the Eshowe Relief Column, and not the battle of Ulundi as glossed by Daphne Child (*Zulu War Journal*, p. 59). The 4th Battalion, NNC then formed part of the 1st Division in its advance up the coast, and from 23 July served with Clarke's Column. Between 11 August and 2 September, the bulk of Clarke's Column (including the 4th Battalion, NNC) was encamped at kwaSishwili, General Wolseley's camp close to the Ulundi battlefield. The NNC 'friend' would then have had the

January, and Ulundi on the 4th July, so the Zulus had ample time to carry off the Isandhlwana loot to Ulundi, and no doubt in the confusion of the distribution my pair of boots had got separated and this single boot thrown away. It is quite safe to say that no-one else in the whole of the Forces had boots of similar cut, and my friend, like all other Kaffirs being an observant individual, knew directly he saw it who it had belonged to, and at once brought it away in the hope of being able to find me again and hand it back. This only shows what a good fellow the kraal Kaffir is, and he in particular was.

Ulundi is about eighty miles as the crow flies from Isandhlwana[46] and about two hundred via the Coast road to Maritzburg, so the Zulu army had the honour of carrying my boot (or boots) for over 150 miles,[47] and this good chap had tramped with it another 200 miles on an off-chance. To him, of course, it was of no value whatever, but to me that boot is greatly treasured, both for the remarkable circumstances under which I got it back and as a reminiscence of my days with the 3rd N.N.C. It is now stored with other belongings at Messrs Curtiss & Sons, at Portsmouth.[48] The pocket handkerchiefs, I'm sorry to say, I had to make use of, so they are no more. My good friend, it is needless to say, was amply rewarded for what he had done.

---

opportunity to scour the battlefield and retrieve Harford's distinctive boot and handkerchiefs.

46 The distance is closer to 65 miles.

47 The Zulu army would have carried Harford's boot only from Isandlwana to oNdini, so why Harford doubles the distance it covered from his 80 miles to 150 miles is not clear. The distance from oNdini to Pietermaritzburg via the coastal road is indeed about the 200 miles the NNC 'friend' is said to have 'tramped'. Yet here is another mystery. Clarke's Column, of which he was apparently a member, marched back inland from kwaSishwili to Greytown, and not along the coast. Was the 'friend' in fact a deserter?

48 The firm of Curtiss & Sons, furniture removals and storage, was established in Portsmouth in 1871 and is still going strong.

One of the first persons I met after getting into Maritzburg was Captain Stubbs *[Major Stabb]*, 32nd Regiment, who was President of the Board on claims for losses at Isandhlwana.[49] He asked me why I had sent in no claims for anything, but evidently it had been mislaid as I had personally forwarded all claims from the Contingent, to which mine was attached. So I made him out another, and hereby hangs a curious tale showing the inexplicable ways of the War Office. As far as my claim was concerned, it was just two years before I heard anything more about it, and then, when the Regiment was in Bermuda,[50] I received an official letter from the War Office, requesting me to give my reasons for claiming £25[51] on account of articles lost at Isandhlwana. This struck me as a most extraordinary request, and I showed the letter to the Colonel,[52] to whom I explained that although I had only claimed compensation for an ordinary Field Kit as laid down in Sir Garnet Wolseley's *Soldiers' Pocket Book*,[53] I had really

49 Major Henry Sparke Stabb (not Stubbs) (1853–88), 32nd Regiment, had seen action in the Indian Mutiny, 1857–8. On Special Service in 1879, he served on the staff of the 2nd Division, was present at the battle of Ulundi, and was then Commandant of Fort Victoria until the end of hostilities. He subsequently was president of a board for the investigation and settlement of all claims preferred by colonists and others for losses received by them during the war.

As in the case of the NNC soldier who returned his belongings to him, Harford's encounter with Stabb must have taken place in early October after Clarke's Column arrived in Pietermaritzburg, and not in June as the narrative suggests. Why Harford opted to alter the chronology is unclear, except that he perhaps believed it suited the narrative better to describe the two incidents where he did, rather than when they actually occurred.

50 The 99th Regiment was stationed in Bermuda from January 1880 to June 1881.

51 Purchasing power today of about £3,850.

52 Colonel Welman.

53 Wolseley, *The Soldier's Pocket-Book*, pp. 8–12: 'Field Equipment for Officers'. To modern eyes, the amount of officer's 'Field Kit' appears extraordinarily lavish.

lost over £150 worth of things,[54] including my two guns[55] which were worth £50 alone[56] …. (As Staff Officer to the Contingent, having been furnished with a wagon to myself, I had taken many more things with me than I was entitled to by regulations.) He said, "Have you any receipts left of your purchases for the campaign? If so, I should send them all in and simply say that you had only put in for the cost of a regulation Field Kit, but had lost considerably more, as would be seen by the receipts you enclosed for perusal."

The total now, including the two guns, was close on £200,[57] and another six months went by before anything more was heard of the matter, until one morning I received a cheque for £88.10.6½d.[58] How the sum had been arrived at it was impossible to say, but anyhow it was a most welcome surprise and came just at the right moment as the high cost of living in Bermuda was ruining us all, our Mess bills running to about £20[59] a month for absolutely nothing at all.

Such a thing as a scare was unknown to us at Rorke's Drift, though parties of Zulus continued to prowl about in the vicinity long after Isandhlwana, but on my ride down to the Coast I found everywhere—Greytown, Maritzburg and Durban—still suffering from nerves and most of the streets with their barricades still standing. There was one laager between Helpmekaar and Greytown, (known afterwards as "Fort Funk"), where nearly a month after Isandhlwana a night scare took place, when several thousands of rounds of ammunition were expended on what proved

54 Purchasing power today of about £23,100.

55 Harford's two prized shotguns (see pp. 97–8 and p. 98 n. 11 above).

56 Purchasing power today of about £7,700.

57 Purchasing power today of about £30,800.

58 Purchasing power today of about £13,630.

59 Purchasing power today of about £3,080.

in the morning to be nothing but a derelict ox which a fool of a sentry had mistaken for a party of Zulus.[60]

As I passed through the Umvoti County, Captain Townshend's *[Townsend's]* old coffee plantation at Avoca and the adjoining sugar and other estates recalled many happy memories,[61] and the familiar calls of the birds and other denizens of the bush made me long to go round and have a look at some of my old haunts again. The faithful Jim was awaiting my arrival at Verulam, and the whole of the road from here to the Tugela abounded with reminiscences of the glorious time I spent with Dr Ray in 1864

60 There is no corroborative evidence about such a night alarm taking place towards the end of February at a laager between Helpmekaar and Greytown. The Umvoti Laager, occupied by a few families after Isandlwana, was situated south of Greytown and was in any case abandoned on 12 February; while the Hermannsburg Laager to the north-east of Greytown, which was manned by mounted volunteers throughout the war, ceased to shelter any civilians by early April. It never experienced an alarm. However, there was a scare at the Greytown Laager itself on 2 February when there were rumours of a Zulu incursion and the townsfolk took refuge there for the night. They did so again on the afternoon of 4 February when a young officer of the garrison of the 2/4th Regiment, amused by the pusillanimous state of the civilian population, for a lark rang one of the town's church bells which had been designated an alarm signal.

61 Captain H. Townsend's (not Townshend's) Avoca plantation in Victoria County was eight miles north up the coast from the town of Durban. Today it is the name of a northern suburb of the hugely expanded city. Townsend, who had formerly been an officer in the 99th Regiment, was a Captain in the Victoria Mounted Rifles with its headquarters in Verulam, a justice of the peace for Victoria County and a member of the Chamber of Agriculture for Natal. (In holding these positions of status in the colony, Townsend and Harford's father were very alike.) Harford recalled that in his youth, 'I very often went to stay there [at Avoca] collecting birds and insects and occasionally lending a hand at the coffee pulping operation. Captain and Mrs Townsend were the most hospitable and unconventional of hosts and the free and easy life of planters at that time was very delightful and precisely to my liking.' (Payne et al., *Harford*, p. 30.)

at the Lower Post, now known as Fort Williamson,[62] riding and shooting all over the country and leading a real Colonial life.[63] The same delicious scent from the veld perfumed the air as in those days, and imbued one with indescribable feelings of life and sport. The country was very little changed from what I had remembered of it, except for alterations caused by floods and storms especially along the river courses, and I felt that I would give a good deal to be able to live my early life at the Lower Post and Avoca over again, with its adventures and splendid training for the rough-and-tumble of the world's existence, which has ever since stood me in such good stead. I can never sufficiently thank or show my gratitude to my dear old friends, Dr Ray and Captain Townshend, for having given me really the opportunity of my life in learning to ride and shoot and the art of roughing it and being able to do everything for oneself.

I found my Regiment, together with the 88th, Royal Irish Regiment *[Connaught Rangers]*, encamped close to the Tugela River on the Zululand side,[64] and was told by everyone how stout and fit I looked. I think they expected to see a scarecrow arrive, knowing what a rough time the 3rd Column had had of it, but a hard life suits me down to the ground, though not so with most people. The C.D. [seedy][65] appearance of the majority of my brother officers,

62 The earthwork Fort Williamson on the Natal (south) bank of the lower Thukela was begun in 1861 during the short-lived Zulu 'Invasion Scare' of that year. Neglected thereafter, by 1870 the fort was in disrepair.

63 Dr Ray was an old friend of Harford's parents who was the regimental medical officer of the detachments of the 11th Regiment and the Cape Mounted Rifles stationed at Fort Williamson.

64 The 1st Brigade of the 1st Division, comprising the 2/3rd, 88th and 99th Regiments, had been encamped there since mid-April (see pp. 121–2 n. 31 above). Harford made a slip in designating the 88th (Connaught Rangers) Regiment the 'Royal Irish Regiment'. That title belonged to the 18th Regiment, which took no part in the Anglo-Zulu War.

65 'Seedy' meaning shabby-looking, or out of sorts.

who had been living in luxury, getting everything they required, showed very clearly that living in camp, with little or nothing to do and every want supplied, did not make for health, and I could not return the compliment.[66]

Jim became a great favourite with everyone, officers and men, and I was horrified one morning when he turned up dressed in a blue patrol jacket, red silk sash and glengarry cap presented to him by the Colonel, thinking himself no end of a swell. He was very proud of his appearance, which I was not, as Jim in his "moocha" *[umutsha]*[67] and Jim in his "Kitchen Kaffir" get-up were not the same sort of individual.[68] Nevertheless, I am glad to think he was not spoilt.

Within forty-eight hours of my resuming my duties as Adjutant there was a midnight scare created by a Colour Sergeant, whose voice as I lay in my tent was quite familiar to me though I hadn't

66 The 1st Brigade, 1st Division had been engaged in improving the earthwork Fort Tenedos (first begun by No. 1 Column on 13 January 1879) along with other defensive arrangements on both sides of the Lower Thukela. One company of the 99th Regiment garrisoned Fort Tenedos. On 23 April men of the 1st Brigade began the construction of the earthwork Fort Crealock on the north bank of the Matigulu River as a supply depot on the 1st Division's proposed line of advance, and first garrisoned it on 10 May. In mid-June three companies of the 99th garrisoned Fort Crealock. Meanwhile, on 29 April the 2nd Brigade, 1st Division began to construct the earthwork Fort Chelmsford on the south bank of the Nyezane River in advance of Fort Crealock and completed it on 10 May. During the latter part of April, all of May and the first two weeks of June, the 1st Brigade was engaged in convoy duty, bringing up sufficient supplies to Fort Chelmsford to last the 1st Division two months. (The last of these convoys on which men of the 99th Regiment served was on 4 June.)

67 *Umutsha*; *imitsha* (plural): loin covering of long pieces of twisted skin hanging like tails.

68 This is a derogatory term for a male domestic servant, dressed in some form of European clothing, usually a 'kitchen boy' suit with a short-sleeved loose top, sometimes a waist sash, and trousers ending just below the knees.

heard it for more than a year.[69] I heard him rush out of his tent, saying, "Here they come! Here they come, right down the hill!", and in a very few moments the whole Regiment were in the trenches. The 88th Regiment, who were close on our right, took up the scare and almost at once commenced blazing away at what was found later on to be a clump of palms whose nodding tops had been mistaken against the skyline, in the darkness, for moving Zulus. Our men, luckily, saw nothing to fire at. I was determined that, as far as I was concerned, this should be the last. Everyone's rest disturbed, and standing to arms all night in the trenches, with the certain knowledge that there could be no enemy within 200 or 300 miles was absolutely ridiculous, so I got the whole of the N.C.O.'s together at the first available moment and lectured them pretty strongly on the matter. I gave strict orders that not a soul in the camp was to be disturbed until I had been made acquainted with the details, and that all reports from sentries or outposts were to be brought to me quietly.

This interview had its effect only a very few nights after, when a young officer in command of an outpost near the river sent up an urgent message reporting that hundreds of Zulus were crossing the Tugela a little distance above his post, so I went down to have a look for myself and see what was happening. On reaching the spot, I came upon the youngster in a great state of excitement. "There they are, Sir. There they are! You can see them crossing. They've got lanterns." The phantom Zulus were nothing but myriads of fire-flies, and a sight well worth having been turned out of bed to see, but at the same time I had to give my young friend a good lecture on the trouble that he might have caused. With only a little over a

69 Harford officially resumed his duties as Adjutant of the 99th Regiment on 23 July 1879, although it is evident that he had been performing these duties ever since early June when he rejoined his regiment. It has not proved possible from the available sources to confirm or give a date to this false alarm.

year's service, and never having been out of England before in his life, such a thing as flies being able to emit light was a novelty that never entered his head, and it was curious that none of the N.C.O.'s or men of the picquet could not have put him straight.

It would be far better if Latin and Greek were eliminated from the examination papers for youngsters destined for the Service, and a year's residence in India or one of the Colonies insisted on instead, on which questions of some practical use could be set. This would not only be an advantage to the individual, but be a very great gain to the Service and go a long way to prevent regrettable incidents. Money wasted by parents in sending their sons, as a preliminary, to serve in the Militia and subsequently for cramming, could be spent to better purpose (and the cost of such a measure would be far less).[70]

The nervousness of the Headquarters staff, who apparently also entertained the idea that sundry Zulu impi's were lurking about only waiting an opportunity to attack our camp, was very clearly shown one day soon after I had rejoined the Regiment. Lieutenant Neville *[Nevile]* and I went out for a shoot, to try and get a Rietbuck,[71] and passed over some ground that I knew very well and had shot over with John Dunn when staying with Dr Ray. On our return I found

70 The Royal Commission appointed to inquire into the Present State of Military Education (1868–9, 1870) concluded that prospective officers for the cavalry, Guards and line should receive some professional instruction, and that all admissions to the Royal Military College, Sandhurst be determined by open competition in which the candidates could sit papers in Latin and Greek. Soon thereafter, the War Office instituted examinations through which the successful candidates could gain their commissions direct, without attending Sandhurst. With the abolition of purchase in 1871, promotion to Lieutenant and Captain was by examination. Yet this only established eligibility for promotion which, in fact, normally continued to be based on seniority.

71 The southern reedbuck, or rietbok (*Redunca arundinum*) is an antelope. The male bears forward-curving horns and the female none.

a letter awaiting me from the Adjutant-General,[72] expressing the G.O.C.'s surprise that a good soldier like Lieutenant Harford should have gone out shooting in the neighbourhood of the camp, etc. etc., and that such must not occur again. Anything more idiotic could scarcely be conceived. For reconnoitring work no better means could have been devised than to give encouragement to every sportsman in the camp to scour the country for game, but now we were condemned to stew in our tents.

72 The DAG of the 1st Division was Major A.L. Walker,* 99th Regiment. The GOC was Major-General Crealock (see pp. 121–2 n. 31 above).

CHAPTER 6

The Capture of Cetewayo

From the Tugela the 99th moved to Fort Chelmsford, a little further up the coast,[1] and before we had been there many days I was offered the appointment of 2nd Staff Officer to the Column that Colonel *[Lieutenant-Colonel]* Mansfield Clarke* was organising at Port Durnford for the purpose of hunting down Cetewayo.[2]

---

1 Between 17 and 19 June the 1st Brigade, 1st Division, including all eight companies of the 99th Regiment under Colonel Welman, moved forward to Fort Chelmsford, where on 19 June they were joined by Major-General Crealock and the Divisional Staff.

2 Harford is eliding events. While the HQ of the 99th Regiment (including Harford), along with four companies, remained in garrison at Fort Chelmsford, on 1 July the remaining four companies advanced up the coast with the 1st Brigade, 1st Division to Port Durnford and commenced Fort Richards (on which construction ceased when peace negotiations were opened with the amaZulu). On 4 July the battle of Ulundi was fought, and on 9 July Lord Chelmsford resigned his command in South Africa to General Wolseley. On 10 July Wolseley began reducing the strength of the 1st Division. What concerned him was that King Cetshwayo had fled north after the defeat of his army at Ulundi and was still at large. Unbeknown to the British, Cetshwayo had taken refuge at ekuShumayeleni, an *umuzi* on the isiKhwebezi River belonging to Mnyamana kaNgqengelele, the *inkosi* of the Buthelezi people and the king's chief *induna*. Cetshwayo holed up there for a month, attempting fruitlessly to enter into negotiations with the British. For his part, Wolseley was apprehensive that Cetshwayo might be trying to rally his *amabutho* to continue the struggle, and understood that the leading men of the Zulu kingdom would be reluctant to accept a settlement

It was a great piece of luck, and fortunately the Colonel[3] had no objection to my going, though I'm afraid it inconvenienced him a little, my leaving again so soon after rejoining.[4] Not knowing what arrangements our Brigadier was making with regard to our feeding,[5] I took with me a fairly substantial supply of tinned meat, jam, etc. in case of accidents. Colonel Mansfield Clarke, however, had made

---

that ended the war so long as Cetshwayo was still at liberty. Wolseley therefore decided he must advance to the environs of the now burnt-out oNdini and from there send out patrols to apprehend the fugitive monarch. On 21 July, before embarking at Port Durnford to settle affairs in Natal prior to marching to oNdini overland, Wolseley arranged that when the 1st Division was finally broken up – it ceased to exist on 23 July – a brigade under Lieutenant-Colonel Clarke should be formed from the units not being sent back to Natal, and should move north to oNdini to rendezvous with him there. Clarke's Column, joined by Harford, began its advance on 24 July, marching from Port Durnford to the lower drift across the Mhlathuze River.

The total strength of Clarke's Column, including wagon drivers and other support personnel, amounted to 2,159 white troops (including No. 10 Battery, 7th Brigade, RA, with two Gatling guns, N Battery, 6th Brigade, RA, with two 9-pounder guns, a detachment of Royal Engineers, the 57th Regiment, 3/60th Rifles and 80th Regiment (five companies), No. 2 Squadron Mounted Infantry, No. 1 Troop, Natal Horse (also known as de Burgh's Horse, recruited from NCOs of the disbanded 3rd NNC) and two troops of Lonsdale's Horse; and 1,257 black troops (Jantze's Native Horse, Mafunzi's Mounted Natives, the 4th Battalion, NNC and a detachment of NNPC). The column was accompanied by 198 wagons, 54 carts and 6 ambulances, and carried supplies for 14 days.

3 Colonel Welman of the 99th Regiment.

4 When the 1st Division ceased to exist on 23 July 1879, the 99th Regiment returned to Natal and the HQ and several detachments marched into Pietermaritzburg on 26 August. The regiment was to form the permanent garrison in Natal and was redeployed at various posts. The HQ and two companies were stationed at Fort Napier in Pietermaritzburg, with two companies at Greytown, one at Rorke's Drift, one at Fort Pearson at the Lower Thukela, one at Durban and one at Port St John's.

5 Harford is referring to Lieutenant-Colonel Clarke who had been the Brigadier of the 2nd Brigade, 1st Division and was now Brigadier of Clarke's Column.

ample arrangements, as the Admiral *[Commander Campbell]*,[6] who was a great friend of his, was on the eve of sailing for Home and had made him a present of enough stores to last several months. All the same, my things came in handy to start off with, and I think pleased the Brigadier, though he said he was sorry that I should have gone to such expense.

I never learned who it was who had so kindly recommended me for the billet, but on reporting myself, Colonel Clarke received me most kindly, saying that he had heard a good deal about me and hoped that I would keep up the reputation that I had brought. Never was there a stricter or more exacting C.O., and never was there a better soldier to serve under, and the result was that the Column worked like clockwork. The Intelligence staff under Captain Murray;[7] R.E. *[61st Regiment]*, Captain Blood;[8] Mounted Infantry and Colonial troops, Major Percy Barrow,* 19th Hussars; N.N.C., Captain Barton,* 7th Royal Fusiliers; Mule battery, Major Duncan, R.A.;*

6 By 'the Admiral', Harford means Commander (Acting Captain) H.J.F. Campbell, RN, of HMS *Active* who came on shore on 20 November 1878. He was in command of *Active*'s Naval Brigade that took part in the operations of No. 1 Column and was present at Nyezane and the blockade of Fort Eshowe. Subsequently, he was in command of the Naval Brigade of 795 sailors forming part of the 1st Division (the crews of HMS *Active, Shah, Boadicea* and *Tenedos*) and superintended the landing of stores at Port Durnford. On 21 July Campbell and the Naval Brigade embarked on the transport *City of Venice* for Durban.

7 Captain Charles Wyndham Murray, 61st Regiment, *psc*, was on Special Service in 1879 as Major-General Crealock's ADC. In May he was appointed DAQMG in the Intelligence Branch of the 1st Division, and then in July in the same capacity to Clarke's Column. He was attached to the Mounted Troops under Major Barrow* and was present during the search for Cetshwayo. He then reconnoitred the route to be traversed by Clarke's Column from kwaSishwili to Middle Drift. He was promoted Brevet Major.

8 Captain Bindon Blood, 30th Company, RE, commanded the Royal Engineers of the 1st Division during its advance to Port Durnford, and then those of Clarke's Column. He was promoted Brevet Major.

Major Tufnell, 3rd/60th Rifles;[9] Major Tredenick *[Tredennick]*, 57th Regiment;[10] Major Tucker, 80th Regiment;[11] Commander *[Assistant Commissary-General]* Reeves, A.S.C.;[12] Sergeant-Major *[Surgeon-Major]* Giraud, R.A.M.C. *[AHC]*;[13] Captain Hart,* 81st *[31st]* Regiment. Myself as Staff Officer,[14] and Lieutenant Towers-Clarke,* 57th Regiment, orderly officer, made up the Column, not forgetting Jim,

---

9 Major Arthur Tufnell, 3/60th Rifles, served with the battalion throughout the campaign. When Colonel W.L. Pemberton was invalided home in late April, he succeeded to the command of the battalion and was promoted from Captain to Major. His battalion served with the Eshowe Relief Column and he commanded it during Gingindlovu. He continued in command when the battalion formed part of No. 1 Division and subsequently joined Clarke's Column. He was promoted Brevet Colonel.

10 Major James Richard Knox Tredennick (not Tredenick), 57th Regiment, served in the Second Taranaki War (New Zealand Wars), 1865–6. In 1879, his regiment, newly arrived in Natal from Ceylon (now Sri Lanka) under Lieutenant-Colonel Clarke's command, formed part of the Eshowe Relief Column and he was present at Gingindlovu. From mid-April, when Lieutenant-Colonel Clarke was given field commands as Brigadier of the 2nd Brigade, 1st Division and then of Clarke's Column, he assumed command of the 57th Regiment in the field until the end of the war and took part in the operations of the 1st Division and of Clarke's Column.

11 Major Charles Tucker, 80th Regiment, served in the Anglo-Bhutan (Duar) War, 1865 and in the First Anglo-Pedi War, 1878. In 1879 he commanded the 80th Regiment which formed part of No. 5 Column concentrating in January 1879 at Derby on the Swazi border. In February his regiment garrisoned Luneburg. In April the 80th Regiment at Luneburg was relieved and under Tucker's command joined Wood's Flying Column and fought at Ulundi. On the breakup of the Flying Column, the 80th Regiment formed part of Clarke's Column. Made CB and promoted Lieutenant-Colonel.

12 Assistant Commissary-General (not Commander) Henry Spencer Edward Reeves, Senior Commissariat Officer with Clarke's Column.

13 Surgeon-Major (not Sergeant-Major) Charles Hervé Giraud, Army Hospital Corps (not the RAMC, which was not formed until 1898), served in the Second Anglo-Sino War of 1860. He was stationed at the Cape from 1873. In 1879 he served as Senior Medical Officer with Clarke's Column.

14 Harford's official designation on Clarke's staff was Staff Officer, subordinate to the Principal Staff Officer, Captain Hart.

who ingratiated himself with everyone and became quite a character in his regimental get-up.

Towers-Clarke and I had all our meals with the Brigadier in his tent—Captain Hart preferring to live separately. "Towers" and I shared a tent, which was always pitched by the side of the Brigadier's.

Our first objective was Ulundi, where Sir Garnet Wolseley had taken up temporary headquarters,[15] and all went well till we reached Entonjaneni *[Mthonjaneni]*, a high hill some fifteen or twenty, miles from Ulundi, on the top of which Lord Chelmsford had encamped the night before the battle.[16] But very fortunately for us our Brigadier preferred to camp on the plains at the foot of it,[17] for during the night a terrific hurricane accompanied by a deluge of rain came on, which swept over the whole of Natal, simply devastating the country and completely demolishing our camp.[18] When daylight came, the scene was one of vast desolation, only one tent in the whole camp was left standing and that was the Brigadier's which Captain Hart, Towers-Clarke, myself, our servant and Jim had held on to all night by means of extra ropes and constant hammering in of pegs. How we managed

15 After leaving Port Durnford on 21 July, Wolseley had proceeded via Durban to Pietermaritzburg, where he remained until 30 July. Then, with an escort of a squadron of the 1st King's Dragoon Guards, he had ridden north via Rorke's Drift to the Mthonjaneni heights. On the afternoon of 7 August he joined Clarke's Column at the foot of Mthonjaneni, and on 10 August established his kwaSishwili camp close by the burnt-out oNdini.

16 In fact, Chelmsford's force had laagered on Mthonjaneni on 27 June and moved forward on 1 July to form a laager on the right bank of the White Mfolozi River. On 4 July Chelmsford crossed the river from this laager and fought the battle of Ulundi.

17 On its march, Clarke's Column had reached St Paul's Anglican mission on 30 July, the Anglican mission at KwaMagwaza on 3 August, and the Mthonjaneni heights on 6 August. On 7 August it descended to the plain below, where it encamped and where General Wolseley joined it.

18 The severe storm began on the evening of 7 August and lasted throughout the two following days, making it impossible for Clarke's Column to resume the advance until 10 August.

it, I don't know, but we did it, which was the great thing. I can only say it was the worst night I ever spent in my life, and I think I might say with certainty that not a living soul in that camp but would not have expressed the same sentiments. Many of the tents had been blown to ribbons, and some carried off for miles. Cactus and other trees were rooted up everywhere,[19] but the most serious of the damage that was done was the loss of over 300 oxen, which lay dead in their spans by the side of their wagons, which of course meant that until they could be replaced the Column was at a standstill.[20] The tent that Towers-Clarke and I shared, with all our belongings … had completely disappeared, and it was only after hours of searching that, bit by bit, we recovered most of our things again—and in a nice state they were.

Several buck were caught during the night by men of the different Regiments as they were being blown through the camps, and how it was that Major Barrow managed to prevent the ponies and mules of his mounted troops from stampeding was a miracle.

By way of digression, Captain Moir, of my regiment, told me a good story with reference to this same storm which swept away the camp where he was at the time, further down the coast.[21] Private Geoghegan, an Irishman, the Company Cook, determined that his company should not go without their "gun fire" tea,[22] sat on a pot over the fire all night and kept it going—for which thoughtful expedient he got a sovereign! It was the only bit of fire in the camp.

19 The 'cactus' trees Harford saw uprooted were most likely tall, succulent 'candelabra trees' (*Euphorbia ingens*) that grow in the valley of the White Mfolozi, and possibly the large, single-stemmed aloes (*Aloe marlothii*) that thrive in the same thornveld habitat.

20 The unremitting rain and accompanying freezing weather killed 452 draught-oxen belonging to Clarke's Column within 60 hours. When the column finally moved forward, 195 sick oxen had to be left behind, along with 54 wagons for which there were now no draught animals.

21 A severe storm swept the camp of the 1st Division at Port Durnford between 2 and 4 July, and prevented General Wolseley landing there from HMS *Shah*.

22 The name for early morning tea in the British Army.

This crushing loss of oxen of course greatly exercised the Brigadier's mind, and it was a lucky thing for us that the Commander-in-Chief[23] was so close at hand, as he at once directed the officer commanding at Fort Victoria,[24] which was only a few miles off, to hand over all his cattle to our Column, an item which was anything but appreciated by the troops at the Fort. This enabled us, after a little over a week of uncommonly stiff work, digging huge, deep trenches and burying the dead animals, to move on to Ulundi.[25] Here we were hung up for a considerable time, why I can't remember, but there was plenty of work to be done and in the course of my duties I became well acquainted with General *[Brigadier-General]* Sir [George] Pomeroy Colley, the Chief of the Staff,[26] and *[Lieutenant-]*Colonel Eastlake *[East]*, Deputy *[Adjutant and]* Q.M. General.[27]

---

23 General Wolseley.

24 The rhomboid-shaped, earthwork Fort Victoria was built on 7 August by the 57th Regiment close by the camping ground of Clarke's Column below the Mthonjaneni heights. It was garrisoned by the HQ and three companies of the 57th Regiment, so the officer commanding there would have been Major Tredennick.

25 Clarke's Column moved forward on 10 August and encamped at the White Mfolozi. The following day (11 August) it crossed the river and joined Wolseley's kwaSishwili HQ camp near oNdini. Evidently, it left behind work parties at Fort Victoria to bury the dead oxen, and Harford, as Staff Officer, was engaged in the unsavoury task.

26 Brigadier-General Sir George Pomeroy Colley (1835–81), Staff, KCSI, CMG, was an intellectually brilliant soldier who had been Professor of Military Law and Administrations at the Staff College, 1871–3. As a member of Wolseley's staff, he saw service in the Third Anglo-Asante War, 1874. He rejoined Wolseley's staff on his special mission to Natal in 1875. In 1876 he was appointed military secretary to the Viceroy of India, and in 1878 his private secretary. From July 1879 he was on Special Service as Wolseley's Chief of Staff until the conclusion of the war and was appointed CB.

27 Lieutenant-Colonel Cecil James East (not Eastlake) (1837–1908), late 57th Regiment and AQMG, Intelligence Department, joined Chelmsford's staff on Special Service in June 1879 as DA and QMG and was present as the senior

In my spare time I went over the battlefield of Ulundi and picked up one or two relics in the shape of shields, assegais, etc. A few days after we arrived, Jim came to me to say that he knew the spot where Cetewayo's crown and other paraphernalia presented to him on the occasion of his Coronation by "Somtseu" were buried, and asked if he might go and make a search. I told him certainly, but I would like to go with him, but he said that he would rather go at first by himself and if he found that they had not been taken away he would go with me to get them. However, it turned out that they had been removed, and squatting down, snapping his fingers to emphasise matters, he declared that it had only been done that very day, as the earth from the hole was quite fresh.[28] I should much like to have gone with him afterwards, to have a look at the spot, but I never got the chance.

---

staff officer at Ulundi. He continued as DQMG on Wolseley's General Staff until the end of the campaign and was promoted Brevet Colonel.

28 'Somsteu', or *Somtsewu* in isiZulu, was the Zulu nickname for Sir Theophilus Shepstone.

King Mpande died in late 1872 and his heir, Cetshwayo, was acclaimed king in a traditional Zulu ceremony in August 1873. However, Cetshwayo agreed to undergo a further 'coronation' ceremony by Shepstone to cement diplomatic relations with Natal and strengthen his own hand against dissident *amakhosi*. The grand pageant, orchestrated by Shepstone under the protection of an armed escort of the Natal Volunteer Corps, took place on 1 September 1873 at the emLambongwenya *ikhanda*. Shepstone invested Cetshwayo with a scarlet and gold mantle, and placed an extraordinary, befeathered coronet with embroidered fabric streamers and ear-flaps, devised by the master-tailor of the 75th Regiment (then in garrison in Natal at Fort Napier) on his head. (There is a photograph of the 'crown' and other items from Cetshwayo's household in the Campbell Collection, University of KwaZulu-Natal, Album C66-046.) As Jim reported, the coronet and other trumpery finery had indeed been looted, but some items must have reached Britain because one of the smaller crimson-dyed ostrich plumes (now much faded) that had formed part of the coronet is preserved in the Royal Commonwealth Institute Library in the Cambridge University Library (ORCS.4.13).

Several small expeditions consisting of officers and men acting independently were traversing the country in the hope of capturing Cetewayo,[29] and as it seemed likely that our Column would be at Ulundi for some little time, Captain Stewart, 3rd Dragoon Guards, who had joined us on special service, came to my tent one afternoon and told me that if he could get Sir Garnet Wolseley's sanction he proposed to start an expedition of his own, consisting of officers only, to hunt for Cetewayo, and asked if I would come as Interpreter. Needless to say, I said that I should be only too delighted, if Colonel Clarke would allow it, and I also begged that my co-Adjutant, Towers-Clarke,[30] might be one of the party; to which he agreed. Happily, both Sir Garnet Wolseley and Colonel Mansfield Clarke quite fell in with Stewart's venture, and the following officers formed the expedition:

---

29 Cetshwayo, on learning that patrols were out hunting him, took fright and fled north from ekuShumayeleni where he had been hiding out and made for the fastness of the Ngome forest. On 13 August Major Barrow led out a patrol from kwaSishwili – consisting of a troop (approximately 70 men) of the 1st King's Dragoon Guards and 60 men of the 2nd Squadron Mounted Infantry – north across the Black Mfolozi River, only just a couple of steps behind the fugitive Cetshwayo. Barrow failed to catch him, however, and returned on 17 August to kwaSishwili, leaving a detachment under Captain Lord Gifford* to maintain the pursuit north of the Black Mfolozi. A further detachment of the 1st King's Dragoon Guards patrolled in the opposite direction towards the Nkandla forest south-west of KwaMagwaza, where for a short while it was mistakenly believed Cetshwayo was intending to take refuge; while Captain Arthur Godolphin Yeatman-Biggs, RA, DAAG Line of Communications, in command of an expeditionary force of 50 mounted gunners and Royal Engineers and a company of the 5th Battalion, NNC, set out from Port Durnford on 17 August to patrol the St Lucia Bay district to the east lest Cetshwayo head in that direction. Traversing much the same terrain as Captain Stewart's party (see pp. 144–56 below), they rode into the kwaSishwili camp on 31 August, just in time to see the captive Cetshwayo being brought in.

30 Lieutenant Towers-Clarke was Orderly Officer; Harford was Staff Officer.

Captain Stewart, the Chief; myself, Interpreter; Lieutenants *[Captains]* Hutton,[31] Smith[32] and (name forgotten) 3/60th; Lieutenant Shepherd *[Captain Sherrard]*, 80th;[33] and Towers-Clarke, 57th Regiment.[34] We took no food of any sort with us, intending to live on what we could get or find at the Kaffir kraals *[imizi]*, but Stewart carried a flask of brandy in case of accidents. Our transport consisted of a mule and my Helpmekaar pony to carry cooking utensils, blankets, etc. The mule had to be led, and all except Stewart and I took their turn at this, and a nice lot of trouble he gave us on many occasions. My pony either followed like a dog or was driven along with a whip. Our time was limited to three weeks, when the Column would be on the move again.[35] On the day of our departure, Major McCalmont, 7th Hussars, and I think it was Lieutenant Creagh, R.A., two of Sir Garnet's A.D.C.'s, turned up and said that they were coming with us. But the first night out, with only boiled pumpkin for dinner and nothing but boiled mealies to look forward to the next

31 Captain Edward Thomas Henry Hutton, 3/60th Regiment, served with the Eshowe Relief Column and fought at Gingindlovu. He was Major-General Crealock's ADC during the 1st Division's advance to Port Durnford and then served with his regiment in Clarke's Column.

32 Captain Charles Holles Smith, 3/60th Regiment, joined the 1st Division in May 1879, took part in the advance to Port Durnford and subsequently served with Clarke's Column.

33 Harford doubtless meant Captain James Ormsby Sherrard (not Shepherd), 80th Regiment. In 1878 he saw service with his regiment in the First Anglo-Pedi War, then in 1879 served with it in its operations, first with No. 5 Column, then with No. 4 Column and Wood's Flying Column, and finally with Clarke's Column.

34 It seems Captain Stewart's expedition was larger than Harford suggests. Wolseley noted in his journal that he was sending out Stewart 'and a party of about 12 to 20 volunteers, mostly officers … on a roving commission in search of this biped game' (i.e. Cetshwayo). (Preston (ed.), *Wolseley's Journal*, p. 89: 16 August 1879.)

35 Captain Stewart's expedition started out on 17 August and rejoined Clarke's Column on its way between kwaSishwili and the Black Mfolozi on about 24 August, having been away for a week.

day, so damped their ardour that when we continued our journey at daybreak they decided to return to camp—and were considerably well chaffed on their sudden change of mind.[36]

First of all we headed towards St. Lucia Bay,[37] travelling over some beautiful country and coming across lots of game, buck, zebra, buffalo, etc. We had a rifle and a few rounds of ammunition with us, our only armament, but reserved it for use only if we got hard up for food, otherwise had we been on a shooting expedition we could have had some splendid sport. Being still at war, nearly all the kraals we visited in the hope of learning something of Cetewayo's whereabouts were denuded of men, none but the very old and the women and children remained, and from these neither information or supplies of any sort could be obtained. When we asked for milk, etc., the invariable reply was, "How are we to get milk when our men are all away fighting?" However, we always got as much food in the shape of mealies and Kaffir corn[38] as we required, by opening the pits in the centre of the cattle kraals (where they always store their crops)[39] and by picking up an odd pumpkin now and again in the fields, all of which we paid for to avoid trouble of any sort.

---

36 Brevet Major Hugh McCalmont, 7th Hussars, had served with Wolseley on the Red River Expedition in 1870 and as his ADC in the Third Anglo-Asante War, 1873–4. On Special Service during the last phase of the war in 1879, he served as one of Wolseley's four ADCs on his personal staff. Lieutenant Arthur Gethin Creagh, RA, was likewise on Special Service in 1879 as one of Wolseley's four ADCs. McCalmont led out his own patrol between 21 and 26 August in pursuit of Cetshwayo; while Creagh joined Captain Lord Gifford's party in the chase. He was promoted Brevet Lieutenant-Colonel.

37 Captain Stewart's small party of officers initially moved in a south-easterly direction towards the coast with the purpose of intercepting Cetshwayo should he attempt to escape towards the Nkandla forest. Failing to find him, Stewart's party swung north-west across the Mfolozi.

38 Sorghum.

39 The amaZulu stored their grain and seed for the following season in deep pits with carefully disguised funnel-shaped mouths in the *isibaya* (the enclosure for livestock) in the middle of every circular *umuzi*.

Only at one kraal not far from the Coast, after we had been out for about a week, did we find not only signs of abundance but also a considerable amount of activity. It was a very large kraal, and a great number of Kaffir women were continually leaving it all the time we were there, laden with baskets of food, most of which, we noticed, was cooked. This raised our hopes considerably, as we felt certain that the supplies must be for the King's party, and a careful watch was kept on the direction the women went. There were several men at the kraal, too, but they showed no signs of hostility in any way and gave us all we wanted except information about the whereabouts of the King, concerning which they pleaded absolute ignorance. It was at this kraal that I obtained the wooden milk pail now at Curtiss's.[40]

Sleeping the night there, we decided to follow the route the women had been taking, and made our way across country towards the junction of the White and Black Umfolozi Rivers. Nothing more was seen of any parties of women, and we very soon lost trace of their tracks in the broken country we passed over. It was a three or four days' journey to the river, and from the numerous kraals

40 Harford's splendid carved wooden milk pail (*ithunga* in isiZulu) is over two feet tall. He deposited it, along with his boot recovered at oNdini, with his storage agents, Curtiss & Sons of Portsmouth.

In Zulu culture, the carving of wood was an exclusively male occupation and objects such as milk pails, meat dishes and staffs were strongly associated with men, cattle and the ancestors. When a milker (who was always a man) approached the cattle to be milked, he had to hold the milk pail above his head to emphasise he was honouring the cattle and the ancestors. Because *amathunga* had to be carried in this way, they were carved from soft, unseasoned light woods and not from heavier hardwoods used for the likes of spoons and meat dishes. Certain designs of Zulu wood carving were restricted to items for use in the *imizi* of people of high status. One such is the motif on Harford's *ithunga* of rows of small blocks, known as *amasumpa*, or warts, confirming his milk pail as a prestige item of museum quality, especially since its provenance is known.

we visited en route not a word could we learn about the King's whereabouts in any shape or form.

The morning we reached the Umfolozi, where we had to find a crossing for ourselves, the recognised drifts being some miles away, we had rather an amusing but at the same time a rather uncomfortable experience. After choosing a spot, we first of all had to clear a space through the thick mass of reeds that bordered the river's edge and make a sort of roadway into the water for the ponies, and having nothing but our pocket knives to cut them down it was a long business. Then the next thing was to get our animals over it, but none of them would face it, my pony taking to his heels for all he was worth with half of our belongings on his back. He went a long way up the stream, and it took ages to catch him again. Eventually, however, after much persuasion and a tremendous lot of bother, all were got across except the mule who carried the other half of our traps. He absolutely refused to budge an inch. Coaxing, whacking, shoving, hauling were all tried with no effect, when someone hit on the brilliant idea of cutting a lot of monkey-rope,[41] of which there was any quantity, climbing up the high trees, and twisting it into a miniature cable long enough to pass round him and reach well into the river, so that some of us could get in and pull while others shoved from behind. At last we got him into the water, when he went along without much trouble till about halfway across. Then, without any warning, he suddenly took it into his head to lie down, with the result that our blankets, pots and pans, etc. all went under water.

The only thing we could do now was to unload our traps mid-stream, carry them piecemeal to the opposite bank and put them to dry as quickly as possible in the sun, and as the animal still remained immovable we fastened one end of the coil of monkey-rope round his neck and, passing the other end round the trunk of

41 Thick-stemmed forest creepers.

a tree on the bank, pulled him up on his legs and literally dragged him out. It was impossible to help laughing after the whole thing was over, but we had had a most uncomfortable experience. Luckily, our blankets soon dried, so we were all right for the night. A more beautiful spot than the point at which we crossed could not be well imagined, a long stretch of still water bordered with thick masses of feathery reeds and overhung by magnificent trees whose branches almost touched the water. Add to this the delicious scent of some of the flowering shrubs, and the bird life, with the warm atmosphere and wild peacefulness of the surroundings, and you could not wish for anything better or more heavenly.

The next day, one of the first kraals we visited belonged to a hunchback Induna, probably, if not for certain, the only born-so deformity in Zululand who was looked upon with great reverence by the Zulus. He owed his life to the fact that his birth as a deformity had been predicted by the Witchdoctors *[izangoma]*, who had also foretold that he was to become a powerful chief. Consequently, he was not, as is the invariable custom, put out of the way at birth.[42]

We were now not far from the kraal of Somkele *[Somkhele]*,* and had a most unforgettably adventurous day. The country now was almost treeless, and we rode over nothing but a sea of rolling, grassy hills. As we were about to visit a chief almost as powerful as Cetewayo himself, and one who Cetewayo really feared, Stewart, who had brought a white mackintosh with him, put it on despite the heat, to distinguish his dress from ours. He and I usually rode together a little distance ahead of the others, and when we were within a mile or so of Somkele's abode a large party of Zulus appeared coming towards us over a distant rise, fully armed with assegais and shields, which didn't look at all pleasant. When they

42 In earliest times, Zulu children born with abnormalities were never allowed to live; while when twins were born one of them was killed by having a lump of earth placed in its throat. However, it is not clear to what extent infanticide was still being practised in the historical period.

got to within a few hundred yards of us, just as they were topping some rising ground, they suddenly discarded their assegais, slipping them under the long grass. Stewart didn't quite notice this, but I did, knowing the trick well.

When we met, they carried nothing but their shields, and a couple of indunas came up to us and explained that they had been sent by Somkele to ask what we were doing in his territory. Stewart then informed them that he was on a mission from the Great Queen and required an interview with Somkele, and that our mission was a peaceful one. Seeing that we were unarmed I think put them at their ease, and we asked them to conduct us to the kraal. But before going on, we asked the Indunas why their men had left their assegais behind in the grass, and told them that we had seen them throwing them away, to which they replied that we must have been mistaken, so we said, "All right, we will take you to the spot", and on getting to the place, there were the assegais, all beautifully hidden. "Now", we said, "How do you account for this?" "Oh", they replied, "We know nothing about it. These must be assegais belonging to the herd boys." "Well", we said, "You must have them all picked up at once, before we go any further." And a goodly lot were collected.

This having been satisfactorily accomplished, we sent the party back to the kraal with a message to Somkele to say that a representative of the Great Queen had come to see him and wished to have a talk with him. In an instant the whole party bounded off like a herd of springbuck, in a great state of delight, apparantly, [sic] at carrying the news. Deeming it wise to take precautions in case of accidents, Stewart arranged that he and I, on arrival at the kraal, should carry on the preliminaries and while so doing the others of our party should take up positions round the outside and watch for any hostile movements.

The kraal had an enormous circumference, and contained a great number of huts in double rows, the centre space being quite 200 yards wide, if not more. The whole being enclosed with a thick, thorny

Zeriba *[zariba]*.[43] As we rode up to the entrance gate, which was only a wooden hurdle to keep the cattle out, hundreds of heads peeped over the zeriba to watch our arrival. We were met almost at once by one of Somkele's Indunas and told that he was too ill to receive us. This, of course, was nonsense, and we sent in a message to say that we were sorry to hear that he was ill, but that as the representative of the Great Queen could not possibly leave without having had an interview with him, we hoped that he would make it convenient to see us. For quite a couple of hours messages were bandied backward and forward to the effect that he couldn't see us and that we insisted on seeing him, when presently the gate was removed and we were informed that Somkele was prepared to receive us.[44]

I shall not forget the scene in a hurry. A roadway led straight through to the top end of the kraal, on either side of which squatted at least 1000 warriors in full fighting costume. Through these Stewart (with his mackintosh on) and I rode, and as we did so an audible murmur—whether of approval or not, I cannot say—ran through their ranks. Beyond them, at the end of the road, sat Somkele, with an old worsted shawl of many colours thrown over his shoulders and surrounded by his Ministers and Indunas. Having saluted him, he simply waved his hand at us and said, "Get down." However, on looking round I saw that no mats had been placed for us, and mentioned the fact to Stewart, so we said, "When you have provided a place for us, we will get off our horses", and pointed out that the bare ground was not quite the place for a representative of the Great Queen to be asked to take a seat.

Royal mats were at once brought out, and we got off our ponies, which were immediately taken away. We were now absolutely in Somkele's hands, to treat us as he wished. It must be remembered

43 A zariba is a hedged or palisaded enclosure or stockade.

44 To this day, it is customary for amaZulu of high status to demonstrate their power by keeping supplicants, visitors or assemblies waiting, sometimes interminably.

that we were still at war with the Zulu nation,[45] so that it was impossible to say what situation might arise. Just as we were on the point of settling down, up tramped one of Somkele's chiefs from a neighbouring kraal (accompanied by several Indunas, who had, no doubt, been hastily summoned for the occasion), and took his place by Somkele's side. A more magnificent specimen of humanity it would be impossible to conceive. Much over six feet in height, powerfully and perfectly built, and as straight as a dart. Somkele, too, was a fine specimen, but had become fat and unwieldy-looking.

With the arrival of the lastcomer the company was evidently complete, as utshwala[46] was handed round and a nice bowlful handed to us after Somkele had had a good pull out of it himself, as is the etiquette, to show that it had not been tampered with.[47] As soon as an opportunity presented itself, Stewart explained to Somkele that it would be better if we could discuss our affairs with him alone and not in the presence of Chiefs and Indunas, which rather alarmed him, I think, at first, but in the end he was good enough to send away everyone except one or two of his special Ministers, which was more than we really expected. It was rather a delicate matter starting the subject of the whereabouts of his uncle,[48] but with Stewart's diplomacy, although the interview was a long one, the discussion was carried on throughout in the most amicable manner. Somkele was a past master in the art of evading compromising questions, and we utterly failed in getting any information out of him.

45 The final submission of the Zulu leaders to Wolseley was not made until 1 September, when they accepted the terms of his settlement. However, Somkhele, along with the other coastal *amakhosi*, had already submitted to Major-General Crealock on 5 July.

46 Sorghum beer.

47 In other words, poisoned.

48 In fact, Somkhele was King Cetshwayo's first cousin.

On the conclusion of the interview Stewart, who always had very grand ideas, said to me, "Harford, we will hold a levée",[49] and the officers who were outside were sent for and formally introduced, the difference in their uniform being explained as Somkele wanted to know why we were not all dressed alike. As each officer was presented, old Somkele felt the cloth of their uniform and in one case said, "Give me that coat", but of course was told that that was impossible as none of us had any other change of clothing. The levée over, Stewart produced his silver flask with the brandy, and offered Somkele a drink. The old chap quickly grabbed at it and took a good pull, exclaiming, "Canteen![50] Oh! Umnandi impela".[51] Then, handing it to each of his ministers in turn without losing hold of it, and only just enabling them to get a taste, polished off the remainder himself, smacking his lips and informing Stewart that he intended to keep the flask, carefully stowing it away behind him. This was awkward, but after a great deal of explanation that it was a gift and could not be parted with, was eventually given up.

During this time one of Somkele's warriors came up and asked if any of us had been at Isandhlwana, and on telling him that I was out with the Contingent at Isipezi at the time of the fight, he caught hold of both my hands and shook them firmly in a great state of delight, saying it was a splendid fight. "You fought well, and we fought well", he exclaimed, and then showed me eleven wounds that he had received, bounding off in the greatest ecstasy to show how it all happened. Rushing up towards me, he jumped, fell on his stomach, got up again, rolled over and over, crawled flat, bounded on again, and so forth, until he came right up to me. His movements

49 A levée is a formal assembly held by the sovereign, or by his or her representative, at which men only are received and introduced.

50 A canteen is a soldier's flask for carrying water or liquor, or the place in a military camp where it is sold. By association, the amaZulu called alcohol such as brandy 'canteen', or *enkantini*.

51 'Truly delicious.'

being applauded by the warriors squatting in the centre of the kraal with a loud "Gee!"

I now had a look at his wounds. One bullet had gone through his hand, three had gone through his shoulder and had smashed his shoulder-blade, two had cut the skin and slightly into the flesh right down the chest and stomach, and one had gone clean through the fleshy part of the thigh. The others were mere scratches in comparison with these, but there he was, after about eight months, as well as ever and ready for another set-to.[52] Could anything more clearly show the splendid spirit in which the Zulus fought us? No animosity, no revengeful feeling, but just sheer love of a good fight in which the courage of both sides could be tested, and it was evident that the courage of our soldiers was as much appreciated as that of their own.

To compensate Somkele for not letting him keep the brandy flask, Stewart presented him with a round, metal-backed 3d lookingglass[53] and a razor strop, which by the merest chance he happened to have in his pockets. The glass delighted the old chap beyond everything, and at once he held it up close to his face to have a look at himself, and exclaimed, "Ow! I never knew that I was so ugly!" Except for a large mole on his chin, out of which grew a single curly hair, his face was quite smooth, and of this hair he was particularly proud and sat there gently pulling it, with the glass held close up to it for a long time.

It was now getting late and we thought we had better be moving on, and before doing so Stewart asked for a couple of guides to accompany us for a few days, which request, after some little

52 This warrior was very lucky to have recovered from such serious wounds, especially his shattered shoulder-blade. For while Zulu *izinyanga*, or traditional healers, could successfully treat uncomplicated flesh wounds, splintered bones and the massive tissue damage and internal injuries inflicted by rifle bullets were beyond their skills.

53 Thruppenny, of little value.

hesitation, was acceded to. Just as we were about to start a small procession of mostly izintombe (girls)[54] and one or two youths made their appearance bringing a beautiful cow, two sheep, a couple of goats, and several baskets of mealies and pumpkins as a present for Stewart's acceptance, and at the same time Somkele placed his old kraal, which was some three or four miles away, at our disposal for the night as no-one was living there. Everything was gratefully accepted, and we departed, leaving the guides to join us in the morning.

By the time we reached the kraal a thick, misty drizzle had developed, but we found no difficulty in shaking ourselves down most comfortably in a splendidly roomy and beautifully-built hut, as well as finding excellent shelter for the animals. The remarkably friendly and hospitable manner in which Somkele had received and treated us made us a little suspicious, however, of his real intentions, so we took all the precautions we could in case of accidents, by keeping our ponies saddled and by two of us doing sentry over the hut while Stewart slept and the rest of us patrolled the vicinity throughout the night. But kindly Providence had been with us, and we had belied the good will of our host.

Travelling on now, we continued our search for any sort of information we could get as to Cetewayo's whereabouts, visiting all the kraals where it was at all likely we might get in touch with him. One day we really thought he was in our hands. The kraal was evidently a rich one, and the few men and numerous women about resented every attempt on our part to examine any of the huts, and made an awful fuss. At the hut that I went to look into, a very dear old Kaffir lady, a particularly handsome woman with beautifully fine features, quite unlike a Kaffir and with snow-white hair, sat in the doorway and absolutely refused to move or let me look in till, by dint of a great deal of persuasion, and the assurance that I had

54 An *intombi*; *izintombi* (plural): a full-grown unmarried girl.

no desire to leave the kraal till we had made certain that they were not harbouring the King, she got up and allowed me to have a look. No trace, however, of the King could be found, but in several of the huts a good many guns and other weapons were stowed away, and these we ordered to be collected and taken at once to Headquarters at Ulundi.

Another day, on reaching a kraal where we intended to sleep the night, Stewart and I were lying on the ground just at the edge of the zereba *[zariba]* outside, cooking our meal, when only a few feet from us, stretched almost at full length in the dried scrub, was a snake that I had often heard of and much wanted to see, and that very few white men have ever come across. It was the Idhlozi *[idlozi]* of the Kaffirs, a beautiful creature, vivid green with jet black marking, between two and three feet long, and thick like a puffadder. I would have given anything to have been able to bottle it, and the opportunity was such as could scarcely ever occur again, no Kaffirs, either men or women, being about. Being held sacred, and looked upon as the incarnation of some ancestor of the kraal, to kill one, if it became known, would certainly mean an assegai put through you, so having no collecting material we left our friend alone.[55] By a curious coincidence, one morning a day or two after leaving Somkele's, three if not four of the expeditionary parties that

---

55 An *idlozi*; *amadlozi* (plural): the shade of a departed ancestor. But Harford was not entirely wrong in calling the non-venomous spotted bush snake (*Philothamnus semivariegatus*) he encountered an *idlozi*. For the Zulu name for the snake is an *inyandezulu*; *izinyandezulu* (plural) which means 'slaughtering cattle for the departed ancestor'. In Zulu religious belief, the living and the dead were bound together as a single community in which the *amadlozi* were the senior members. The *amadlozi* watched over the living, who in turn consulted them in everything they did, propitiating them with offerings of sacrificial meat, water and snuff when they sensed their disfavour (for example, when people fell ill), and contacting them through blood sacrifice. When an *idlozi*, who was supposed normally to live below the ground, wished to revisit the world of the living it did so manifested in the form of an *inyandezulu* such as Harford saw, and wisely left unharmed.

were out passed within sight of each other, only a few miles apart. But only Major Maurice, R.A., accompanied by an orderly, came up to us, and this worthy, having pumped us with regard to our movements, put spurs to his horse and rode off, declining to give us any further information than that he had got very reliable news as to Cetewayo's whereabouts. The execrations that followed him as he went off can be imagined. Stewart, who knew his character, could only say, "That's Maurice all over!"[56]

We were then in what is known as "Lion Country", and heard afterwards that one of the parties had lost three horses that night, which had been killed and dragged several hundred yards from their bivouac to be eaten.

It was very evident that the various expeditions had been following much the same scent, and no doubt their movements concerning which Cetewayo was kept well informed, led him to take refuge in the Ngome forest[57] where eventually "Clarke's Column" succeeded in capturing him.[58] Our three weeks nearing to the end,[59] we began working our way back to Ulundi, visiting kraals en route to search for arms and giving orders wherever we found any for them to be taken to Headquarters as we had no means of breaking them up.

---

56 Brevet Major John Frederick Maurice (1841–1912), RA, had served as Wolseley's private secretary in the Third Anglo-Asante War, 1873–4. In 1879 he accompanied Wolseley to South Africa on Specia Service as his DAA and QMG for intelligence duties on his General Staff. Between 17 and 24 August he was with Captain Lord Gifford's patrol in search of Cetshwayo, and on 26 August Wolseley sent him off northwards towards the Phongolo River in command of his own patrol. Wolseley well understood (as did Stewart) that while Maurice was loyal, energetic and intellectually brilliant, he was also eccentric, volatile and argumentative, and concluded that 'no man could be more unsuited for the duties of a staff officer or for leading men.' (Preston (ed.), *Wolseley's Journal*, p. 96: 24 August 1879.)

57 The dense Ngome forest in north-central Zululand grows on broken hilly terrain, making it an ideal place to take refuge.

58 On 28 August 1879.

59 In fact, Harford was out on patrol for a week (see p. 144 n. 35 above).

On the day we were due to rejoin the Column,[60] Towers-Clarke and I picked up our two servants and a mule cart left for us at a point some little distance from Ulundi, as the Column had gone on. Here Stewart and the other officers parted from us; we had had a most delightful and adventurous journey of some 300 miles[61] over most wonderfully picturesque country, depending on Providence for food, while still at war with its inhabitants, always, except on one occasion, sleeping in the open veld and never once seeing any sign of hostility.

Being late in the afternoon, and no chance of reaching the Column that night as there was no road and we had nothing to guide us as to the route the Column had taken, (except when the grass had been trodden down by the troops and here and there wagon tracks on the hard soil), we decided to drive on till it was dark and get on again at dawn. We had the advantage of half moon for a short while, and as that set we hauled up under a lovely flat-crown tree for the night. Here, while our servants were taking the traps out of the cart, the mules being unharnessed, and Towers-Clarke and I arranging our bivouac, I saw a large animal which I took to be a wolf[62] coming steadily down from a knoll close to

60 On 23 August, as part of the operations to capture Cetshwayo, a portion of Clarke's Column, consisting of the 3/60th Rifles (400 infantry), two companies of the 4th Battalion, NNC (300 men) and 300 mounted men, carrying ten days' provisions, set out northwards under Clarke's command from kwaSishwili for the wagon drift across the Black Mfolozi. Fifty 1st King's Dragoon Guards under Major Marter* joined the column. Clarke's orders were to bring pressure on the region in which Cetshwayo was moving and to burn *imizi* and carry off cattle if necessary. He was also to visit and lean upon three northern *izikhulu* whom Wolseley intended making independent chiefs in his settlement of Zululand, if they were sufficiently compliant: Somkhele (already visited by Stewart's patrol); Zibhebhu kaMaphitha,* the Mandlakazi *inkosi*; and Mgojana kaSomaphunga, the Ndwandwe *inkosi* and husband of Cetshwayo's sister.

61 Probably closer to 250 miles.

62 Harford means a hyena. The hyena the first Dutch-speaking settlers at the Cape encountered was the brown hyena (*Parahyaena brunnea*) with its long

us, and pointed it out to Towers. Then, as it was too dark to see clearly, and being curious to know what sort of animal it was, I stole very quietly towards it and stood perfectly still to watch. Presently, as it got nearer, I saw it was a lioness, and called to Towers to let me have one of our servants' rifles as quickly as he could. In the meantime she had walked up to within a yard of me, and I could have almost caught hold of her. There she stood with her great eyes looking from side to side, not taking the slightest notice of me.

The servants, having very foolishly laid their rifles at the bottom of the cart, were unable to get them out till everything had been unloaded, and long before that had been done, Her Majesty had quietly walked off. However, I carefully watched the direction she had gone in, and presuming that she had not gone far, as undoubtedly it was the mules that she was after, as soon as I got hold of a rifle I went off and lay down where I thought I might get a shot as she circled round. I did fire at something that I thought looked like an animal moving in the grass in front of me against the skyline, but when we went to look round before we started in the morning, saw nothing even like a track in the grass. It would have been a splendid thing if we could have arrived in camp with a lioness in our cart, and most certainly we should have done so if the men's rifles had been handy.

Our Column was now following no specified route, consequently an enormous amount of road-clearing had to be done, especially over streams and vleis[63] as with ox-wagons a good semicircular sweep is required for the long spans of oxen to work round and get the strain to enable them to pull the wagon straight across. The

shaggy coat and pointed ears, which they dubbed the *strandwolf* (beach wolf). Thereafter, colonists usually referred to a hyena as a 'wolf', even though the spotted (laughing) hyena (*Crocuta crocuta*) Harford would most likely have encountered in Zululand looked very different from the brown hyena, having rounded ears and short coat.

63 *Vlei*, a marsh in Afrikaans.

Intelligence officer, who always kept a day ahead of the Column, selected the route and sent his sketch-map in every evening with all bad places specially marked, and it was my duty to go off each morning at daybreak with a company of one of the regiments, suitably equipped with axes, shovels, etc., to get these bad places put straight before the Column came up. I enjoyed the work immensely, and if only it had been possible to combine sport with duty could have bagged numbers of guineafowl and partridge. At one vlei in particular, I remember, the party had been working for several hours and just as they had finished out flew quite forty or fifty guineafowl from a thickly covered tree, close above our heads.

As a rule our company grounds were reached about eleven o'clock, and occasionally one was able to get out with the gun. One afternoon Major Duncan, R.A. and I took a turn out to look for buck, and on beating down a ravine where he was one side and I on the other, I saw his spaniel working very excitedly in a thick bit of scrub a little way behind him, and called out to him to look out as I thought that there was something there. In a few minutes the dog jumped out, uttering a little whine as if he had pricked himself in the thorns, and we went on. Then, as we got further down the dog lagged behind considerably, and I said to Duncan, "Your dog is a long way behind. I think he's got a prickle in his foot, as I heard him whine as he got out of that bush. We'd better go back and see." So we went back, and found his head all swollen and a trickle of blood running from the tip of his nose. Seeing at once that he had been bitten by a snake, Duncan took him in his arms and I carried the guns and we made for the camp as hard as we could go.

By the time we got in, the animal's head was quite the size of a football, his eyes were closed up and his tongue an enormous size. Duncan at once got his medicine-chest and produced a bottle of salvolatile, rubbing some on his nose, and with the greatest difficulty getting some down his throat. We continued this treatment every now and then till the last thing at night, adding an occasional drop of milk. For three or four days the dog remained in a state of stupor, but eventually pulled through all right—most probably it was a Mamba that had bitten him. Had it been a Puffadder it is improbable that he would have recovered.[64]

The Column worked its way along in accordance with the reports received from various quarters by the Intelligence department, until one morning a Kaffir arrived at our bivouac and informed the Brigadier that he knew the place in the Ngome bush where Cetewayo was hiding, and could show him the way to the kraal. Young Oftebro,* our interpreter, who was the son of a missionary and who had lived among the Zulus all his life, knew the country well and was also a personal friend of Cetewayo's, so without any delay Colonel Mansfield Clarke sent him off to accompany a squadron of the King's Dragoon Guards under Major Marter* and a company of N.N.C. under Captain Barton, Royal Fusiliers, to effect the King's capture. When the party had started,[65] I shall never forget the kind way in which Colonel Clarke said to me, "You know, Harford, I would have sent you, but Oftebro knows every inch of the

64 Harford's scientific knowledge of butterflies and beetles evidently did not extend to snakes. From the description, it is evident that the spaniel was bitten by a puff adder (*Bitis arietans*). Puff adders have cytoxic venom that causes immense swelling, pain and necrosis that would send a dog into a state of shock. In most cases a dog would not survive a puff adder bite, and Major Duncan's was extremely fortunate to have done so. It certainly would not have lived if it had been bitten by a black mamba (*Dendroaspis polylepis*) – the habitat of green mambas is confined to the coastal bush – whose venom is extremely toxic. Besides, the snake in question could not have been a mamba since its venom, unlike a puff adder's, does not cause local swelling. Salvolatile (smelling salts), a solution of ammonium carbonate in alcohol, is a stimulant administered to restore consciousness after a faint, and would have had no effect in combatting the snake toxin in the dog's body.

65 Major Marter's force set out in the morning of 27 August. Besides the squadron of the King's Dragoon Guards and the company of the 4th Battalion, NNC, an officer and ten men of the 2nd Squadron Mounted Infantry and Lonsdale's Horse joined the party.

country as well as the King himself, and his thorough knowledge of the language is most important", (or words to that effect).

The fact of Major Marter's party capturing Cetewayo was a great blow to Lord Gifford's* expedition,[66] which had run him to earth and were on the point of bagging him, but not knowing the lie of the country had got to a place where they couldn't move without being seen by day and were holding on till it got dark. Marter's party, being led by experts, took a route completely concealing their movements, almost under Gifford's nose, and rapidly surrounding the kraal captured him.[67] In telling me the story afterwards, Oftebro said that as soon as the kraal had been surrounded and our troops were closing in on it, one or two shots were fired, but Cetewayo saw that the game was up. He himself then went up to the hut that the King was in, and spoke to him from outside, and directly Cetewayo heard his voice he said, "Is that you?" … (calling him by his Zulu name), and after a few minutes' conversation, quietly gave himself up.

66 Lord Gifford had been a member of Major Barrow's party of mounted men who had ridden out on 13 August from Wolseley's camp in pursuit of Cetshwayo, and when Barrow returned to camp on 17 August, he and a detachment continued the search north of the Black Mfolozi. On the night of 26 August, he set out in the same direction as Marter.

67 By 3 p.m. on 28 August Marter's men had surrounded the secluded kwaDwasa *umuzi* belonging to Mkhosana kaSangqana, a Buthelezi *induna*, deep in a valley in the Ngome forest. They took the occupants of kwaDwasa completely by surprise and they put up no resistance. Cetshwayo himself surrendered with considerable dignity. Besides the king, Marter made prisoners of Mkhosana, eight men, a lad, five women and a girl (*umndlunkulu*, or women of the king's *isigodlo*, his private enclosure in his *ikhanda*). At 4 p.m. Marter, with the prisoners on foot and under military escort, began the march to Clarke's camp at the Black Mfolozi. The party camped out that night, and the following day the march was resumed towards the kwaNdasa *ikhanda*. Shortly before reaching it, three of Cetshwayo's male attendants and one women bolted. Two of the men were shot but the others made good their escape. Marter was infuriated and roughly threatened Cetshwayo with death if he made a similar attempt.

At dawn, almost at the first streak of light the following morning, a Kaffir messenger from Major Marter appeared with a note fastened in the slit of a small stick. The Brigadier, Towers-Clarke and I were sleeping under our wagon. The Brigadier lay between us, I being on the outside. On handing me the stick, the bearer whispered, very quietly, "He is caught!", and I woke the Brigadier, handing him the stick without a word. "Marter's got him", he said, as he jumped up, and went off to tell the news to Captain Hart, and in a very few minutes it was known throughout the camp. A cart had also been asked for, for the conveyance of the King and his wives, which was immediately sent off under the guidance of the messenger.[68] On the way in, I believe, some of the followers gave a lot of trouble and had to be fastened to the troopers' horses, but eventually all arrived safely. On arrival in camp, the sight of so many soldiers alarmed them considerably, and Cetewayo looked the picture of fright as they drove up.[69] After alighting from the cart, the King (with his wives hanging on to him as if they thought he was doomed to immediate execution, and absolutely terrified), strode in with the aid of his long stick, with a proud and dignified air and

68 Because the king and his *umndlunkulu* were finding it hard going on foot, Marter requested Clarke to send a mule wagon to convey them, and it arrived at kwaNdasa on the morning of 30 August escorted by two companies of the 3/60th Rifles. The cavalcade arrived at Clarke's camp later that same day.

69 Martin Oftebro, in an interview recorded in 1927 by Carl Faye on an Ediphone with a wax cylinder, remembered that when Cetshwayo's cart reached the eMikwaneni drift over the Black Mfolozi, the king got out and waded across the river on foot. The men of the 4th Battalion, NNC were lined up on the opposite bank and derisively chanted the war-song of the amaNdwandwe, the old foes of the amaZulu. Oftebro recalled that 'this was too much for Cetywayo. His humiliation was complete. At this point I received the impression that Cetywayo for the first time thoroughly realized what it meant to be a captive. He seemed to "fall to pieces". All the "Majesty" went out of him, leaving him extremely dejected.' (Laband and Knight (eds), *Archives of Zululand*, vol. 4, pp. 495–6.)

grace, looking a magnificent specimen of his race and every inch a warrior in his grand umutcha *[umutsha]* of leopard skin and tails, with lion's teeth and claw charms round his neck. Well over six feet, fat but not corpulent, with a stern, severe and cruel countenance, he looked what he was, a savage ruler.

A tent was provided for him and his wives, and a guard mounted over it of the 60th Rifles, and for the two days he remained in camp Colonel Clarke very kindly paid me the compliment of giving them over into my charge. After that, they were driven to Maritzburg in a mule wagon in charge of Lieutenant *[Captain]* Poole, R.A.,[70] with a mounted escort.[71] Cetewayo had brought with him when he came in two very nice grass baskets filled with utshwala, and on his departure I handed one to Colonel Clarke, and the other I brought home, (the last he drank out of), and gave to Dr Ray.

---

70 Captain Joseph Ruscombe Poole, RA, was on Special Service as Brigade Major with the South African Field Force. He escorted the captive King Cetshwayo from Wolseley's camp to Cape Town, where he was his sympathetic custodian at the Castle until late December 1880, when he was recalled to serve in the First Anglo-Boer War (the Transvaal Rebellion). He was killed at the battle of Laing's Nek, 28 January 1881.

71 Early on the morning of 31 August Cetshwayo and the other prisoners were taken from Clarke's camp to kwaSishwili, where they arrived at 10 a.m. Cetshwayo was humiliatingly treated not as a fallen king, but as a common criminal. Wolseley refused to see him. At 2 p.m. Cetshwayo and his party of three men and five women set off under escort in an ambulance wagon drawn by ten mules for a destination undisclosed to him. Harford was mistaken in stating that Cetshwayo was driven to Pietermaritzburg, but his error is understandable because those were Poole's original instructions and Wolseley had announced them to his officers. In the event, Wolseley sent a message after Poole once he had gone only a few miles ordering him to change direction and take Cetshwayo to Port Durnford instead of Pietermaritzburg. There, on 4 September, the fallen king was embarked with his party on the steam transport *Natal* and conveyed as a state prisoner to Cape Town, where he was imprisoned in the Flagstaff Bastion of the Castle.

Having captured the King and thus virtually ended the campaign, the Column had to see the completion of the surrendering of arms, demanded and ordered by the Government. One powerful and recalcitrant chief, Sibebu *[Zibhebhu]*,* gave us a lot of trouble, doing all he possibly could to evade the authorities. At last, after repeated demands, the Brigadier sent him a message to say that if his orders were not complied with by a certain day and hour, troops would be sent to enforce them. On the day and hour named, as no Sibebu or arms were forthcoming, Major Marter's squadron of the King's Dragoon Guards, accompanied by the Brigadier himself with me as Staff Officer (and last, but not least Jim, who had begged to be allowed to come out), rode off towards Sibebu's kraal[72] to give him a fright. Having gone some three or four miles, a swarm of Kaffirs, some of them mounted, could be seen in the distance coming towards us, so we halted to await their arrival.[73]

Just as they topped a hill rising in front of us, a most ridiculous scene occurred. Sibebu and his mounted escort were riding a little distance ahead of the men bringing in the arms, and as they came over the rise Major Marter gave the command to his men to mount, and these quickly wheeled to the right, so as to face the Zulus. The movement, being so suddenly and quickly executed, so alarmed

---

72 Zibhebhu's ekuVukeni *umuzi*.

73 On 26 July 1879, Wolseley had issued orders that those Zulu chiefs who had not already submitted were to be invited to do so, and that if they did not comply by 10 August they would be treated as enemies and punished. Wolseley's instructions to Clarke on 23 August (see p. 157 n. 60 above) included that he put pressure on Zibhebhu, who had promised on 13 August to come into Wolseley's camp but had not yet done so. As described by Harford, Clarke accordingly sought Zibhebhu out, and on 28 August, duly chastened, Zibhebhu appeared at kwaSishwili with bundles of firearms and a herd of cattle in token of his submission. The problem with Harford's account is one of chronology. He places the visit to Zibhebhu at ekuVukeni *after* Cetshwayo's capture on 28 August, whereas the encounter definitely took place beforehand, shortly after Clarke's Column reached the Black Mfolozi, most likely on 24 August.

Sibebu and his mounted followers that the whole lot of them either fell or scrambled off their ponies, imagining, no doubt, that our men were going to charge. It was very funny, and impossible to keep from laughing. On seeing that our troops remained in position, Sibebu came up to Colonel Clarke and offered all sorts of excuses for not having delivered up the arms before, but the Brigadier gave him very clearly to understand what he thought of his conduct.

Now followed a little incident which I was quite unprepared for. Jim came quietly up, and asked if he might be allowed to speak to Sibebu. This rather astounded me, and Colonel Clarke having no objcction the two greeted each other most cordially, snuffed together and showed every sign of intimate acquaintance. Jim told me later on that he was his brother-in-law, having married one of his sisters. It was a curious coincidence their coming together again in this way.

Now that Sibebu had been successfully dealt with, the Column's mission was at an end,[74] and in accordance with orders from

74 It is curious that in his memoirs Harford does not mention the ceremony at kwaSishwili on 1 September, which he witnessed. At 4.30 that afternoon Wolseley spelled out to 200 assembled Zulu notables, ranged in four rows before his tent, the terms of his settlement of Zululand. The monarchy was to be abolished, alongside the *ibutho* system which had been its mainstay, and the former kingdom was to be divided up between 13 appointed chiefs under the nominal supervision of a British Resident.

Elsewhere in Harford's papers, however, he did record his impressions of the ceremony (see Payne et al., *Harford*, p. 166). He wrote: 'I was present at the meeting – at which the 2 field Guns, belonging to Captain *[Brevet Major Stuart]* Smith's battery [N Battery, 5th Brigade, RA], captured by the Zulus at Isandhlwana and taken off at once to Ulundi – and which were recovered by troops of No. 1 Column [the 2nd Division], at the battle of Ulundi, (found in a donga) – were specially brought to the spot where the meeting took place. And the Union Jack, erected on a staff, between them – and a table on which was a map delineating the boundary areas, allotted to the various chiefs was placed, which each chief, on his name being called, came up and signed. [All the appointed chiefs, except for John Dunn, were illiterate, and a cross was substituted for a signature.] The meeting took place on a

Headquarters we proceeded to Maritzburg *[Pinetown]* for dispersal—and a very pleasant march it was, passing over a lovely country, via Kwamagwaza *[KwaMagwasa]* English Mission Station[75] and Greytown.[76] From one of our camps we were only a few miles from Eshowe, so I took a hurried ride up to have a look at the place and find poor Davison's grave and get a sketch of it.

Just to show one of the barbarous customs practised by the Zulus, I give an incident, gruesome as it is, which occurred at our Kwamagwaza camp. As is the case in all campaigns, a certain number of animals have to be left behind when the troops march

---

hillside and I thought, at the time, that the chiefs showed great want of respect, in their demeanour and appearance, and to be in an uncommonly sullen mood.' One wonders how Harford thought the truculent chiefs ought to have behaved. With gratitude? After all, they were experiencing the bitterness of defeat and witnessing the fragmentation and signing away of the Zulu kingdom.

75 On 11 July 1879 the Flying Column, on its withdrawal after Ulundi, built a fort near the deserted Anglican mission station at KwaMagwasa, and called it Fort Roberston after the absent missionary, Rev. R. Roberston. It was subsequently renamed Fort Albert by Clarke's Column when it encamped nearby on 3 August on its march to join Wolseley at kwaSishwili.

76 Clarke's Column had returned to kwaSishwili on 31 August from its camp at the Black Mfolosi. At 7.30 a.m. on 2 September Wolseley reviewed Clarke's Column, which then commenced its march back to Natal by way of Middle Drift across the Thukela. The column of some 3,000 men with its train of 120 wagons, field bakery and hospital extended for over a mile on the march. On 3 September John Dunn, whom Wolseley had appointed one of the 13 chiefs, joined the column which was to march through his new chiefdom. Clarke's instructions, conveyed through Brigadier-General Colley on 1 September, were to ensure that Dunn received the submission of his new subjects and, at the same time, to overawe several recalcitrant Zulu chiefs along the middle Thukela and force them to comply with the terms of Wolseley's settlement. As the column advanced, Clarke sent out armed patrols to exact submissions, to round up and confiscate cattle the amaZulu had captured in raids across the Natal border, and to break up surrendered firearms. Clarke's Column arrived in Pinetown by way of KwaMagwasa, Greytown and Pietermaritzburg on 7 October, when it was officially broken up.

off, being too exhausted to go on. As a rule … they revive and soon pick up again, when sometimes they are driven in and more often than not are annexed by the people who find them. Three or four had to be discarded at Kwamagwaza. For some reason, (I forget now what), some short time after the Column had marched I had to return to the camping-ground, and as I rode in I saw clumps of Kaffirs sitting round the oxen that we had been unable to take on. I went up to see what they were about, thinking that they had despatched them and were going to have a feast, but to my horror found that they were calmly carving out a large shield from the back of each ox and skinning it off while the poor beasts were still alive, some extraordinary superstition being attached to this particular method of obtaining a shield! Having a good hunting-crop with me, I used it pretty freely on one or two that I rode down, but this was useless as directly I got out of sight again they would only be back again like vultures to carry on with their work. The only consolation one had was that within an hour or two they would all be slaughtered and by the following morning nothing but their bones left.

Nothing more being required of me after arrival at Maritzburg, I rejoined my Regiment at Pinetown,[77] where they and the 24th Regiment were encamped on the open ground just outside the boundaries of our old farm, Stapleton Grove. Jim and I parted at Maritzburg with many regrets on both sides, I to rejoin the 99th and he to return to his kraal.

A copy of Colonel Mansfield Clarke's farewell orders to his staff is in one of my boxes at Curtiss's,[78] and when personally wishing

77 With the breakup of Clarke's Column on 7 October, Harford's services as Clarke's Staff Officer were no longer required, and he was ordered to rejoin his regiment. Pinetown was the main military depot in Natal.

78 The printed *Column Orders* of 7 October 1879 stated: 'The exertions of his [Clarke's] Staff Officers – Captain Hart, 31st Regiment, and Lieutenant Harford, 99th Regiment … have on all occasions been such as to merit

him goodbye, he very kindly said that if ever he could be of any use to me, to be sure and let him know. I owe a very great deal to his kindness when he became Adjutant-General at the War Office, later on.[79]

We remained at Pinetown for a considerable time, awaiting orders, and eventually embarked on the 31st December, for Bermuda.[80]

While at Pinetown I was able to renew many old acquaintanceships and visit old shooting and collecting haunts. The features of the country round about were not much changed, except that many

---

the Brigadier's warmest approbation, and he will have much pleasure in bringing their good services to the notice of the General commanding.' The day before, On 6 October, Clarke wrote a personal note to Harford: 'Now that we are to part company, I write to thank you for all the good work you have done for me since you have been with the column. I have at all times found you unwearying in the performance of your various duties and it has given me great pleasure to recognise this formally in Column Orders and in a special report I have made to the Chief of Staff [Brigadier-General Colley].' (Payne et al., *Harford*, pp. 167, 168.)

79 Clarke (who was promoted General in 1902 and who succeeded as third Baronet Clarke of Dunham Lodge in 1899) was in fact never AG at the War Office as Harford mistakenly wrote, but QMG to the Forces from 1899 to 1903. Previously, he had been Commandant-General of the Colonial Forces at the Cape, 1880–2, and Commander-in-Chief of the Madras Command of the Indian Army, 1893–8. He would go on to be Governor of Malta, 1903–7. What the nature of Clarke's 'kindness' to Harford was is not known, but it may have been due to his influence while QMG that Harford, who had been gazetted Colonel of the Wiltshire Regiment on 7 January 1902 and who went on half pay the following day, was on 15 December 1902 appointed to the command of the 62nd Regimental District.

80 The 99th Regiment embarked on HMS *Himalaya*, an iron steam-screw troopship with sails on three masts. Displacing 4,690 tons, it could accommodate up to 2,000 troops. While stationed in Bermuda, Harford continued to serve as Adjutant until being gazetted Captain on 30 March 1881. Troops involved in one or more of the campaigns in South Africa between 25 September 1877 and 2 December 1879 were eligible for the South Africa Medal. The date bar fixed to the medal specified in which operations the recipient had been engaged, and Harford's showed 1879 for the Zulu campaign.

springs and streams had dried up and notably the Umbilo River, which was the boundary of the side of our farm, and the beautiful rivulet which ran into it from the other.[81] A very amusing incident took place a few days after I arrived in the camp, when our old friend known as "Drunken Davidson" came to pay me a visit.[82] It was just at our orderly-room hour, when prisoners, orderly N.C.O.'s and others were waiting for the Colonel to arrive, that a wild horseman came charging into the camp, shouting at the top of his voice, "I want to see Mr. Charles Harford!", repeating this many times over. He was told by the Sergeant-Major that I was in the orderly-room tent and very busy. However, recognising my old friend's voice, for many scores of times when a boy he had woken me up at all hours of the night shouting almost the same words, I went out to greet him. To the great amusement of the assembled officers, N.C.O.'s and men, he fell on my neck and kissed and hugged me and shouted out his joy at meeting the son of Captain Charles Harford once more, making all sorts of grimaces and roaring with laughter and joking as was his wont.

At this moment Major Walker,* who was doing the Colonel's work that morning, (and to whom I had often related stories of old Davidson's wild escapades), came up, and taking in the situation asked him to take a seat in the tent and wait till I had finished my work and orderly-room was over. So he stalked in and sat down at my table at the back of the tent, as quiet as a mouse, with one arm leaning on the table and looking very wise. Presently, seeing my glengarry cap on the table, he at once put it on, and as this could be seen by everyone outside, even the prisoners couldn't help laughing. It caused the C.O. to look round and see what the joke was about, and he also couldn't help smiling and chuckling to himself. The

81 Today, the UmBilo river system is shockingly polluted by the release of sewage and chemicals into its now discoloured and toxic waters, and the eThekwini municipality seems unprepared to take corrective action.

82 Untraced.

whole scene was most ridiculous, but to appreciate it one wants to have seen the man and watched his monkey-like sudden changes of countenance and facial expression. Directly I was free I took him to my tent, where we talked over old times and, after tossing off half a tumbler of neat whisky, he galloped off to give someone else a treat.

In 1881, after having been eighteen months in Bermuda, we were suddenly ordered to South Africa for service against the Boers, but on reaching Cape Town found that peace had been declared.[83] The Regiment was sent into camp at Wynberg,[84] which at that time was one of the most beautiful spots in Cape Colony, and except for the few farms and vineyards in the vicinity remained in a state of nature.

---

83 On 16 December 1880 the Boers of the Transvaal Territory, annexed by Britain in April 1877, rebelled and declared their independence. The British failed to repress the Transvaal Rebellion, also known as the First Anglo-Boer War, and after a string of military defeats at Boer hands, agreed to an armistice on 21 March 1881. The Pretoria Convention of 3 August 1881 formally ended the war. Meanwhile, the British government had been rushing military reinforcement to South Africa from India, Ceylon (Sri Lanka) and Bermuda. In June 1881 the 99th Regiment had just been ordered to leave Bermuda for Jamaica, Barbados and Trinidad and was about to embark when it received fresh orders to proceed to the Cape on the troopship HMS *Orontes*. The regiment was stationed in Wynberg, close to Cape Town, for ten months. Then, in April 1882 it embarked once more on HMS *Himalaya*, bound this time for Bombay (now Mumbai), and was stationed at Rawalpindi in the Punjab (now in Pakistan), where it was rejoined by the families left behind in Bermuda in June 1881.

Meanwhile, Harford's regiment had changed its name. On 1 July 1881 the Childers Reforms came into effect and the United Kingdom was divided into regimental districts, each allocated a two-battalion regiment usually bearing a 'county' title. Regimental numbers were abolished, and previously single-battalion regiments, such as the 99th, were paired to become the 1st or 2nd battalions of the new regiments. The 99th Regiment thus became the 2nd Battalion, The Duke of Edinburgh's (Wiltshire Regiment). It was paired with the 62nd (Wiltshire) Regiment of Foot, which became the 1st Battalion.

84 Wynberg, now a southern suburb of the city of Cape Town, was then a small garrison town, and the regiment's encampment was on a level, open stretch of lawn-like ground.

Here I was able to renew my acquaintance with Cetewayo, who with his wives was in exile living in a home provided for them by the Government a mile or two out on the Cape Flats—a more or less dreary residence but very comfortable.[85] Occasionally I went out to have a talk with him, which I think he appreciated, and when the Regiment got settled down and band days were instituted, finding that the authorities had no objection, he was given a standing invitation to our weekly "At Homes". This pleased him immensely, particularly as a bottle of champagne was always opened for his special benefit. He was generally the first guest to arrive, and coming early as he did, almost always had to sit with me in our orderly-room while I went on with my work.

---

85 Cetshwayo had continued to be held in state custody at the Castle in Cape Town through special legislation passed in July 1880 by the Cape Parliament, but in February 1881 he was transferred to civil custody. Cetshwayo and his *umndlunkulu* were accommodated on the farm Oude Molen on the bleak Cape Flats, a few miles east out of Cape Town. There he enjoyed greater freedom. He could run cattle and engage in outdoor recreations like coursing jackals and rabbits with the dogs he had been given, and hunting birds with his thrown knobkerrie. He took regular carriage rides and permission was soon granted him to visit the theatre and attend social functions such as the regimental 'At Homes' described by Harford.

Elsewhere in his writings (see Payne et al., *Harford*, p. 190) Harford complacently decided that Cetshwayo 'seemed to be quite content with his lot, being well looked after and allowed to go about'. The truth was otherwise. These diversions only helped distract Cetshwayo, who was falling into a mood of despondency as no end to his captivity seemed in sight, and as news of brewing civil war in Zululand reached his ears. He repeatedly petitioned the British government for his restoration as king to bring stability to Zululand and in August 1882 he was finally permitted to visit London to plead his case. As a result, he was returned to Zululand in January 1883, but only to the central portion of his former kingdom. Many Zulu notables who had benefited from Wolseley's settlement resisted his restoration and civil war broke out. By July 1883 Cetshwayo had been defeated and he died a refugee under British protection on 8 February 1884.

On one occasion, when I told him that the High Commissioner and his wife, Sir Hercules and Lady Robinson,[86] were coming, he was greatly excited, and kept on asking when I thought they would arrive, and getting up to look out of the tent when there was anything like the rumble of a trap. The fact was that he had taken a violent fancy to Lady Robinson, who was an uncommonly pretty lady,[87] and rumours were current that he had already made tender enquiries as to whether Sir Hercules would part with her for fifty cows!! Whether this ever reached Lady Robinson's ears I never heard, but no doubt somebody would have told her the joke.

Cetewayo always took the greatest interest in inspecting the Band instruments and hearing the different sounds that were got out of them, and, greatly to the amusement of the men, went round asking them to blow hard. His favourite instrument was a double bass, to which he invariably placed his ear while the boy who played it blew for all he was worth. Of course at these "At Homes" Cetewayo wore European clothes, which detracted greatly from his appearance as a Monarch; Cetewayo in his Royal savage dress of leopard tails and skins, and Cetewayo in a tailor-made suit of European clothing, were two distinctly different individuals, scarcely to be identified with one another.

86 Sir Hercules George Robert Robinson (1824–97), KCMG, was High Commissioner for Southern Africa and Governor of the Cape (1881–9), having previously been (in sequence) Governor of Hong Kong, New South Wales, and New Zealand. He married in 1846 the Hon. Nea Arthur Ade Rose D'Amour Annesley (1823–1904), daughter of the tenth Viscount Valentia.

87 Elsewhere in his writings (see Payne et al., *Harford,* p. 190), when Harford described Cetshwayo's infatuation with Lady Robinson, he realistically ascribed it not to her being (as he had chivalrously put it in his reminiscences) 'uncommonly pretty', but to her being 'a particularly stout woman' and thus conforming to the culturally determined sexual preference of a Zulu man.

Biographical Notes

Where individuals have been mentioned more than once in the text, information about them is to be found here. When first named in the text, and also when they appear in the footnotes before they do in the text, they are marked with an asterisk (*). Other persons mentioned in the text are identified in the footnotes.

The information provided aims to place the individual in the context of the Anglo-Zulu War and is not intended to be a full biography. The information supplied is: name; dates (where known); rank, regiment, orders and decorations at the beginning of the Anglo-Zulu War; record of past service; service during 1879; orders, decorations and promotion in recognition of service during the Anglo-Zulu War. Subsequent career not noted.

Barrow, Percy Harry Stanley (1848–86). Captain, 19th Hussars. He was Brigade Major of Cavalry at the Curragh from 1877 until March 1878, when he was sent to South Africa on Special Service to form a squadron of Mounted Infantry. In 1879 he served first with No. 1 Column in command of No. 2 Squadron, Mounted Infantry and was present at Nyezane. Then, he was in command of the Divisional Troops of the Eshowe Relief Column and fought at Gingindlovu, where he was wounded. He next commanded the Mounted Troops of the 1st Division, and subsequently – as Major (Local) – the Mounted Troops with Clarke's Column. CMG. Brevet Major.

Barton, Geoffrey (1844–1922). Captain, 7th Fusiliers. He saw action in the Third Anglo-Asante War, 1874. On Special Service throughout

1879, he was Staff Officer to Colonel Durnford of No. 2 Column and during Isandlwana was stationed with the 1/2nd NNC near Middle Drift. Subsequently, he was commander of the 4th Battalion, NNC, serving successively with the Eshowe Relief Column, when he was present at Gingindlovu, then with the 1st Division and finally with Clarke's Column. Brevet Major.

Bellairs, William (1828–1913). Colonel (not General), Staff, CB. He saw service in the Crimean War, 1854–6, and held staff appointments in the West Indies, Ireland, Canada and Gibraltar, 1857–77. During the Ninth Cape Frontier War, 1877–8, he served as DAG on the Headquarters Staff. On Special Service in 1879, he first served as DA and QMG on Chelmsford's Headquarters Staff. He was absent with Chelmsford's reconnaissance-in-force during Isandlwana. Afterwards, he returned to Pietermaritzburg and remained there until April 1879, when Major-General Clifford took command of the Line of Communication and Base, freeing him to join the 2nd Division in the field as DA and QMG. During Ulundi, he commanded the garrison holding the double laager on the south bank of the White Mfolozi River. He then served as DAG on General Wolseley's General Staff.

Bengough, Harcourt Mortimer (1837–1922). Brevet Major, 77th Regiment. He saw service in the Crimean War, 1854–5. On Special Service in 1879, he commanded the 2/1st NNC with No. 2 Column and was stationed out of the action at kwaMahamba Drift during Isandlwana. He subsequently proceeded to Umsinga to protect the border from Zulu invasion and built and garrisoned Fort Bengough. In March 1879 the 2/1st NNC was reconstituted under Bengough's command as the 2nd Battalion, NNC. In May it joined the 2nd Division in its advance and fought at Ulundi. Then, from July to early September it served with Baker Russell's Column in pacification operations. Brevet Lieutenant-Colonel.

Black, Wilsone (1833–1909). Major, 2/24th Regiment. He saw service in the Crimean War, 1854–6, and in the Ninth Cape Frontier War, 1878. In 1879 he initially commanded the Lines of Communication,

Greytown and Middle Drift, and was then attached to Chelmsford's personal staff. He was absent with Chelmsford's reconnaissance-in-force during Isandlwana. Subsequently, he was stationed until early August in command of the companies of the 2/24th Regiment constituting part of the garrison at Rorke's Drift. He led the patrol on 4 February 1879 that retrieved the Queen's Colour of the 1/24th from the Mzinyathi River, and then commanded the reconnaissances of the Isandlwana battlefield in March and May. In June he commenced the burial of the dead at Isandlwana. CB. Brevet Lieutenant-Colonel.

Bromhead, Gonville (1845–91). Lieutenant, 2/24th Regiment. He saw service in the Ninth Cape Frontier War, 1878. In 1879 he was in command of B Company, 2/24th Regiment during the unsuccessful Zulu attack on Rorke's Drift. After the defence of the post, he remained on garrison duty throughout the remainder of the campaign. VC. Brevet Major.

Brownrigg, Henry John (1828–1904). Deputy Commissary-General, Commissariat and Transport Department. He saw service in the Crimean War, 1854–5, and in the Ninth Cape Frontier War, 1877–8. During 1879 he was initially in charge at Helpmekaar of the North-East Frontier and after Isandlwana was made responsible for replacing the transport lost in the battle. He next served with the 2nd Division as Commissary-General and subsequently took charge of the northern depots and lines of communication of Clarke's and Baker Russell's columns.

Cetshwayo kaMpande (c. 1832–84). Zulu king. He took part in the Swazi campaign of 1852. When his father, King Mpande, fearing his growing power, began to favour his half-brother Mbuyazi to succeed him as king, Cetshwayo defeated and killed Mbuyazi at Ndondakusuka in 1856. Mpande recognised Cetshwayo as his heir in 1861 and he thereafter exercised most of his father's royal prerogatives until he succeeded him in 1872. Cetshwayo's efforts to stave off the Anglo-Zulu War through negotiation failed. He adopted a strategy of defending his country from the British invasion with the intention of negotiating a peace settlement from a position of military strength. A string of defeats foiled this policy. The British captured the fugitive king on 28 August 1879 at the kwaDwasa *umuzi* in the Ngome forest and exiled him to Cape Town.

Chard, John Rouse Merriott (**1847–97**). Lieutenant, RE. In 1879 he was attached as extra subaltern to the 5th Company, RE. He was the senior officer present during the unsuccessful Zulu attack on Rorke's Drift. He then succumbed to disease. After recovering his health in hospital at Ladysmith, he rejoined the 5th Company, RE attached to the 2nd Division. During Ulundi, the 5th Company, RE made up part of the garrison that held the double laager on the south bank of the White Mfolozi River. VC. Brevet Major.

Chelmsford, Sir Frederic Augustus, second Baron (**1827–1905**). Staff, Major-General with local rank of Lieutenant-General. KCB, CB. In January 1878 he was appointed General Officer Commanding Her Majesty's Forces at the Cape of Good Hope, Natal and St Helena, and held that post until his resignation in July 1879. He saw service in the Crimean War, 1855–6, the Indian Mutiny, 1858–9, and in 1868 as DAG to the Abyssinian Field Force. He served as AG of the Indian Army, 1869–74. He commanded during the final stages of the Ninth Cape Frontier War, 1878, and in Zululand in 1879. He was absent on a reconnaissance-in-force during Isandlwana, but commanded at the victories of Gingindlovu and Ulundi. GCB.

Clarke, Charles Mansfield (**1839–1932**). Lieutenant-Colonel, 57th Regiment. He saw action in the Indian Mutiny, 1858, and in the Third New Zealand War, 1861–7. In May 1878 he was appointed commanding officer the 57th Regiment. After Isandlwana, the regiment was sent out from Ceylon (modern-day Sri Lanka) as reinforcements. Under Clarke's command, the regiment joined the 2nd Brigade, Eshowe Relief Column, and fought at Gingindlovu. After the relief of Eshowe, Clarke was appointed Brigadier of the 2nd Brigade, 1st Division and took part in the advance to Port Durnford. After the breakup of the 1st Division, between late July and September he took command of Clarke's Column engaged in the pacification of central Zululand, in the pursuit and capture of King Cetshwayo and in the pacification of the middle border. CB. Brevet Colonel.

Clery, Cornelius Francis (1838–1926). Major, 32nd Regiment. He was Instructor of Tactics at the Royal Military College, Sandhurst, 1871, and Professor, 1872–5. In 1875–7 he was DAQMG on the Headquarters Staff, Dublin, and then at Aldershot, 1877–8. In 1878, as a Special Staff Officer he served briefly in the Northern War in Griqualand West, and in the First Anglo-Pedi War. In 1879 he joined No. 3 Column as Principal Staff Officer to Colonel Glyn. He was absent with Chelmsford's reconnaissance-in-force during Isandlwana, and after the relief of Rorke's Drift was stationed there with the garrison under Colonel Glyn. From May he served with No. 4 Column (subsequently the Flying Column) as Colonel Wood's Principal Staff Officer and was present at Ulundi. Brevet Lieutenant-Colonel.

Cochrane, William Francis Dundonald (1847–1927). Lieutenant and Adjutant of the 32nd Light Infantry. On Special Service in 1879, he served with No. 2 Column on Colonel Durnford's staff as Transport Officer and survived the battle of Isandlwana. In February 1879 he was placed in command of the Natal Native Horse with the local rank of Captain. He served with Wood's No. 4 Column and was present at Hlobane and Khambula. Still in command of the Natal Native Horse, he subsequently served with Wood's Flying Column, took part in the White Mfolozi reconnaissance-in-force, and fought at Ulundi.

Coghill, Nevill Josiah Aylmer (1852–79). Lieutenant, 1/24th Regiment. In 1876 he was appointed ADC to the GOC, South Africa, Lieutenant-General Sir Arthur Cunynghame. He served in the Ninth Cape Frontier War, 1877–8. In 1878 he was appointed ADC to High Commissioner Sir Bartle Frere but rejoined his regiment in January 1879 to serve as Orderly Officer on the staff of Colonel Glyn in command of No. 3 Column. He did not accompany Glyn on the reconnaissance-in-force on 22 January because of an injury to his knee on 20 January, and remained in the camp at Isandlwana. He escaped from the battlefield down the Fugitives' Trail and (despite his injured knee) turned back at the Mzinyathi River, along with Lieutenant Higginson of the NNC, to assist Lieutenant Melvill, who was attempting to carry the cased Queen's Colour of the 1/24th Regiment to safety. He was killed with Melvill on the Natal bank. Posthumous VC awarded in 1906.

Cooper, A.W. Commandant (?). 2/3rd NNC. Late of the 95th Regiment. He was absent with the reconnaissance-in-force during Isandlwana. His demoralised battalion was dismissed on 24 January and Cooper joined the garrison at Rorke's Drift. He took part in Major Black's patrol on 4 February 1879 that recovered the Queen's Colour of the 1/24th Regiment.

Courtenay (not Courtnay), Edward Reginald (1853–1919). Lieutenant, 20th (not 21st) Hussars. He was on Special Service throughout 1879 as Staff Officer to Major Percy Barrow, who was initially in command of the mounted troops of No. 1 Column, and subsequently of those of the Eshowe Relief Column, the 1st Division and finally of Clarke's Column. Courtney fought at Nyezane and Gingindlovu where his horse was shot under him.

Dabulamanzi kaMpande (c. 1839–86). Zulu prince and half-brother of King Cetshwayo, whom he strongly supported in the 1856 war of succession against Mbuyazi. He developed close contacts with colonial hunters and traders in south-eastern Zululand, where he lived at his *umuzi*, eZuluwini. In 1879 he was with the uncommitted Zulu reserve at Isandlwana, and although he held no official command, he asserted his royal status to lead the unsuccessful assault on Rorke's Drift. Retiring in disgrace to eZuluwini, he coordinated the Zulu blockade of Fort Eshowe and led the Zulu right horn at Gingindlovu. He surrendered to the 1st Division on 12 July.

Dalton, James Langley (c. 1834–87). Acting Assistant Commissary, Commissariat and Transport Department. He saw service in the Eighth Cape Frontier War, 1851–3, in the Red River Expedition in Canada,

1870, and in the Ninth Cape Frontier War, 1877–8. In 1879 he was posted to No. 3 Column. He was present at Rorke's Drift, where it seems he did more to organise its defence than the regular officers present, and was severely wounded. After his recovery, he was posted to Fort Napier in Pietermaritzburg as Senior Commissariat Officer with the permanent rank of Sub-Assistant Commissary. VC.

Dartnell, John George (1837–1913). Brevet Major, retired from the 27th Regiment by sale of commission, 1869. He saw service in the Indian Mutiny, 1857–9, and in the Anglo-Bhutan (Duar) War, 1865. In 1874 he was appointed Commandant of the Natal Mounted Police and Inspector of Volunteer Forces, Natal. In 1879 he was with No. 3 Column on Chelmsford's Headquarters Staff as commander of the NMP and the Natal Mounted Volunteers and was away skirmishing during Isandlwana. He was Commandant of Natal Colonial Defensive District No. 1 from December 1878 to July 1879. During February, when stationed at Ladysmith, he supervised defence preparations in Natal before returning to Rorke's Drift as a member of the garrison. He took part in Major Black's cross-border reconnaissances from Rorke's Drift in March, April and June.

Davison, Arthur Stewart Fielding (1856–79). Lieutenant, 99th Regiment and Adjutant since 30 November 1878. In 1879 he served with No. 1 Column and was present at Nyezane. On 27 March 1879 he died of typhoid fever during the siege of Eshowe.

Degacher, Henry James (1835–1902). Lieutenant-Colonel, 24th Regiment. CB. He commanded the 2/24th throughout 1879. He was absent with Chelmsford's reconnaissance-in-force during Isandlwana. Subsequently, he commanded and fortified the Rorke's Drift post. In April he moved with three companies of the 2/24th to the Dundee camp, where he remained in command while the battalion was scattered at posts along the border to protect the lines of communication and the Dundee District during the advance of the 2nd Division.

Dillon, Martin Andrew (1826–1913). Major-General. AMS to the Duke of Cambridge at the Horse Guards. He saw service in the Indian Mutiny in 1857–8, in 1860 in the Second Anglo-Sino War and in 1868 as AAG to the Abyssinian Field Force. He was not made KCB until 1887.

Duncan, Alexander William (1837–96). Major, O Battery, 6th Brigade, RA. He saw service in the Third Anglo-Asante War of 1873–4. In 1879 he served with the 1st Division in its advance to Port Durnford, and then with Clarke's Column. Brevet Lieutenant-Colonel.

Dunn, John (1830–95). He entered Zululand in 1853 as a hunter and trader, and King Cetshwayo assigned him a large chiefdom in south-eastern Zululand. Harford knew him during his childhood days in Natal. In 1879 Dunn threw in his lot with the British and served with the Eshowe Relief Column as Chelmsford's Intelligence Officer and fought at Gingindlovu. He then commanded John Dunn's Scouts with the Divisional Troops of the 1st Division and was critical in negotiating the submission of the coastal Zulu chiefs. He advised General Wolseley on his settlement of Zululand and was appointed one of the thirteen chiefs that replaced the Zulu monarchy.

Erskine, the Hon. David (1816–1903). A younger son of the second Baron Erskine of Restormel Castle in the county of Cornwall, he was commissioned in 1835 into the 51st Light Infantry and saw service in Malta, Tasmania and India before selling out in 1858 with the rank of Major. Like many another former officer, he took up a post in the colonial administration and emigrated to Natal, where he served as Colonial Secretary from 1858 until his retirement in 1875, and was the Lieutenant-Colonel of the Natal Volunteer Corps from 1862 to 1871. Then, from 1878 to 1880 he was the Resident Magistrate of Walvis Bay, annexed to the Cape Colony in March 1878. He subsequently retired to England with his family, where he mismanaged his investments and was eventually declared insolvent. On 26 September 1870 in Pietermaritzburg he married, as his second wife, Emma Florence Mary Harford ('Sissy'), Harford's eldest sister, by whom he had four children. Trooper Robert

Erskine of the Natal Carbineers, the youngest of his five children by his previous marriage to Anna Maria Spode, was killed on 4 November 1873 at the Bushman's River Pass during the Langalibalele Rebellion.

Fynn, Henry Francis, Jnr (1846–1915). The son of a Natal pioneer, he was fluent in isiZulu and was a Natal civil servant. The Resident Magistrate of the Umsinga Division of Weenen County since 1876, in 1879 he accompanied No. 3 Column as Chelmsford's interpreter and political adviser. He was absent with Chelmsford's reconnaissance-in-force during Isandlwana. He then resumed his magisterial duties.

Gabangaye kaPhakade (?). Harford calls him 'Ingabangi'. He was the eldest son and heir of Phakade, the *inkosi* of the amaChunu who were refugees from the Zulu kingdom living in Weenen County, Natal. The amaChunu formed six companies of the 2/3rd NNC but Phakade was too old and infirm to lead them. Gabangaye, who was also advanced in years, commanded them in his stead. Harford describes him as a 'witchdoctor', but he was most likely acting as an *imbongi*, or praise-singer, when the NNC advanced into Zululand, rather than an *isangoma*, or diviner inspired by the ancestral spirits. Both *izangoma* and *izimbongi* would have been attired outlandishly to colonial eyes in skins and feathers, leading one such as Harford to lump them together as 'witchdoctors'.

Gifford, Edric Frederick Gifford, third Baron (1849–1911). Captain, 57th Regiment. VC. He saw service in the Third Anglo-Asante War of 1873–4, when he was awarded the VC. On Special Service in 1879, he served with the 1st Division and then as one of General Wolseley's four ADCs on his personal staff. He took a leading part in the hunt for the fugitive King Cetshwayo between 13 and 28 August. After the king's capture by Major Marter from underneath his nose, he was sent home with despatches.

Glyn, Richard Thomas (1831–1900). Colonel, 24th Regiment. CB. He saw service in the Crimean War, 1854–5; the Indian Mutiny, 1857–8; the Diamond Field Revolt of 1875 in Griqualand West; and the Ninth

Cape Frontier War, 1877–8. In December 1878 he was given command of No. 3 Column. He was absent with Chelmsford's reconnaissance-in-force during Isandlwana. Afterwards, he was placed in command of the garrison at Rorke's Drift until May, when he took up command of the 1st Brigade, 2nd Division. He was present at Ulundi in command of the Infantry Brigade of the 2nd Division.

Hamilton-Browne, George ('Maori Browne') (1844–1916). Commandant, 1/3rd NNC. In 1878 he volunteered as an officer in Pulleine's Rangers, an irregular unit raised in the Ninth Cape Frontier War. He next saw action in 1879 with No. 3 Column at kwaSogekle but was absent with the reconnaissance-in-force during Isandlwana. When the 3rd NNC was disbanded at Rorke's Drift, he formed its white NCOs into a mounted unit that became the nucleus of the Natal Horse. He remained in garrison at Rorke's Drift and participated in cross-border raiding until March 1879, when he was ordered to the Cape Colony to assist in raising Lonsdale's Horse (Mounted Rifles). He joined the Eshowe Relief Column with Lonsdale's Horse and was present at Gingindlovu. He was then sent back to the Cape with irregulars due to be discharged. His unreliable memoirs, *A Lost Legionary in South Africa*, were published in 1912.

Harness, Arthur (1838–1927). Brevet Lieutenant-Colonel, RA. He commanded N Battery, 5th Brigade, RA, throughout 1879. He marched with No. 3 Column and was absent with Chelmsford's reconnaissance-in-force during Isandlwana. Subsequently, he was stationed at Helpmekaar. In April he joined the Divisional Troops of the 2nd Division and fought at Ulundi. In August he joined Baker Russell's Column. CB.

Hart, Arthur Fitzroy (1844–1910). Captain, 31st Regiment. He saw service in the Third Anglo-Asante War, 1874. On Special Service in 1879 as Staff Officer to the 2nd Regiment, NNC with No. 1 Column, he was present at Nyezane. He was then Staff Officer with the Eshowe Relief Column and fought at Gingindlovu. He next served as Brigade Major of the 2nd Brigade, 1st Division, and finally as Principal Staff Officer of Clarke's Column. Brevet Major.

Jameson, Robert (1840–1919). He came to Natal in 1859 and founded a company in Durban manufacturing jams, condiments and preserves. He was a keen amateur botanist and arboriculturist. A member of the Durban Town Council in 1876–81 and for long periods thereafter, he was mayor in 1895–6. As an officer in the Durban Mounted Rifles under Captain Theophilus Shepstone, he served with No. 1 Column in 1879. During Nyezane his unit was held in reserve, guarding the baggage train, and was sent back to the lower Thukela with all the other mounted troops when Colonel Pearson decided to stand fast at Fort Eshowe. Thereafter, the Durban Mounted Rifles were engaged in keeping communications open along the Thukela border from the coast to Middle Drift.

Jim (his Zulu name is not recorded) (?). He was Harford's personal servant throughout the campaign. He was the brother-in-law of Zibhebhu kaMaphitha, the *inkosi* of the Mandlakazi people in the Zulu kingdom. Jim had known the young Harford when employed on his father's farm, Stapleton Grove. Recruited into the 3rd NNC, in January 1879 he recognised Harford at Sand Spruit and remained with him during his service with No. 3 Column, in garrison at Rorke's Drift, with the 1st Division and with Clarke's Column. They parted company in Pietermaritzburg in October 1879.

Jones, Walter Parke (1844–83). Captain, 5th (Field) Company, RE. In 1879 he was initially stationed at Helpmekaar, where he designed the fort in the aftermath of Isandlwana, and then at Dundee, where in May he designed Fort Jones for the protection of the 2nd Division's supply depot. He and his company subsequently joined Wood's Flying Column and were present at Ulundi. Brevet Major.

Lonsdale, Rupert LaTrobe (1849–88). Commandant, 3rd Regiment, NNC. He sold his commission of Lieutenant in the 74th Regiment in 1874 and settled in the Cape Colony. During the Ninth Cape Frontier War he volunteered and commanded a unit of Mfengu levies, 1877–8. Offered the command of the 3rd NNC with No. 3 Column, he was with the reconnaissance-in-force during Isandlwana. When the 3rd NNC was disbanded, Chelmsford sent him to the Cape to raise three troops of white irregular cavalry, known as Lonsdale's Horse (Mounted Rifles). The unit joined the Divisional Troops of the 1st Division in its advance to Port Durnford. Two troops then served with Clarke's Column, and one with Baker Russell's Column. CMG.

Marter, Richard James Coombe (1838–1902). Major, in command of the left wing of the 1st Dragoon Guards. In April 1879 he joined Major-General Marshall's Cavalry Brigade attached to the 2nd Division and was heavily engaged in extensive raiding of Zulu territory and in escorting convoys. He was present at the skirmish at Zungeni on 4 June. His two squadrons were subsequently divided between Baker Russell's Column and Clarke's Column. He commanded the squadron serving with the latter column and was employed in pacification operations and in tracking down the fugitive King Cetshwayo. Marter led the patrol that finally captured the king in the Ngome forest on 28 August and brought him into Wolseley's camp on 31 August. Brevet Lieutenant-Colonel.

Matshana kaMondisa (?). Initially the *inkosi* of a section of the Sithole people living south of the Mzinyathi River in Natal, in 1858 he fell foul of the colonial authorities and fled to Zululand. King Mpande appointed him *inkosi* of the Sithole people living at the confluence of the Mzinyathi and Mangeni rivers. At the outbreak of war in 1879, King Cetshwayo's advisers mistrusted Matshana because of his previous connections with Natal, and did not entrust him with a military command. So, instead of joining the Zulu army marching to confront No. 3 Column, he and his fighting men remained in his own district south-east of Isandlwana and skirmished on 21–22 January with the British reconnaissance-in-force attacking his stronghold on the Phindo heights. It seems probable that he was acting in concert with the main Zulu army and was engaged in drawing part of the British forces away from the Isandlwana camp it intended to attack. After Isandlwana, the war largely passed him and his people by. On 20 August he surrendered at Rorke's Drift to H.F. Fynn Jnr.

Melvill, Teignmouth (1842–79). Lieutenant and Adjutant, 1/24th Regiment. He served during the Ninth Cape Frontier War, 1877–8. In 1879 he was present with his battalion in the camp of No. 3 Column at Isandlwana. When the British line collapsed, he rode out of the camp down the Fugitives' Trail with the battalion's cased Queen's Colour. He was unhorsed in the flooded Mzinyathi River and lost the Colour, but was assisted to the Natal bank by Lieutenant Coghill and Lieutenant Higginson of the NNC where he and Coghill were killed. Posthumous VC awarded in 1906.

Mills, Charles (1825–95). Permanent Under-Secretary in the Colonial Secretary's Office, Cape Colony, between 1872 and 1882. He was made KCMG only in 1885, six years after Harford met him.

Moir, Alexander McArthur (1844–1885). Captain, 99th Regiment. In 1879 he served with the Eshowe Relief Column and was present at Gingindlovu. He then served with his regiment in the 1st Brigade, 1st Division and took part in the advance to Port Durnford.

Nevile (not Neville), Charles Cavendish (d. 1884). Lieutenant, 99th Regiment. He served in 1879 with No. 1 Column and was present throughout the Zulu blockade of Eshowe. He subsequently served with the 1st Brigade, 1st Division in its advance to Port Durnford. Captain.

Norris-Newman, Charles Louis Marie (1852–1920), known as 'Noggs'. A journalist and adventurer, in 1879 he was the special correspondent of the *Standard*, syndicated to the *Times of Natal* and the *Cape Standard and Mail.* He attached himself to No. 3 Column and was present at kwaSogekle but was absent with Chelmsford's reconnaissance-in-force during Isandlwana. He joined the Eshowe Relief Column and saw action at Gingindlovu. He then joined the 2nd Division and was present at Ulundi. The book of his experiences, *In Zululand with the British*, was published in 1880.

Oftebro, Martin (1858–1942). He was a son of Rev. Ommund Christiansen Oftebro (1820–93) of the Norwegian Missionary Society active in Zululand who, when his relationship with King Cetshwayo deteriorated, in 1878 abandoned his mission station at Eshowe. Martin Oftebro accompanied Major Marter's patrol on 26–28 August as an interpreter and was present at Cetshwayo's capture at kwaDwasa in the Ngome forest.

Raw, Charles (d. 1888). Lieutenant, in command of No. 1 Troop, Sikali's Horse, Natal Native Mounted Contingent. He survived Isandlwana, and once Sikali's Horse had dispersed home after the battle, he remained with the garrison at Rorke's Drift and took part in the patrols on 3–4 February that located and buried the bodies of Lieutenants Coghill and Melvill, and retrieved the Queen's Colour of the 1/24th Regiment from the Mzinyathi. Thereafter, in late February he joined the reconstituted Edendale Horse that became a troop in the Natal Native Horse, and served with No. 4 Column when he was present at Hlobane and Khambula, and with Wood's Flying Column when he fought at Ulundi.

Reynolds, James Henry (1844–1932). Surgeon, Army Hospital Corps, MB. After service in India and St Helena, in 1877 he was attached to the 1/24th Regiment in the Cape and took an active part in the Ninth Cape Frontier War, 1877–8. When in 1879 No. 3 Column advanced into Zululand, he was left in charge of the field hospital established at Rorke's Drift. During the Zulu attack, he assisted in the defence of the post and treated the wounded at a makeshift dressing station. After the battle, he remained with the garrison at Rorke's Drift and was invalided out with dysentery. VC. Surgeon-Major.

Russell, John Cecil (1839–1909). Brevet Major, 12th Lancers. He served in the Third Anglo-Asante War, 1873–4. In 1879 he was on Special Service and given command (with the local rank of Lieutenant-Colonel) of No. 1 Squadron, Mounted Infantry in No. 3 Column. He was with the reconnaissance-in-force during Isandlwana. In March 1879 he was transferred to No. 4 Column. He was in command of the rear section of No. 4 Column engaged at Hlobane. Colonel Wood fastened the blame for the debacle on him for not coming up in support of the section under the command of Lieutenant-Colonel Redvers Buller, and he was transferred to Pietermaritzburg as Commandant, Remount Establishment.

Shepstone, Sir Theophilus (1817–93), KCMG. A highly influential colonial official, he had been Diplomatic Agent to the Native Tribes in Natal, 1845–55, and Secretary for Native Affairs, Natal, 1856–76. From 1877 to 1879 he was Administrator of the Transvaal Territory.

Sihayo kaXongo (c. 1824–83). The *inkosi* of the Qungebe people in south-western Zululand and *induna* of the iNdabakawombe *ibutho*, he was an especial favourite of King Cetshwayo's and a member of his council. A cross-border incident led by several of his sons in July 1878 was seized upon by the British as one of their justifications for their invasion of the Zulu kingdom, and he and his family were much blamed in Zululand for provoking the war. On 12 January 1879, No. 3 Column destroyed his kwaSogekle *umuzi* in the first action of the war.

Smith, George (1845–1918). Reverend, a missionary in Natal with the Society for the Propagation of the Christian Gospel with his parish at Weston. In 1873 he volunteered to serve as chaplain with the colonial forces suppressing the Langalibalele Rebellion. In 1879 he volunteered to serve as a military chaplain with No. 3 Column. He took part in the defence of Rorke's Drift and subsequently accompanied the 2nd Division as chaplain. Chaplain to the Forces in the Army Chaplain's Department.

Somkhele kaMalanda (c. 1840–1907). The *inkosi* of the Mphukunyoni people. He was a first cousin of King Cetshwayo, and an *induna* of the uThulwane *ibutho*. As an *isikhulu* he dominated the Zulu north coast and lived in quasi-royal style surrounded by his own *izinduna* and warriors. He had been averse to going to war in 1879 and was among the coastal *amakhosi* who made their opportune submission on 5 July 1879 to Major-General Crealock at an impressive parade of the 1st Division. In his settlement of Zululand, General Wolseley appointed him one of the thirteen chiefs that replaced the Zulu monarchy.

Stewart, Herbert (**1843–85**). Captain, 3rd Dragoon Guards. Most of his earlier military career was spent in India in staff appointments, and he entered Staff College in 1877. He was also a barrister in the Inner Temple and was a first-class cricketer. On Special Service in 1879, he served from April to July as the highly commended Brigade Major in the Cavalry Brigade attached to the 2nd Division. Thereafter, he was 'Specially Employed' on the Lines of Communication and Base with Clarke's Column.

Thompson (**?**). Lieutenant, 1/3rd NNC. No such person appears in the list of officers of the 3rd Regiment, NNC, but there is a Sergeant Rupert Thompson mentioned in the incomplete rollcall of NCOs.

Towers-Clarke, Alexander (**1856–1914**). Lieutenant, 57th Regiment. In 1879 he served with his regiment in the Eshowe Relief Column, was present at Gingindlovu, took part in the advance of the 1st Division to Port Durnford as Orderly Officer to Lieutenant-Colonel Clarke, and finally continued with Clarke's Column as his Orderly Officer. He made several road surveys in Zululand, notably that from St Paul's to Middle Drift.

Upcher, Russell (**1844–1936**). Brevet Major, 2/24th Regiment. In September 1878 he was appointed Commandant of Durban. In January 1879, while marching to join No. 3 Column in Zululand, he received news of Isandlwana and retired on Helpmekaar. He assumed command of the 24th Regiment from 23 January to 11 May 1879. He advanced with the 2nd Division but was left in command of the Mthonjaneni laager during the battle of Ulundi.

Wainwright, A.F. (**?**). Lieutenant, 2/3rd NNC. He was absent with Chelmsford's reconnaissance-in-force during Isandlwana. With the disbanding of the 3rd NNC, he was one of the former officers and NCOs of the 3rd NNC stationed at Rorke's Drift (the nucleus of the Natal Horse) riding out on patrol, and took part in the recovery of the Queen's Colour of the 1/24th Regiment.

Walker, Albert Lancelot (1840–1918). Major, 99th Regiment. He saw active service in the Second Anglo-Sino War of 1860. He proceeded on Transport Service to South Africa in November 1878 and was initially Officer Commanding at Stanger on Line of Communications to No. 1 Column and the Eshowe Relief Column. He continued as DAG to the 1st Division until the end of the war. Brevet Lieutenant-Colonel.

Walsh, Henry Alfred (1853–1918). Lieutenant, 1/13th Light Infantry. He served with the Mounted Infantry in the First Anglo-Pedi War of 1878. Throughout 1879 he commanded a troop of No. 1 Squadron, Mounted Infantry. Serving first with No. 3 Column, he was absent with the reconnaissance-in-force during Isandlwana. He was in garrison at Helpmekaar until mid-March, when No. 1 Squadron joined No. 4 Column, and he was present at Hlobane and Khambula. No. 1 Squadron advanced with Wood's Flying Column, and he fought at Ulundi.

Welman, William Henry Dowling Reeves (1827–1906). Lieutenant-Colonel, 99th Regiment. He commanded the regiment throughout the campaign. He was in command of the 2nd Division of No. 1 Column that remained in support during Nyezane, and was present throughout the blockade of Eshowe. Subsequently, he advanced up the coast to Port Durnford, when the 99th Regiment formed part of the 1st Brigade, 1st Division. CB.

Williams, Cecil Charles (1855–79). Lieutenant, 58th (not 27th) Regiment. He proceeded on Transport Service to South Africa in November 1878 and joined No. 4 Column at Utrecht. In February 1879 he was appointed Staff Officer to Major W. Knox Leet, the Commandant of Wood's Irregulars. He was killed at Hlobane fighting with the 2nd Battalion, Wood's Irregulars.

Wolseley, Sir Garnet Joseph (1833–1913). Lieutenant-General, Staff, GCMG, KCB, KCMG, CB. He saw service in the Second Anglo-Burmese War, 1852–3; the Crimean War, 1854–5; the Indian Mutiny, 1857–8; and the Second Anglo-Sino War, 1860. He then commanded during the Red River Expedition, 1870, and the Third Anglo-Asante War, 1873–4. Subsequently, he was Administrator of Natal, 1875, and High Commissioner and Governor of Cyprus, 1878–9. In May 1879 the British government sent him to South Africa on Special Service as High Commissioner in South-Eastern Africa, Governor of Natal and the Transvaal, and Commander-in-Chief of the Forces in South Africa with the local rank of General. He arrived too late for Ulundi, but pacified Zululand after Lord Chelmsford's resignation and imposed his settlement on the defeated kingdom. GCB.

Wood, Henry Evelyn (1838–1919). Brevet Colonel, Staff, VC, CB. He served in the Crimean War, 1854–5; the Indian Mutiny, 1858; the Third Anglo-Asante War, 1873–4; and the Ninth Cape Frontier War, 1878. On Special Service in 1879, he commanded No. 4 Column and was present at the defeat at Hlobane and the victory at Khambula. With the local rank of Brigadier-General he commanded the renamed Flying Column and fought at Ulundi. KCB.

Zibhebhu kaMaphitha (c. 1841–1904). He was the powerful *inkosi* of the Mandlakazi people of north-eastern Zululand, who had strong trading contacts with the colonial world. He advised against war with Britain, but in 1879 fought gallantly throughout the campaign. He held a subordinate command at Isandlwana, where he was wounded, and again at Khambula. He commanded the mounted scouts who drew the British reconnaissance-in-force into an ambush at the White Mfolozi the day before Ulundi, and also fought in that battle. On 26 August he submitted to General Wolseley, who appointed him one of the thirteen chiefs that replaced the Zulu monarchy.

List of Regiments

Regiments of Heavy Cavalry
1st King's Dragoon Guards
2nd Dragoon Guards (Queen's Bays)
3rd (Prince of Wales's) Dragoon Guards

Regiments of Light Cavalry
7th (The Queen's Own) Hussars
12th (The Prince of Wales's Royal) Lancers
17th (Duke of Cambridge's Own) Lancers
19th Hussars
20th Hussars
21st (Empress of India's) Lancers

Regiments of Foot
3rd (East Kent – The Buffs) Regiment of Foot
4th (The King's Own Royal) Regiment of Foot
7th (Royal Fusiliers) Regiment of Foot
11th (North Devonshire) Regiment of Foot
13th (1st Somersetshire) (Prince Alfred's Light Infantry) Regiment of Foot
14th (Buckinghamshire – The Prince of Wales's Own) Regiment of Foot
18th (The Royal Irish) Regiment of Foot
21st (Royal Scots Fusiliers) Regiment of Foot
24th (2nd Warwickshire) Regiment of Foot
27th (Inniskilling) Regiment of Foot
31st (Huntingdonshire) Regiment of Foot
32nd (Cornwall) Light Infantry

51st (2nd York, West Riding, The King's Own Light Infantry) Regiment of Foot
57th (West Middlesex) Regiment of Foot
58th (Rutlandshire) Regiment of Foot
60th (The King's Royal Rifle Corps) Regiment of Foot
61st (South Gloucestershire) Regiment of Foot
62nd (Wiltshire) Regiment of Foot (From 1 July 1881: 1st Battalion, The Duke of Edinburgh's (Wiltshire Regiment))
74th (Highlanders) Regiment of Foot
75th (Stirlingshire) Regiment of Foot
77th (East Middlesex) Regiment of Foot (Duke of Cambridge's Own)
80th (Staffordshire Volunteers) Regiment of Foot
81st (Loyal Lincoln Volunteers) Regiment of Foot
85th (Bucks Volunteers) (The King's Light Infantry) Regiment of Foot
88th (Connaught Rangers) Regiment of Foot
95th (Derbyshire) Regiment of Foot
99th (Duke of Edinburgh's) Regiment of Foot (From 1 July 1881: 2nd Battalion, The Duke of Edinburgh's (Wiltshire Regiment))

Glossary

isiZulu–English

In accordance with modern practice, words in isiZulu are entered under the stem (here capitalised) and not under the prefix

isAngoma (pl. **izAngoma**) diviner inspired by ancestral spirits

isiBaya (pl. **iziBaya**) enclosure for livestock

imBongi (pl. **izimBongi**) praise-singer

iButho (pl. **amaButho**) age-grade regiment of men or women; warrior

inDaba (pl. **izinDaba**) matter of discussion; important meeting

iDlozi (pl. **amadlozi**) ancestral spirit

inDuna (pl. **izinDuna**) appointed officer of state, headman, councillor

isiGodlo (pl. **iziGodlo**) king's or great nobleman's private enclosure at upper end of *ikhanda*; women of his establishment who lived there

iKhanda (pl. **amaKhanda**) royal military homestead where *amabutho* were stationed

isiKhulu (pl. **iziKhulu**) great one of the realm, nobleman

inKosi (pl. **amaKhosi**) chief, king

uMnyama (sing. only) spiritual force of darkness or evil influence

iMpi (pl. **iziMpi**) military force

umNdlunkulu (sing. only) maids-of-honour; girls of royal *isigodlo*

iNyanga (pl. **iziNyanga**) traditional healer; herbalist

iThunga (pl. **amaThunga**) milk pail

inTombi (pl. **izinTombi**) a full-grown unmarried girl

umuTsha (pl. **imiTsha**) loin covering of long pieces of twisted skins or fibres hanging like tails

uTshwala (sing. only) sorghum beer

umuZi (pl. **imiZi**) homestead of huts under a headman

Gazetteer

The first column has Harford's spelling where it differs from the present; the second column contains the present-day spelling; the Zulu name commonly used today is in brackets.

Persons

Cetewayo	Cetshwayo
Isikota	Sikhotha
Matyana	Matshana
Sibebu	Zibhebhu
Sirayo	Sihayo
Somkele	Somkhele
Umbelazi	Mbuyazi
Umkungu	Mkhungo

Rivers

Amange	Mangeni
Bashee	Batshe
Umfolozi	Mfolozi
Buffalo River	(Mzinyathi)

Mountains

Entonjaneni	Mthonjaneni
Isandhlwana	Isandlwana
Isipezi	Siphezi
Itchiane	Shiyane
Malakata	Malakatha

Places

Etchowi	Eshowe
Kwamagwasa	KwaMagwasa
Simonstown	Simon's Town

Select Bibliography

Printed Primary Sources

Anon., *Historical Records of the 2nd Battalion, 24th Regiment for the Campaign in South Africa, 1877-78-79: Embracing the Kaffir & Zulu Wars*. Secunderabad, Deccan: 2nd Battalion, 'The South Wales Borders', January 1882.

Ashe, Maj. Waller and Capt. the Hon. Edmund V. Wyatt-Edgell, *The Story of the Zulu Campaign*. London: Sampson Low, Marston, Searle, & Rivington, 1880. (Reprinted Cape Town: N & S Press, 1989.)

British Parliamentary Papers:

LII of 1878–9 (C. 2242). S.A. Correspondence, 1878–9.

LIII of 1878–9 (C. 2252), (C. 2260), (C. 2316), S.A. Correspondence, appointment of Wolseley, 1878–9.

LIV of 1878–9 (C. 2454). S.A. Correspondence, Ulundi, 1878–9.

L of 1880 (C. 2482), (C. 2505), S.A. War, Correspondence, 1879–80.

LI of 1880 (C. 2676), S.A. Correspondence, 1879–80.

Brown, R.A. (ed.), *The Road to Ulundi: The Water Colour Drawings of John North Crealock (the Zulu War of 1879)*. Pietermaritzburg: University of Natal Press, 1969.

Child, Daphne (ed.), *The Zulu War Journal of Colonel Henry Harford, C.B.* Pietermaritzburg: Shuter & Shooter, 1978.

Clarke, Sonia, *Invasion of Zululand 1879: Anglo-Zulu War Experiences of Arthur Harness; John Jervis, 4th Viscount St Vincent; and Sir Henry Bulwer.* Houghton: The Brenthurst Press, 1979.

—— *Zululand at War 1879: The Conduct of the Anglo-Zulu War.* Houghton: The Brenthurst Press, 1984.

Durnford, Lt Col Edward C.L., *Isandhlwana, 22nd January, 1879: A Narrative, Compiled from Official and Reliable Sources*. London: P.S. King, 1879.

—— *Isandhlwana: Lord Chelmsford's Statements Compared with the Evidence*. London: P.S. King, 1880.

Elliott, Major W.J., *The Victoria Cross in South Africa: Isandhlwana and Rorke's Drift*. London: Dean & Son, 1882.

Emery, Frank, *The Red Soldier: Letters from the Zulu War, 1879*. London: Hodder and Stoughton, 1977.

Forbes, Archibald, 'Lord Chelmsford and the Zulu War', *The Nineteenth Century*, 7 (February 1880), pp. 216–34.

Hallam Parr, Capt. Henry, *A Sketch of the Kafir and Zulu Wars: Guadana to Isandhlwana*. London: C. Kegan Paul, 1880.

Hamilton-Browne, Col G., *A Lost Legionary in South Africa*. London: T. Werner Laurie, 1912. (Reprinted Uckfield: The Naval & Military Press; London: National Army Museum, 2010.)

Harness, Lt Col Arthur, 'The Zulu Campaign from a Military Point of View', *Fraser's Magazine*, new series, 21 (April 1880), pp. 477–88.

Hart, the late Lieutenant-General H.G, edited by his son, *The New Annual Army List, Militia List, Yeomanry Cavalry List, and Indian Civil Service List for 1880 (Being the Forty-First Annual Volume), Corrected to the 31st December 1879*. London: John Murray, 1880.

—— *The New Annual Army List, Militia List, Yeomanry Cavalry List, and Indian Civil Service List for 1881 (Being the Forty-Second Annual Volume), Corrected to the 30th December 1880*. London: John Murray, 1881.

Illustrated London News, 1878, 1879.

Knight, Ian, *The National Army Museum Book of the Zulu War*. London: Sidgwick & Jackson in association with the National Army Museum, 2003.

Laband, John (ed.), *Lord Chelmsford's Zululand Campaign 1878–1879*. Stroud: Alan Sutton Publishing for the Army Records Society, 1994.

—— and Ian Knight, *The War Correspondents: The Anglo-Zulu War*. Stroud: Sutton Publishing, 1996.

—— (series ed.) and Ian Knight (volume ed.), *Archives of Zululand: The Anglo-Zulu War 1879*, 6 vols. London: Archival Publications International, 2000.

London Gazette, 1879.

Mackinnon, J.P. and S.H. Shadbolt, *The South African Campaign of 1879.* London: Sampson Low, Marston, Searle, and Rivington, 1880.

Moodie, Duncan C.F. (edited by John Laband), *Moodie's Zulu War.* Cape Town: N & S Press, 1988 (a reprinted selection from D.C.F. Moodie, *History of the Battles and Adventures of the British, the Boers, and the Zulus.* Adelaide: George Robertson, 1879).

Natal Almanac and Yearly Register 1868. Pietermaritzburg: Davis & Sons, 1867.

Natal Colonist, 1879.

Natal Mercury, 1879.

Natal Witness, 1879.

Norris-Newman, Charles L., *In Zululand with the British throughout the War of 1879.* London: W.H. Allen, 1880. (Reprinted London: Greenhill Books; California: Presidio Press, 1990.)

Payne, David, Emma Payne and Adrian Greaves, *The Writings, Photographs and Sketches of Henry Charles Harford 1850–1937.* Wales: The Ultimatum Tree Ltd, 2008.

Preston, Adrian W. (ed.), *The South African Journal of Sir Garnet Wolseley 1879–1880.* Cape Town: A.A. Balkema, 1973.

Rattray, David, *A Soldier-Artist in Zululand: William Whitelock Lloyd and the Anglo-Zulu War of 1879.* Rorke's Drift: Rattray Publications, 2007.

Rees, Wyn (ed.), *Colenso Letters from Natal.* Pietermaritzburg: Shuter & Shooter, 1958.

Richards, Walter, *Her Majesty's Army: A Descriptive Account of Various Regiments Now Comprising the Queen's Forces, from Their First Establishment*, 3 vols. London: H. Virtue, n.d. [c. 1880].

Smith-Dorrien, Sir Horace, *Memories of Forty-Eight Years' Service.* London: John Murray, 1925.

Stevenson, Lee, Ian Knight and Alan Baynham-Jones, *Rorke's Drift by Those Who Were There: Eyewitness British and Zulu Accounts*, 2 vols. Barnsley: Greenhill Books, 2023.

Times of Natal, 1879.

War Office, Intelligence Division, *Narrative of the Field Operations Connected with the Zulu War of 1879.* London: Her Majesty's Stationary Office, 1881. (Reprinted London: Greenhill Books; California: Presidio Press, 1989.)

Webb, Colin de B. and John Wright (eds), *A Zulu King Speaks: Statements Made by Cetshwayo kaMpande on the History and Customs of His People.* Pietermaritzburg: University of Natal Press; Durban: Killie Campbell Africana Library, 1978.

Wolseley, Colonel Sir Garnet J., *The Soldier's Pocket-Book for Field Service*, 2nd edn. London: Macmillan, 1871.

Printed Secondary Sources

Atkinson, C.T., *The South Wales Borderers, 24th Foot, 1637–1937.* Cambridge: Cambridge University Press, 1937.

Beckett, Ian F.W., *Rorke's Drift and Isandlwana.* Oxford: Oxford University Press, 2019.

Best, Brian, 'Zulu War Medals', *Journal of the Anglo Zulu War Historical Society*, 3 (June 1998), pp. 35–8.

Cannadine, David, *Oxford Dictionary of National Biography Online* (www.oxforddnb.com).

Castle, Ian, *Zulu War: Volunteers, Irregulars and Auxiliaries.* Oxford: Osprey, 2003.

—— and Ian Knight, *Fearful Hard Times: The Siege and Relief of Eshowe, 1879.* London: Greenhill Books, 1994.

Doke, C.M. and B.W. Vilakazi (compilers), *Zulu–English Dictionary*, 2nd edn. Johannesburg: Witwatersrand University Press, 1972.

Dominy, Graham, 'Fort Napier: The Imperial Base that Shaped the City', in John Laband and Rob Haswell (eds), *Pietermaritzburg 1838–1988: A New Portrait of an African City.* Pietermaritzburg: University of Natal Press and Shuter & Shooter, 1988.

—— *Last Outpost on the Zulu Frontiers: Fort Napier and the British Imperial Garrison.* Urbana, Chicago and Springfield: University of Illinois Press, 2016.

Droogleever, R.W.F., *The Road to Isandhlwana: Colonel Anthony Durnford in Natal and Zululand.* London: Greenhill Books, 1992.

French, Major the Hon. Gerald, *Lord Chelmsford and the Zulu War.* Oxford: John Lane the Bodley Head, 1939. (Reprinted Barnsley: Pen & Sword Military, 2014.)

Gon, Philip, *The Road to Isandlwana: The Years of an Imperial Battalion.* Johannesburg: Ad. Donker, 1979.

Greaves, Adrian, *Rorke's Drift*. London: Cassell, 2002.

— and Ian Knight, *Who's Who in the Zulu War. Vol. I: The British; Vol. II: Colonials and Zulus*. Barnsley: Pen & Sword Military, 2006, 2007.

Guest, W.R., 'Review of *The Zulu War Journal of Colonel Henry Harford, CB.*, edited by Daphne Child', *Natalia*, 8 (December 1978), pp. 80–1.

Hooper, Lindsay, 'Domestic Arts: Carved Wooden Objects in the Home', in Marilee Wood (coordinator), *Zulu Treasures: Of Kings and Commoners. A Celebration of the Material Culture of the Zulu People*. Ulundi and Durban: KwaZulu Cultural Museum and the Local History Museum, 1996.

Knight, Ian, *Nothing Remains but to Fight: The Defence of Rorke's Drift, 1879*. London: Greenhill Books, 1993.

—— *Go to Your God like a Soldier: The British Soldier Fighting for Empire, 1837–1902*. London: Greenhill Books, 1996.

—— *A Companion to the Anglo-Zulu War*. Barnsley: Pen & Sword Military, 2008.

—— *Zulu Rising: The Epic Story of Isandlwana and Rorke's Drift*. London: Macmillan, 2010.

Krige, Eileen Jensen, *The Social System of the Zulus*, 2nd edn. Pietermaritzburg: Shuter & Shooter, 1974.

Laband, John, *The Rise and Fall of the Zulu Nation*. London: Arms and Armour, 1997. (First published as *Rope of Sand: The Rise and Fall of the Zulu Kingdom*. Johannesburg: Jonathan Ball, 1995.)

—— *The Atlas of the Later Zulu Wars 1883–1888* (Pietermaritzburg: University of Natal Press, 2001).

—— *Kingdom in Crisis: The Zulu Response to the British Invasion of 1879*. Barnsley: Pen & Sword, 2007. (First published Manchester: Manchester University Press, 1992.)

—— *Historical Dictionary of the Zulu Wars*. Lanham: The Scarecrow Press, 2009.

—— *The Shadow of Isandlwana: The Life and Times of General Lord Chelmsford and his Disaster in Zululand*. Barnsley: Greenhill Books, 2023.

—— and Rob Haswell (eds), *Pietermaritzburg 1838–1988: A New Portrait of an African City*. Pietermaritzburg: University of Natal Press and Shuter & Shooter, 1988.

—— and Jeff Mathews, *Isandlwana*. Pietermaritzburg: Centaur Publications and KwaZulu Monuments Council, 1992.

—— and Paul Thompson, *War Comes to Umvoti: The Natal–Zululand Border 1878–79*. Durban: Department of History, University of Natal, Research Monograph No. 5, 1980.

—— and Paul Thompson with Sheila Henderson, *The Buffalo Border 1879: The Anglo-Zulu War in Northern Natal*. Durban: Department of History, University of Natal, Research Monograph No. 6, 1983.

—— and Paul Thompson, *Field Guide to the War in Zululand and the Defence of Natal 1879*, 2nd revised edn. Pietermaritzburg: University of Natal Press, 1987.

—— and Paul Thompson, *Kingdom and Colony at War: Sixteen Studies on the Anglo-Zulu War of 1879*. Pietermaritzburg: University of Natal Press; Cape Town: N & S Press, 1990.

—— and Paul Thompson, *The Illustrated Guide to the Anglo-Zulu War*. Pietermaritzburg: University of Natal Press, 2000.

—— and Paul Thompson, 'African Levies in Natal and Zululand, 1838–1906', in Stephen M. Miller (ed.), *Soldiers and Settlers in Africa, 1850–1918*. Leiden and Boston: Brill, 2009.

Lock, Ron and Peter Quantrill, *Zulu Victory: The Epic of Isandlwana and the Cover-Up*. London: Greenhill Books, 2002.

Morris, Donald R., *The Washing of the Spears: A History of the Rise and Fall of the Zulu Nation under Shaka and Its Fall in the Zulu War of 1879*. London: Jonathan Cape, 1966.

Peers, Chris, *Rorke's Drift and Isandlwana 22nd January 1879: Minute by Minute*. Barnsley: Greenhill Books, 2021.

Snook, Lt Col Mike, *How Can Man Die Better: The Secrets of Isandlwana Revealed*, revised edn. Barnsley: Frontline Books, 2018.

Spiers, Edward M., *The Late Victorian Army 1868–1902*. Manchester: Manchester University Press, 1992.

Thompson, Paul S., *Black Soldiers of the Queen: The Natal Native Contingent in the Anglo-Zulu War*. Tuscaloosa: University of Alabama Press, 2006.

Verbeeck, J.A., 'Saving the Queen's Colour', *Natalia*, 8 (December 1978), pp. 46–53.

Acknowledgements

A new, comprehensive edition of Charlie Harford's memoir of the Anglo-Zulu War was the brainchild of Michael Leventhal, the publisher of Greenhill Books, and I am very grateful that he gave me the opportunity to take on this enticing assignment. As ever, his enthusiastic support has encouraged me throughout.

I am much indebted to those involved in the production of this book, especially to Jessica Cuthbert-Smith, the production manager at JCS Publishing Services Ltd, for her meticulous copyediting, and to her associate, Steve Williamson, who was responsible for typesetting and proofreading.

The cartographer Peter Wilkinson has once again (as in several previous projects) patiently borne with my rough sketches and changes of mind to produce an elegant and clear-cut map of Harford's peregrinations during the Anglo-Zulu War.

Illustrations play an essential part in this book. I am especially grateful to Dr David Payne, his daughter Emma Payne and Dr Adrian Greaves for their gracious permission to include indispensable images from *The Writings, Photographs and Sketches of Henry Charles Harford*, and to Nicky Rattray for generously allowing me to reproduce some of William Lloyd's superb Anglo-Zulu War watercolours which first appeared in *A Soldier-Artist in Zululand* by the late David Rattray. Ian Knight has been as openhanded as ever in providing me with images from his private collection, as have Alexander Haimann and Ron Sheeley from theirs. Mbalenhle

Zulu, the Senior Librarian at the Campbell Collections of the University of KwaZulu-Natal, Durban, has supplied me with the images I requested with her accustomed friendly efficiency. Susan Elliott, the Production Editor at the University of KwaZulu-Natal Press, kindly granted me permission to use material from *The Road to Ulundi*, edited by R.A. Brown and published by the University of Natal Press in 1969. Rebecca Naidoo, the Museum Officer at the Durban Local History Museums, located some hitherto unpublished Harford watercolours and drawings for me.

In editing Harford's memoir, I have called upon the researches of many other historians in the field, although any mistakes or misconstructions are mine alone. Most especially, I could not have provided the details concerning Harford's life and career without the book by David and Emma Payne and Adrian Greaves. And the footnotes would have been the poorer without recourse to the invaluable pioneering work by the late Professor Paul Thompson on the Natal Native Contingent with whom Harford served.

As a Research Fellow in the Department of History at Stellenbosch University, I am most grateful for the gracious and unstinting assistance by the Chair, Professor Sandra Swart, and by Leschelle Morkel, the Administrative Officer. I am also beholden to Stellenbosch University for the financial assistance provided by the Faculty Research Fund towards the cost of permissions for reproducing many of the illustrations in this book.

It is now forty-five years since I first brought out a book, and through all these years Fenella has sustained me as I abstractedly worked away on my latest project, acting as a perceptive sounding board, and proffering sound advice. My appreciation is heartfelt, as ever.

Index

Words from Nguni languages are entered under the root rather than under the prefix.